Cold War in the Working Class

SUNY Series in American Labor History

Robert Asher and Amy Kesselman, Editors

The three general officers of the UE (left to right) James Matles,
Director of Organization; Albert Fitzgerald, President; Julius
Emspak, Secretary Treasurer

Cold War in the Working Class

The Rise and Decline of the United Electrical Workers

Ronald L. Filippelli
and
Mark McColloch

STATE UNIVERSITY OF NEW YORK PRESS

Production by Ruth Fisher
Marketing by Bernadette LaManna

Published by
State University of New York Press, Albany

For information, address State University of New York Press,
State University Plaza, Albany, N.Y., 12246

Library of Congress Cataloging-in-Publication Data

Filippelli, Ronald L.
    Cold war in the working class : the rise and decline of the United
    Electrical workers / Ronald L. Filippelli and Mark McColloch.
        p.   cm. — (SUNY series in American labor history)
    Includes bibliographical references and index.
    ISBN 0–7914–2181–3 (hardcover). — ISBN 0–7914–2182–1 (pbk.)
    1. United Electrical and Radio Workers of America—History.
    2. Trade-unions—Electric industry workers—United States—History.
    I. McColloch, Mark. II. Title. III. Series.
    HD6515.E32U654   1995
    331.88'1213'0973—dc20   93–50828
                                                                        CIP

10 9 8 7 6 5 4 3 2 1

For Our Children

Contents

Acknowledgments

Like Saul on the road to Damascus, the writers of a scholarly book need Samaritans to ease the passage. The journey of discovery can be long and difficult, but the help of so many companions along the way is a large part of the reward.

We thank the following librarians and archivists for their assistance: David Rosenberg of the UE Archives at the University of Pittsburgh; Ronald Becker and James Quigel of the Department of Special Collections and Archives of the Rutgers University Libraries; Carole Prieto of the Special Collections at the Washington University Libraries; Dawne Dewey of the Special Collections and Archives Department of the Wright State University Libraries; Archie Motley of the Chicago Historical Society; and Debra Bernhardt of the Robert Wagner Labor Archives, New York University Libraries. Thanks also go to the staffs of the Pennsylvania Historical Collections and Labor Archives at Pennsylvania State University, the Columbia University Oral History Collection, the Walter Reuther Archives at Wayne State University, the Roosevelt University Library, the Urban Archives at Temple University, the National Archives, and the archives of the Federal Bureau of Investigation.

The National Endowment for the Humanities, American Council of Learned Societies, the New Jersey Historical Commission, the University of Pittsburgh at Greensburg, and The College of the Liberal Arts and the Institute for the Arts and Humanistic Studies of the Pennsylvania State University provided funds and other assistance that facilitated the writing of this book.

Special thanks also go to the scholars who, through their advice and other assistance, contributed to whatever merit the book might have. They include Robert Zieger, Gerald Eggert, Robert Asher, Charles Stephenson, and Paul Buhl. Of course, shortcomings are entirely the responsibility of the authors. Clay Morgan and Ruth Fisher of the SUNY Press are models of what scholarly editors and publishers should be. Finally, we thank our families for their support and understanding during this project.

Introduction

The Cold War's chilling effect on American society struck deep into the heart of the American labor movement in 1949 and 1950 when the Congress of Industrial Organizations (CIO) expelled 11 unions representing more than a million members because of "Communist domination." It was the climax of a self-dismemberment unparalleled in American labor history—a dismemberment from which the American labor movement has never fully recovered. While the Cold War brought intense pressure and left an indelible mark on many American institutions, none were as profoundly affected as America's industrial unions.

Eliminating Communists from the labor movement was one of the excesses committed in the name of national security during the Cold War. Politicians, government agencies, religious groups, veterans organizations, and the labor movement itself played major roles. The argument that Communist influence in key industrial unions posed a serious threat to national security was widespread. Congressman Fred Hartley articulated the fears of millions when he argued that "A single Communist in a position of power within the labor movement could act under the direction of Russian agents so as to seriously hinder this country's ability to defend its people and wage war against its enemies." The dimension of the national paranoia explains the intensity of the responses. Each of the Communist-led unions faced a host of enemies. FBI surveillance became commonplace. Congressional committees held over 100 hearings dealing with Communist influence in the labor movement between 1946 and 1956. Criminal indictments for contempt of Congress saddled most left-wing unions and their officers with crushing legal expenses. In addition there were Smith Act indictments, Internal Revenue Service audits, deportations, denials of security clear-

1

ances, Strategic Activities Control Board hearings, and NLRB proceedings.[1]

Although government involvement was the most visible part of the purge, elements of the business community used the opportunity to roll back the gains workers had made during the New Deal and World War II. The National Association of Manufacturers and the Chamber of Commerce spent millions propagating the belief that the Wagner Act and the union shop were Moscow's doing. Companies practiced what they preached. Over a million workers in private industry underwent private security checks resulting in the loss of work for thousands.[2]

Labor too played its part. Anti-Communist unions in both the AFL (American Federation of Labor) and the CIO cooperated with government and industry in the hunt for Communists at the workplace. By 1954, 59 of 100 unions barred Communists from holding office, 41 included supporters in the ban, and 40 barred Communists from membership.

There is no question of the success of these efforts. By the time the CIO merged with the AFL in 1955, nearly 200,000 trade-union leaders from some 250 unions had formally sworn that they did not belong to the Communist Party or believe in communism. The American labor movement emerged as unquestionably the most conservative in the world.[3]

Although the subversive danger ultimately proved to be illusory, the position of several of the left-wing unions in key defense industries gave it plausibility. Of no union was this more true than the UE, the biggest of the left-wing unions, with virtually wall-to-wall unionization of the major electrical manufacturing firms. On the eve of the 1949 CIO convention at which the purge of the left-wing unions began, the *New York Times* noted that "the largest nut that the CIO has to crack is the UE (United Electrical, Radio and Machine Workers of America), its third largest affiliate. This union, well entrenched in General Electric, Westinghouse and other large radio and electrical manufacturing companies is a strong, well disciplined organization."[4]

The *Times* correctly assumed that the key to the success of any anti-communist purge lay in the willingness of the CIO to expel an affiliate that, by any standard, was a successful trade union, and that, along with the United Auto Workers (UAW) and the United Steelworkers (USW), constituted the "big three" of industrial unionism. It was also correct in assigning the task to the CIO because, by 1949, a decade-long insurgency within UE, aided by the government, various employers, the media, the Roman Catholic

Church, and a number of other unions, had failed to dislodge the left-wing leadership of the "red fortress." In the end, of course, the power of the CIO and its anti-communist allies prevailed. Raids, indictments of leaders, congressional hearings, and a barrage of propaganda left the UE a mere shadow of its former self by the mid-sixties. But the UE was not the only casualty. Unionism in the electrical manufacturing industry also sustained near fatal blows, leaving workers the main victims of the internecine warfare that employers took advantage of at every opportunity.

A study of the UE as a crucible of the pressures of the Cold War on American labor in particular, and on American non-governmental institutions in general, might suggest tentative answers to a number of questions about the role of the left in the United States. No other left-wing-led institution in American history achieved the power and influence of the UE. None ever demonstrated the broad-based appeal to American workers that the UE did. None ever resisted the anticommunist hysteria of post-World War II America as successfully as the UE, although, of course, it emerged from the struggle greatly reduced and permanently crippled.

How then did the left-wing leaders of the UE organize hundreds of thousands of ordinary American workers? What policies and programs did they pursue? What was the relationship of the job-related trade union interests of the rank and file and the larger political and ideological goals of the leadership?

It is essential to understand the fate of the UE in the context of American history. One of the great paradoxes of the American labor movement is that it is and has primarily been, especially since the 1920s, a working-class movement outside of the broad stream of socialist thought. Most references to unions as the institutional expression of class struggle existed mainly in the early rhetoric of the movement, but rarely in its operating principles. These have always been mainly rooted in the tradition of "pure and simple" economic unionism. Every really successful union leader since Samuel Gompers has acted firmly in this conservative tradition, including the patron saints of industrial unionism—John L. Lewis, Philip Murray, and Walter Reuther. Save for differences of degree rather than of kind, so too did most of the Marxist leaders of the left-wing unions of the CIO.

Basically pure and simple, or "business" unionism, as it developed in the United States, accepted private property and the market as the fundamental, and largely beneficial, pillars of economic life. Capitalism, while fundamentally desirable, had to be tempered by more humane institutions capable of minimizing the negative effects of unrestrained individualism and extreme concentration of economic power. The labor movement is one such institution.

Inherent in this view is the idea that the labor movement exists primarily to improve the economic well-being of its members. The goal of a fundamental reversal of power between capital and labor has largely been absent from the practice of American unionism since the 1920s. Nowhere is this more manifest than in labor's relation to the formal political process. With few exceptions, American labor leaders have rejected independent, working-class political action, choosing instead an ostensibly nonpartisan approach based on "rewarding friends and punishing enemies" in the Republican and Democratic Parties. In practice, however, at least since the presidency of Woodrow Wilson, organized labor has largely come to rest in the Democratic Party, the more social democratic of the two capitalist parties.

By the second administration of Franklin Roosevelt, organized labor's identification as one of the cornerstones of the new Democratic coalition was complete. While this coalition had great benefits from labor's point of view, it also had negative effects, which contributed to the post-war cold war in the labor movement. As a quid pro quo for general Democratic Party support for labor's agenda in the areas of labor law and social entitlements, the leaders of the CIO increasingly found it necessary to enforce a political orthodoxy on what was basically an economic movement.

This de facto integration into the Democratic Party raised few problems during the activist years of the New Deal and the popular front during World War II. But strains began to show after the war when the division of the world into two camps and the concurrent conservative trend in the United States drove the mainstream of organized labor even tighter into the embrace of the Democrats, while at the same time increasingly isolating the minority of communist-led unions.

For the CIO's left wing, the New Deal's active social engineering and intervention in the economy provided fertile ground for an industrial unionism that seemed to have the potential to go far beyond pure and simple unionism to a significant reformation of the power relations between capital and labor. These militants flocked to the CIO banner during the great organizing drives of the 1930s because they saw the industrial union movement as the foundation of this new order. They had contempt for what they considered the narrow, exclusive nature of the craft unions of the AFL. Short of qualified organizers to deal with millions of workers clamoring for organization under the provisions of the NIRA and the Wagner Act,

John L. Lewis and his Committee for Industrial Organization welcomed the skills and dedication of the left wing. From the beginning they played a significant, some would say pivotal, role in organizing and running the CIO.

For the most part the two factions in the CIO coexisted with a minimum of friction. While there were shadings of difference on their attitudes toward collective bargaining, seniority, grievance procedures, and other matters essential to workers on the shop floor, they were largely differences of degree, not of principle. The left wing generally pushed farther on limiting management's prerogatives, and thus its power, on these matters, but the legal constraints of the Wagner Act and its subsequent National Labor Relations Board (NLRB) interpretation established limits beyond which a union, whatever the ideology of its leaders, could not go without relegating itself to outlaw status. That is not to say that these differences in degree were not important to union members. They were extremely important on the shop floor, and the UE's attention to restricting unfettered management power goes a long way toward explaining the union's ability to maintain an extraordinary amount of rank and file support even in the worst days of the anti-communist hysteria.

But the arena of the Cold War was not to be the shop floor. The drama was to be played out on the international stage. An ideologically divided world fearful of nuclear holocaust created strong pressure to choose sides. This was true of unions as well as of nations. The New Deal and World War II had posed no such problems. Ideological differences had been submerged in the service of the two great causes—the defeat of the Depression and of Fascism. With the inception of the Cold War, the common ground shrank and the differences over the organization of the post-war world widened. Two issues proved to be crucial—the Marshall Plan and the 1948 presidential election. On these issues, the leadership of the left wing unions chose to follow a path in keeping with the Communist Party line rather than the Democratic Party line. No such heresy could be tolerated at a time of conservative resurgence that threatened labor's gains of the Roosevelt years. By 1947, CIO president Philip Murray had come to identify labor's survival with the fortunes of the Democrats. Out of this conviction came the imposition of a political orthodoxy on the CIO unions that the left-wing leadership of the UE refused to accept. This refusal to fall into line inside the CIO turned differences of opinion on international affairs into a threat to Murray's ability to deliver the industrial union movement to the Democrats. It also increasingly made the CIO vulnerable to charges that it harbored anti-American elements who threatened the internal security of the United States. Thus, to Murray, external realities had made adherence to CIO policy on non-trade union issues a litmus test for trade union legitimacy. In the final analysis, the CIO split because it could not compromise internally the external pressures which were driving the rest of the nation, and the world, apart.

These pressures were found, to a lesser or greater degree, in many American unions. This is a study of the effects of those pressures in the UE. It recounts the story of the formation and building of the union and the struggle for control of it by left and right-wing factions against the backdrop of the Cold War at home and abroad. It is also the story of the struggle for dominance in the electrical manufacturing industry between the UE and its right-wing rival, the International Union of Electrical Workers (IUE), to which the CIO granted the UE's jurisdiction after the UE departed.

It is important to define the term left-wing as it is used in this book. First and foremost it refers to the Communists. Party members were very active in the formation of the CIO. It is difficult to say how many there were, although about 40 percent of the CIO's unions had significant Communist connections by the end of the 1930s. In 1948, the FBI asserted that of the Party's 59,000 members, approximately 16,000 were in the CIO—less than 1 percent of the total membership. Even if one assumes that all the Party members were in the expelled unions, the percentage rises only to 2 percent. But the numbers do not tell the whole story. Communists were heavily concentrated among the full-time staff and national officers of the left-wing unions and therefore exercised power and influence far out of proportion to their actual percentage of the membership. The IUE, which probably had access to FBI information, claimed that 200 Communists or former Communists were on the UE payroll in 1950.[5] In most cases there was no way to determine whether a person actually belonged to the Communist Party.

The presence of Communists in leadership positions in the CIO's left-wing unions did not guarantee benefits to the Party, however. Most of the members hid their affiliation with the blessings of the Party. The inroads in the labor movement were too precious to risk by going public. This was certainly true of the UE. Secretary Treasurer Julius Emspak, identified in congressional hearings as a secret member of the Communist Party's central committee, denied to the end of his life that he was a Communist. Director of Organization James Matles had been a leader of the Communist-controlled Trade Union Unity League before coming to the UE, but he too went to his grave denying Party membership. Although secrecy was the rule, some UE leaders did reject the role of "submarines" and openly proclaimed their affiliation. The most notable of these was William Sentner, president of the UE's District 8 in St. Louis. For Sentner, open party membership was an affirmation of the rank and file's ability to judge him on his performance as a trade unionist. In addition, he argued that hiding his membership would promote the "lie" of a Communist conspiracy in the labor movement. According to Sentner, when the time came that he no longer served the best interests of the union, he was sure that the rank and file would exercise their democratic prerogative and elect someone else. Other open Communists below the level of the general officers included James MacLeish, president of District 4 in New York; David Davis, business agent for Local 155 in Philadelphia; and Nat Cohen, an executive board member of Local 475. Both Davis and Cohen served openly on the Communist Party's national committee. There were others as well, particularly at the shop steward level, but in general secrecy proved to be the path of least resistance.[6]

Secrecy had several virtues. It facilitated their alliance with the CIO center, especially Philip Murray and Sidney Hillman, although certainly both men knew which of their colleagues were Communists and which were not. This "discretionary" and mutually beneficial arrangement began with John L. Lewis in the earliest days of the CIO. It also minimized friction with the overwhelmingly noncommunist rank and file of the unions and made it easier to function as pure and simple trade unionists. But secrecy combined with the power that the trade union Communists had acquired as leaders of mass organizations also worked to loosen the ties between the party and the trade unionists. If Communists were to lead mainstream American unions in the American industrial relations system, then the union leaders had to have the freedom to function, form alliances, and make compromises that made real party control largely meaningless. Ostensibly the Party functionaries were in charge, and consultation did take place, particularly on major political issues, but in reality the trade union leaders had far outdistanced them in power and respectability. Earl Browder, Communist Party Chairman for much of the heyday of Communist influence in the labor movement, later commented that the UE's James Matles might only attend a meeting of his party unit once a year. Attendance wasn't necessary anyway. The Party was wary of interfering in internal union matters, and there was nothing very complicated about knowing the Party line. Reading the *Daily Worker* was enough to keep up with official Communist political positions.

The Party's decision in the late thirties to abolish its "fractions" or caucuses in the labor movement confirmed this slackening of central discipline. Previously, strategy was centrally decided and strict discipline was enforced in its implementation. But this narrow kind of Leninism no longer suited either the goals of the Popular Front or the leeway necessary for the leaders of important unions.[7]

Party members whose assignments required them to be open Communists sometimes resented the respectability and flexibility that secrecy gave to the trade union leaders. A bitter debate over whether or not the union leaders should "come out" took place during a 1945 meeting of the national board of the Communist Party. Peter V. Cacchione, a Communist elected openly to the New York City Council, charged that "if the trade union leaders have not come out openly as Communists in three-and-a-half years of easy sailing," it was "idealistic" to believe that they would do so in the future. Cacchione noted that the Communist rank and file was critical of the privileges of the union leaders. He blasted those "who make $100 a week, who contribute nothing to the C.P.A., who do not even attend meetings." Nevertheless, the policy did not change.[8] Influence in the industrial labor movement was too precious to risk.

The loosening of the ties between the party and the trade unionists, and particularly the elimination of party caucuses in the unions, ended what little effort had been expended in the CIO unions to convert the rank and file to communism and to seriously recruit new party members. Even the open party members in the shop, many of them stewards, did little to propagate communism, recruit new members for the party, or explain Communist political positions. Selling *The Daily Worker* at the plant gates, often at a plant other than their own, was often as far as it went.[9] It had proven to be easier to become leaders of masses than to build a mass base. Part of the problem was a function of the composition of the industrial working class in the areas where most of the CIO's strength lay. Many of the workers were Catholics, probably over one half in the UE's case. While usually good trade unionists and New Deal supporters, they were socially and culturally conservative. In part it was the narrow nature of American trade unionism, which clearly separated politics from "bread and butter" union issues. Ironically, this worked to the advantage of the Communist leaders because it reinforced the widely held belief that politics were a person's private affair and that union leaders were judged on how they delivered on economic issues. This balance could not be threatened by a sustained effort to recruit members to the Communist Party.[10]

The success and character of the left wing unions can hardly be attributed only to Communist Party members, whatever their numbers or influence. The left-wing also included trade unionists who belonged to no Communist organization, front or otherwise, but who were intellectually and emotionally socialists. Then there were the many individuals who agreed with the Party position on a variety of issues, trade union and otherwise, but who were not Communists, either formally or philosophically. The usual denominator of these individuals is the derisive term, "fellow traveler."

Even accepting the IUE charge in 1950 that there were 200 Communists or former Communists on the UE payroll does not lead one to conclude that so small a group, many of whom were minor functionaries and support staff, could have led so large and diverse a union through deception and manipulation.[11] The contributions of local and district leaders, few of whom were Communists, were at least as important. The district and local autonomy, and self-reliance that characterized the UE sprang naturally from the decentralized character of its initial organization. Unlike the Steelworkers, Auto Workers, Rubber Workers, and Textile Workers, the early organizers of the electrical manufacturing industry received little or no formal support from the CIO. The workers organized the UE by themselves with their own resources. This required a high degree of dedication, and it imparted a sense of rights and responsibilities inside the organization that marked the militants of both the right and left wings.

From the beginning, the UE's structure provided for broad participation by the membership. In collective bargaining, the company-wide conference boards held real authority. Each year the international union and each district met in their respective conventions. The UE's constitution ensured strong district and local autonomy. District officers received their salaries from the district, not the international, and the general executive board could not remove district presidents from office. In fact, the UE international office received the smallest per capita percentage of union dues of any union in the CIO.[12] International representatives were appointed by the general executive board with "due deference given to the wishes of the membership of the district," but they were paid by the District. Local, district, and national officers stood for election annually, and throughout the conflict, virtually no charges of electoral improprieties were raised against the incumbents. Finally, full-time staff made up only 5 percent of national convention delegates.[13]

Contrast that with the United Steelworkers, which held biannual conventions and whose international officers and district directors served for four-year terms. The President, Philip Murray, appointed all staff members and assigned them to the districts. They remained on the international union payroll. Until 1942, Murray appointed all regional and district directors. The Steelworkers' central office maintained control over collective bargaining and the administration of contracts. Indeed, until well into the union's history, all fourth-step grievances were processed at the national level, thus removing the right of the local to decide whether a grievance should be referred to arbitration. In between conventions, Murray and his executive board had almost total discretionary power. While it is true that these extraordinary powers were delegated to them by the biannual conventions, staff representatives on the international payroll usually constituted from one-fifth to one-quarter of all convention delegates.[14]

In the UE, the general adherence to the principles of constitutional processes and local autonomy by both sides allowed the struggle for control, bitter as it was, to avoid the worst excesses that marked civil wars in unions such as the Auto Workers, the Transport Workers, and the National Maritime Union. It is difficult today, shortly after the collapse of the Soviet Union and much of the socialist world, to understand the intensity of the strife that developed between such basically similar men and women over the communist issue. The fear of communism in the period from 1946 to the culmination of the McCarthy era was so emotional that it could not and cannot be defined objectively. Even after the worst of the hysteria had subsided, the left and right-wing unions in the electrical manufacturing industry continued to batter one another unmercifully, rejecting conciliation and cooperation to the grave disadvantage of the workers. To this day, the UE remains outside of the AFL-CIO.

Writing at this time, after the collapse of the Communist system and the thorough exposure of most of its catastrophic failures and crimes, it is hard to imagine how so many talented, dedicated men and women remained loyal to the point of extreme self sacrifice to a regime and a system that perpetrated such massive fraud and suffering. But the judgment of history, let alone its trajectory, was far from clear in the years between the near collapse of capitalism in 1929 and the Cold War. Massive numbers of artists, workers, intellectuals, politicians, and labor leaders both here and abroad cast their vote for a socialist solution in the turbulent years of the mid-20th century. From our privileged vantage point, it is clear that the judgment that men such as James Carey, Walter Reuther, and Philip Murray rendered on the Soviet Union as a threat to basic human values, including trade union freedom, has largely been vindicated. But to hold unpopular, even patently wrong, political views is not a crime in the United States. The left wing of the labor movement was purged for its political ideas, not for any failure as trade unionists.

This study is not meant to be a comprehensive history of the UE and its competitor, the IUE. It is short on details concerning standard of living, the shop floor, community life and other aspects of social history, save where they illuminate the institutional struggle, particularly its left-right dimensions. This book narrates an inexorable conflict that ended in tragedy for workers and trade unionism in the electrical manufacturing industry. The fate of the UE and trade unionism in the electrical manufacturing industry is but one poignant example of the consequences of the phobia about domestic communism between the fall of Berlin in 1945 and the fall of the Berlin Wall in 1989.

—— 1 ——

THE FORMATIVE YEARS

Ralph Cordiner, who became president of General Electric (GE) in 1940, summed up his company's good fortune when he admitted that "General Electric was fortunate to enter the most dramatic and sustained growth business in the Twentieth Century."[1] In the 15 years from 1920 to 1935, no industry in America grew and diversified as rapidly as electrical manufacturing. At the close of World War I, the industry primarily manufactured heavy electrical machinery, equipment, and apparatus. Consumer items such as the radio, the refrigerator, and the washing machine were all but unknown. The two giants of the industry, then as now, were Westinghouse and General Electric. As the electric age progressed, these two companies acquired additional independent electrical establishments and engaged in the manufacture of every conceivable electrical product from the kitchen toaster to giant locomotives. As a result of the demand for these products, consumption of electricity more than doubled during the twenties, and the industrial workforce in electrical manufacturing soared to 343,000 in 1929, nearly double the 1921 figure.[2]

The industry produced approximately 300,000 distinguishable products by the mid-1930s. Much of the growth lay in the production of home appliances—refrigerators, washing machines, toasters, and especially radios. In addition to vastly increasing the size of General Electric and Westinghouse, these products created new corporate giants such as the Philadelphia Storage Battery Company (Philco), the Radio Corporation of America (RCA), Maytag, the General Motors Frigidaire Division, Century Electric, Emerson Electric, and others. Production was located primarily in nine states east of the Mississippi and north of the Mason-Dixon Line, and even in the midst of the Great Depression, output for the industry approached $3 billion.[3]

The capstones of this industrial kingdom were the Schenectady works of the General Electric Corporation and the East Pittsburgh Division of the Westinghouse Electric and Manufacturing Company. They were the crown jewels in two companies that accounted for about one-fourth of the industry's annual sales by the end of the 1930s.[4] General Electric, in addition to its numerous wholly and partly owned subsidiaries and its foreign branches, operated 32 manufacturing plants in 11 states. By 1937, even after the worst ravages of the Depression, General Electric had 75,212 employees, including the chairman of the board. Westinghouse, number two in the industry, had some 52,249 employees spread out over 19 plants in 14 states.[5]

The explosive surge in employment in the twenties made the crash in the industry during the Depression even more dramatic. Between 1929 and 1933, value added in electrical manufacturing fell by 70 percent, almost one-third more than the general drop in American industry. One of the results of the suddenness of the slide was the inability of General Electric and Westinghouse, both known for their innovative and professional personnel practices, to honor the implied promise of employment security that lay at the heart of welfare capitalism. Both companies tried. General Electric experimented with unemployment insurance and both of the electrical giants tried worksharing and shorter workdays as an alternative to massive layoffs. Skilled workers, a precious commodity in heavy electrical equipment plants, were given less-skilled work to do to forestall their layoff and possible loss to the company. Everything failed. By 1933, both companies had laid off approximately half of their workers.[6]

When it became clear that the disaster could not be contained by company action alone, the leaders of the electrical manufacturing industry, in particular Gerard Swope of General Electric, led the small, but influential group of corporate leaders who pushed President Herbert Hoover for public relief programs. Swope was also in the vanguard of the move toward central economic planning based on government-approved cooperation among corporations organized in industry trade associations—an idea that came to partial fruition in 1934 with the passage of the National Industrial Recovery Act.[7]

Although Swope's solution to America's economic problems lay in a partnership between corporations and government, he also acknowledged the need for employee participation in his corporatist vision. In addition to the range of company welfare programs aimed at bringing the worker into the "family" of the firm, Swope, as well as his contemporaries at Westinghouse, instituted elaborate works council systems to give employees a voice in a limited range of company policies and to keep independent unions out. As New Deal legislation chipped away at the legality of these company unions, management at both General Electric and Westinghouse adjusted by granting the councils considerable autonomy, including the right to collective bargaining. In many cases the leaders of these councils were senior skilled workers, many of whom had been active in earlier failed unionization drives. Through their work on the company unions they not only developed a basically stable relationship with management, but they also enhanced their stature as worker leaders. Both factors would have significant effects on the pattern of later industrial relations at General Electric and Westinghouse.

Prior to 1920, a scattering of AFL craft unions had tried to organize in the electrical industry. The International Association of Machinists, the Electricians, Moulders, Patternmakers, Polishers, Blacksmiths, Steamfitters and Carpenters had locals in several General Electric, Westinghouse, and other electrical plants.[8]

A number of strikes took place in the industry prior to and after the World War I, conducted by the various craft unions. These walkouts especially affected General Electric, but most failed because of a lack of craft union solidarity in the face of GE's intransigence. At no time were the craft unions able to gain a real foothold in the industry, or to establish a contractual relationship with any of the electrical companies. By 1920 these unions had been driven out of the industry entirely and protest virtually ceased. Only six strikes occurred in the entire electrical manufacturing industry between 1927 and 1929, involving just 1,800 workers.[9] The experience of the craft unions made them reluctant to renew their efforts to organize the industry, and until 1932 unionization lay dormant. Disillusioned by their experience, the workers, too, showed little interest in a labor movement dominated by the craft concept. Yet despite the meager results and the general disinterest of most workers, some of the older skilled workers remembered the union days and constituted a cadre of union sympathizers ready to serve when events in the nation caused a revival of the trade union movement.

Nevertheless, during the early years of the Depression the American labor movement continued the downward slide that had begun after World War I. Dues-paying membership fell precipitously as numerous union jobs vanished when the economy collapsed. But the collapse also struck hard at the status and legitimacy of employers. No one lost more prestige than the large industrialists who had successfully crushed the labor movement of the World War I period and repelled efforts at new unionization in the twenties through a combination of political power, ruthless suppression, and welfare capitalism. As one observer of the dramatic shift of opinion caused by the Depression stated, "Capitalism laid an egg and lost its prestige."[10] The corporate heroes of the 1920s had fallen, and the nation filled up with embittered and aggrieved workers.

The Great Depression profoundly altered not only the economic and social, but also the ideological climate of the times. Faith in capitalism was shockingly undermined. By 1933, one-fourth of the labor force was unemployed,[11] and one survey of unemployed workers' opinions revealed that nearly one-fourth of them felt a revolution might be good for the country.[12] In this setting, unionization stirred once more at the core of the electrical industry. Small local unions appeared at General Electric's Schenectady, New York, and Lynn, Massachusetts, works as early as 1932, and by 1935 the virus had spread to the big Westinghouse plants in East Pittsburgh and Philadelphia.

The leaders of these early efforts were often highly skilled and well paid workers. Most had considerable seniority, enough to have escaped the layoffs of the deepest part of the Depression, and many were radicals, or came from families in which radicalism, or unionism, or both had been part of the experience of their brothers or fathers. As older, skilled workers, they were conscious of the inroads that new technology and the changing organization of work had made on their status and power in the shops and in their communities. They fit the model of what one scholar has referred to as "autonomous workmen,"—loosely supervised men who possessed a great deal of discretion in the carrying out of their tasks.[13]

These workers, especially the radicals and union supporters among them, had been overwhelmed by the success of welfare capitalism in the twenties. But although without direct influence, save for their roles on the works councils, they kept the flame of unionism alive. When the Depression created the circumstances in which the companies could no longer honor welfare capitalism's implied contract based on good wages and job security, these older workers were the natural candidates to lead the unionization drives at the heavy manufacturing plants of General Electric and Westinghouse.

Radicals such as William Turnbull, an immigrant British socialist at Schenectady GE, and Alfred Coulthard, a skilled patternmaker and socialist at Lynn took the lead.[14] At the RCA plant in Philadelphia, skilled machinists from the Communist-led Metal Workers Industrial Union took the lead. At East Pittsburgh Westinghouse, Logan Burkhart, a skilled generator inspector with previous AFL experience, played the key role. Communist organizer K. M. Kirkendahl led the drive at the General Motors Electrical Division in Dayton, Ohio. In South Philadelphia, IWW supporters such as John Schaeffer and James Price were instrumental in the organization of the Westinghouse turbine works.[15]

But the skilled, union-conscious craftsmen in the heavy manufacturing shops did not constitute the majority of the workers in electrical manufacturing by the 1930s. Many more worked in the small motor and appliance shops, by far the fastest growing segment of the industry. There, in companies like Philco, RCA, Emerson Electric, and Frigidaire, the workers tended to be young, semiskilled, and largely without trade union traditions. A significant proportion of them were women. Unlike the skilled workers, they had little or no autonomy on the job, tied as they often were to sequential assembly operations. Their labor relations environment was considerably different as well. The new firms cared little for the paternalistic employee relations strategies championed by men like GE's Swope. Managers in these companies were often inexperienced in personnel matters. Not surprisingly, organization attempts in this part of the industry were often marked by bitter conflict. Also not surprisingly, this new workforce had grievances about low pay and working conditions that their older, more skilled co-workers did not share. Later, in a number of places, these two groups of workers would come into conflict for control of a number of local unions.

The first organizing breakthrough came in the appliance sector, at the Philco plant in Philadelphia. This huge factory—by 1930 the leader in the manufacture of radios—had never been threatened by unionism.[16] The coming of the National Industrial Recovery Act (NIRA) changed all that. In June 1933, company officials established an employee representation plan in order to comply with the letter of the Act, if not the spirit. It had little success because of the presence in the plant of a small group of workers who had organized themselves as the Philrod Fishing Club. These workers, including a young man named James Carey, had banded together in 1932 for the ostensible purpose of buying a boat. Their real purpose was to raise money for organizing the plant.[17] The group, headed by a committee that included Joe Quinn, George Morgan, Robert Gallagher, and Harry Block, successfully resisted the pressure for a company union.[18]

The company, through an administrative decision, gave the union sympathizers the chance they were waiting for. An order requiring employees to work ten hours a day temporarily to make up for a Fourth of July holiday produced a walkout by some 350 assemblers, testers, and repairmen. The strike began when a score of workers, including most of the members of the fishing club, walked off the assembly line and paralyzed the plant.

The committee thus found itself, unexpectedly, negotiating with one of the corporate giants of America. On July 15, 1933, only a few days after the strike began, Philco signed a contract calling for an eight hour day, forty-hour week, time-and-a-half for overtime and wage increases of up to 30 cents per hour. The agreement also included seniority and a grievance procedure.[19] In only a few days a group of young men, none of the leaders older than 30, had brought a corporate giant to the bargaining table and had signed a contract without equal in American manufacturing.

Such complete surrender on the part of Philco is difficult to understand. At the time a number of unions in the AFL opened a drive to urge their members and allies to buy only union-made goods. One early UE organizer believed that this threat, coupled with Philco's desire to improve its share in the radio market, led to the company's decision to sign. There was also mention of a possible AFL boycott of Philco products, but this was not substantiated and seems unlikely.[20] The concessions probably resulted from a combination of factors, including ignorance on the part of the company as to the lasting significance of their concessions and a desire to resolve trouble with the unions so as to capitalize on the business upturn in 1933.

What followed illustrated the naivete of the parties involved. On August 17, 1933, barely one month after signing the first agreement, Philco signed another agreement that granted the local a union shop. All new employees were obligated to become union members within two weeks of being hired. There was some question as to whether this provision violated Section 7A of the NIRA, in that people would be denied freedom of choice in joining or not joining a union. The union decided, with the knowledge of the company, that a committee would go to Washington to get National Recovery Administration director Hugh Johnson's approval of the provision. They left the plant in their working clothes and after one of their two cars broke down, all ten arrived at the Capital tired from their cramped journey in one automobile. Having made arrangements for sharing one hotel room, they set out to find Johnson, armed with newspaper pictures of the man for identification.[21]

They discovered Johnson conferring with William Green of the AFL and the top management of the automobile industry about industry codes. The committee interrupted the meeting and asked Johnson to read the union shop provision. Johnson hurriedly did so and signed the document. The organization of the largest radio plant in the country was complete. Almost overnight, an 8,000 strong local union organized on an industrial basis had come into being.[22] The agreement they signed proved to be so costly from the company's point of view that five years later Philco management resorted to a lockout to force a roll back of wages.[23]

On August 3, 1933, the AFL agreed to grant the local a federal charter, which gave it something resembling colonial status within the AFL.[24] It was the first formal step toward the creation of the United Electrical Workers.

Even after the enactment of the NIRA, the AFL continued to show little interest in the millions of workers in industrial plants. When forced to act because of the existence of spontaneously organized locals of industrial workers, they relied on the device of the federal charter. The craft unions looked upon this as a method of holding onto the industrial locals until a way could be found to divide them up among the various craft unions. In 1933 and 1934, five such charters were granted to five major plants in the electrical industry as well as to several smaller ones.[25] General Electric at Fort Wayne, Indiana, and New Kensington, Pennsylvania, and Westinghouse at Springfield, Massachusetts, and Essington, Pennsylvania, joined the Philco local as federally chartered unions in the electrical manufacturing industry.[26] Thousands of employees in a number of other large plants in the industry refused to accept federal charters and instead remained independent. These included such giant factories as Schenectady and Lynn General Electric; East Pittsburgh, Westinghouse; and Camden, RCA.

As at Philco, the organization of unions in the heavy manufacturing plants was largely carried out by the workers themselves. This gave them a habit of independence and self-reliance that would characterize electrical industry unionism for much of its history. There was no national organizing drive funded by the CIO as in steel, auto, rubber, and textiles, and no full-time organizers. Skilled workers with some connection to trade unionism or radical politics took the lead. The Lynn General Electric plant serves as an illustration. The company had effectively replaced independent unions with company unions after an AFL recognition strike in 1918. One individual who had learned the lessons of that attempt to organize on a craft basis was Alfred Coulthard, who had been a member of the old Patternmaker's League, an AFL affiliate. Coulthard, a socialist, led the drive which resulted in the organization of an independent electrical union at Lynn. Fellow skilled workers—machinists, tool-and-die makers, electricians—played prominent roles in the campaign. When the AFL offered them a federal charter and eventual dispersion among 21 craft affiliates, they refused.[27]

The history of unionization at GE's Schenectady plant followed a similar pattern. The local emerged from a combination of two small locals. One, established by a group of skilled workers from Eastern Europe, belonged to the Steel and Metal Workers Industrial Union, an affiliate of the Communist-led Trade Union Unity League (TUUL). Most of its members were Communists. Charles Rivers, a Communist and New York State director of the Trade Union Unity League, provided the skilled leadership needed to bring the workers, many of them veterans of a failed International Association of Machinists (IAM) attempt to organize the plant, together. By the time he arrived in Schenectady in 1932, the young Rivers had already served as an organizer with the TUUL's National Textile Workers in Gastonia, North Carolina, and had spent nearly two years working as a machinist in a Soviet factory.[28] William Turnbull, a socialist and a skilled turbine inspector originally from England, started the second group. The two locals merged in 1934 when the Communist Party, as part of its popular front strategy, dissolved the TUUL and ordered its affiliates to move into the mainstream of the labor movement and "bore from within" to gain influence.[29]

The one thing that the federal locals and the independents had in common was a desire to have the AFL grant an industrial union charter covering the entire industry. The Philco local passed a resolution in December 1933, calling for assistance in the formation of a national organization to coordinate organizational activity and better conditions throughout the industry.[30] James Carey played a key role in urging this action. He had been a delegate to the 1933 AFL convention in Washington, D.C., and realized the hostility in the Federation to industrial unionism. Carey also knew that a national charter was of paramount importance to the electrical workers.[31]

In response to Carey's call, representatives of the federal locals and the independents met on December 28 and 29 in New York City. From the meetings emerged the Radio and Allied Trades National Labor Council with Carey as its chairman. Dues were set at $1 for current operating funds and a one cent per month per capita tax for finances.[32] The primary purpose of the organization was to secure closer coordination of all affiliated unions in the radio industry by collecting and disseminating facts on hours, rates, working conditions, as well as production, earnings, and other pertinent information.[33]

The formation of the Radio and Allied Trades Council raised little enthusiasm in the AFL. The conservative craft unions looked with particular suspicion on any liaison with the left-wing leadership of the independents. The federal and independent groups had first made real contact in the summer of 1933, during the NRA code hearings for the electrical industry. They were joined in these informal hearings by a third group, an affiliate of the Communist-led Trade Union Unity League organization, called the Metal Workers Industrial Union.[34]

The men who organized the Metal Workers Industrial Union shared many of the characteristics of the union pioneers in heavy electrical manufacturing. One key group of skilled mechanics had been members of the Micrometer lodge of the International Association of Machinists during the First World War and had witnessed the destruction of their union in the twenties. These men kept the idea of trade unionism alive among the younger workers, one of whom was James Matles, an apprentice machinist who rose to become the dominant figure in the Metal Workers and one of the key leaders of the TUUL.

James Matles was born Eichel Matlis Fridman in Soroca, Bessarabia (Romania) to Jewish parents in 1909. An average student, Matles left school after junior high school and held a variety of jobs as a mechanic and chauffeur until he emigrated to the United States in 1928. From his earliest days in the machine shops of New York, he demonstrated the dedication and leadership qualities that were to make him respected by friend and foe alike during a turbulent union career that would span nearly half a century. In spite of his youth and his limited command of English, Matles' coworkers called on him to negotiate with employers. His militancy and ability did not go unnoticed by William Z. Foster, Communist Party stalwart and head of the Trade Union Unity League, and by 1932 Matles occupied one of the key leadership positions in the TUUL. Matles considered Foster his mentor, and under the direction of the leader of the great steel strike of 1919, he became a fervent believer in industrial unionism. Whether he also became a member of the Communist Party has never been conclusively proven, but right-wing critics later claimed that he joined in 1930 and became a member of the Party's national trade union commission in 1934. But considering Matles' role in the TUUL, it is likely that any decision as to whether or not to formally join the Party depended on tactical considerations and was made by Foster and the other party leaders, not by Matles.[35]

Matles and other leftists such as Charles Rivers and James Lustig successfully organized in the machine and printing shops in New York City by concentrating on the older shops where a high percentage of experienced, skilled workers could be found. Soon, with the support of TUUL affiliates elsewhere, the effort spread to other cities.[36]

At the New York meeting, the newly formed Radio and Allied Trades National Labor Council applied for an AFL industrial charter. The Federation demanded the unseating of the delegates from the independent locals before an industrial charter could be considered.[37] Not wanting to stand in the way of the charter, the independents agreed to withdraw. However, a close working relationship, albeit unofficial, was maintained.

Pressure for and against an industrial charter continued. The Executive Council of the AFL recognized the existence of a peculiar problem in the electrical industry which made it difficult to establish craft unions. At its meeting before the 1934 convention, the Council searched for a method of applying a general policy that would result in the organization of the many skilled workers into their respective craft organizations, and a coordination of these organizations by plants, through shop councils. The shop councils were to contain representatives from the different trade unions, and would enable a single agency to bargain collectively with management for all employees, thus combining the virtues of centralized bargaining with the self interest of craft union membership. The Council viewed the federal local as the first step toward this end.[38]

The federal unions in turn viewed this approach with considerable skepticism. They realized that the ability of the big manufacturers to shift production between plants to avoid pressure would have to be met by the power of one union representing all the workers of a particular company. To further this end, a group of federal labor union delegates met in early October 1934. Twenty-three delegates representing 42 federal locals from a number of branches of the electrical manufacturing industry, including radio, took part.[39] Of those present, 20 delegates were instructed to vote in favor of industrial unionism and three were uninstructed. The meeting formed a committee charged with seeking the advice of John L. Lewis and David Dubinsky, leaders of the Committee for Industrial Organization (CIO), which had been formed in the AFL. Lewis and

Dubinsky strongly supported the group's resolution that the federal unions "not be separated or segregated into craft unions, but be held intact on industrial lines. . . . "[40]

Throughout 1934, the unions in the radio industry continued their efforts to secure a national charter from the AFL. The Federation, however, despite the appeals, contended that it was not sure that such a proposed national union could finance its affairs and refused to grant it recognition as an industrial union. Also, during this period, organizing efforts continued in the electrical industry, both by the federal locals and the independents. Quite regularly, however, when applications submitted by newly organized industrial locals for federal charters were rejected by the Federation, these organizations joined with the independents.[41]

In December 1934, 11 federal locals sent 18 delegates to Buffalo for the purpose of securing national cooperation. The National Radio and Allied Trades Council, a formalization of the group formed a year earlier in New York City, came out of the Buffalo meeting. While it was not the industrial union they wanted, it was one of the first organizations of its kind to be recognized by the AFL.[42] Lewis Hines, the AFL organizer who had been assigned to the federal radio locals as an adviser, ran the meeting. The prominence of two Philco local members, Carey as president and Harry Block as vice-president, demonstrated the continuing influence of the big Philadelphia local in the radio group. The first action of the new council was to renew the application for an industrial charter.[43]

At the beginning of 1934, a development took place that was to have a profound effect on electrical industry unionism. In March of that year, the Trade Union Unity League officially folded. Its demise resulted from the decision by the Communist Party to give up trying to establish a dual union movement in the United States. The new party line called for "boring from within" the AFL and its existing unions.[44]

One of the TUUL affiliates, James Matles' Metal Workers Industrial Union, had developed a close working relationship with the electrical unions, especially the independents. When William Green ordered the federal radio locals to stop cooperating with the independents, including the Metal Workers Industrial Union, because they were dual unionists, the three groups agreed to stop open cooperation because the radio group feared it might jeopardize its chances for a national charter. Covert cooperation continued, however, with Matles remaining very close to the situation.[45]

In early 1935, a convention of all the independents representing the electrical manufacturing industry and the Metal Workers

Industrial Union met. The objective was to organize a national organization which would then seek affiliation with the AFL on an independent basis. Delegates represented unions from Schenectady, Lynn, Pittsburgh, New York, Philadelphia, and elsewhere. Many of the men who would become stalwarts of the UE's left wing participated—men such as James Lustig, Leo Jandreau, Carl Bersing, David Davis, Elmer Van Gelder, and Charles Rivers.[46] Although the federal locals were not represented, they had observers at the meeting. The delegates formed the National Federation of Metal and Allied Unions. It consisted, on paper, of two national unions: one known as the Electrical and Radio Workers and the other as the Machine, Tool and Foundry Workers, the new manifestation of the Metal Workers Industrial Union. William Turnbull from Schenectady GE and Charles Kenneck, a tool-and-die maker from Philadelphia, headed the two affiliates, while Kenneck was chosen president, and James Matles secretary-treasurer of the new federation.[47] Matles, as the only full-time official, exercised effective control. The federation's objective, in line with the Communist Party's revived popular front strategy, was to seek an industrial charter from the AFL in close cooperation with the federal locals.

On July 19, 1935, Matles informed William Green of the existence of the new Federation of Metal and Allied Unions and told him that it was seeking a basis for affiliation with the American Federation of Labor. He asked for a conference between the representatives of the AFL Executive Council, the Federation's Metal Trades Department, and a committee from his group.[48] Green told Matles to communicate directly with John P. Frey, head of the Metal Trades Department.[49]

The representatives of the new federation met on September 5, 1935, with Frey, Arthur O. Wharton of the Machinists, and Daniel Tracy of the International Brotherhood of Electrical Workers. The latter two had definite ideas about what should become of both the new federation and the federal radio locals. Matles's committee presented its demands for an industrial charter for the electrical and radio industry, in line with an understanding with the federal radio locals. They knew that this would not receive a sympathetic hearing, but decided that as far as electrical manufacturing was concerned, there appeared to be no possibility of doing anything with any of the existing craft union organizations.[50] Dodging the issue, Frey, Wharton, and Tracy told Matles and Kenneck that only the AFL Executive Council had jurisdiction over the issuance of a charter.[51] As for the Machine, Tool and Foundry Workers, it was decided that negotiations between that group and the International Association of Machinists should commence.[52] The decision on the electrical industry, it was hoped, would be made by the fifty-fifth annual convention of the AFL scheduled for October in Atlantic City.

Meanwhile, with full knowledge of what was transpiring among the independents, the National Radio and Allied Trades Council continued to seek an industrial charter. The group met in Cincinnati on March 30 and 31, 1934, to discuss the state of unionization in the industry. President Carey read a letter from William Green informing them that it was the opinion of the AFL Executive Council that the time was not ripe to issue a charter to a national union of radio workers. He doubted that the new union could be self-sustaining, but he did not close the door entirely and urged the NR & AT to continue to organize.[53]

After relaying Green's message, Carey told the disappointed delegates that it would be foolish to carry on a "long winded" fight with the Executive Council over the charter. He proposed, instead, to take the matter directly to the Atlantic City convention.[54] The radio locals accepted Carey's reasoning, but also decided that if the AFL convention refused to grant a charter, the NR & AT would continue as an independent organization.[55] At the time of all of this heady talk, the organization had only $133.25 in its treasury.[56]

At an interim meeting on charter tactics in Philadelphia on July 25, it was decided to convene in Atlantic City at the same time as the AFL meetings.[57] Shortly after this meeting, Carey heard from Weldon Caie, national secretary-treasurer of the Electrical and Radio Workers Union, the new organization of the independents, that the goal of the new organization was the amalgamation of all federal unions in the radio field into one industrial union.[58] There was no direct mention of merger with Caie's group, but this had been looked upon as the ideal solution by both groups for several years. Carey invited the Electrical and Radio Workers to send observers to the federal group's Atlantic City meeting. The AFL had also learned of the projected conference, and William Green directed Lewis Hines to attend and keep an eye on the proceedings.[59] By this time Green must have been aware of the danger. The presence of the independents raised the specter of one large industrial union in electrical manufacturing outside of the confines of the house of labor. To Green, already plagued by the CIO, this must have been anything but a pleasant thought.

Thus the stage was set for the drama to be played out in the convention hall on the boardwalk. The pressures of the AFL from the electrical unions were duplicated throughout the country in the other mass production industries—rubber, auto, and steel. The sentiment for industrial unionism had found its spokesmen in the members of the Committee for Industrial Organization (CIO) which, with John L. Lewis of the United Mine Workers as its leader, had brought the old federation close to schism. The Committee vowed to bring the issue of industrial unionism to the floor of the convention, and 30,000 electrical industry workers, both in the federal and independent groups, waited for the convention to render a verdict.[60]

The 1935 AFL convention proved to be one of the most decisive ever held by that body. A dramatic confrontation between industrial and craft unionism took place. The delegates witnessed the spectacle of burly John L. Lewis of the Miners, who was emerging as the charismatic leader of the "progressive forces" within the federation; and the even burlier defender of craft unionism, William "Big Bill" Hutcheson of the Carpenters, come to blows in full view of the assembled throng. The fracas proved to be symbolic of the irreparable split that was fast developing within the AFL.

When the resolution calling for a national charter for the electrical workers was introduced, the possibility of thrashing the issue out on the convention floor proved distasteful to the AFL leadership.[61] John P. Frey and Matthew Woll, secretary and chairman, respectively, of the resolutions committee, made sure that the resolution never reached the floor. The Committee referred it to the Executive Council for action.[62] This move killed the chances for an industrial charter. The Executive Council apparently decided that the time had come to stop allowing the federal locals and the independents to continue organizing along industrial lines lest the movement get out of hand. If there ever was a chance of bringing these groups into an AFL craft union, the leadership of the federation must certainly have sensed that it was rapidly slipping away.

One important product of the 1935 convention was a working relationship between Carey and Lewis. The young leader of the electrical workers attended the meetings of the CIO held in the President Hotel while the 1935 convention was in session.[63] It must have been an exhilarating experience for so young a labor leader to be so close to Lewis, Hillman, and others who were in the process of changing the face of the American labor movement. From this point on the federal locals watched the CIO and waited.

A significant event took place in Atlantic City during the week prior to the AFL convention. The National Radio and Allied Trades had convened at the Chelsea Hotel to decide their strategy. Meeting with them were the invited representatives of the left-wing Electrical and Radio Workers.

The issue of merger between the NR & AT and the independents raised a great deal of animosity at the meetings. Lewis Hines, the AFL's representative, argued vehemently against any merger. He brought up the anti-AFL attitudes of some of the independents, and warned the federal locals that they would be swallowed up by the much larger independent organization. His main objection, however, and the one on which he placed the most emphasis was that some leaders of the independent group were Communists. He called them members of a world-wide movement for the overthrow of patriotism, and while he admitted that the entire group was not tinged with red, there were "active communistic spirits" behind it.[64]

Carey responded with words he would later regret: "Mr. Hines, has said that some of the men who came here representing the independent group . . . were Communists. I know and care nothing about this; we too have been called radicals and Communists and declared to have no place in the labor movement. We have been accused of being radical outsiders."[65] At the time, Carey rejected red-baiting as a bogus and divisive tactic. In the halcyon days of the 1930s, during the organization of America's mass production industries, all were welcome and a man's politics mattered little. Nevertheless, wanting to do nothing to jeopardize the opportunity for the charter at the upcoming AFL convention, the two groups ended talk of merger but agreed to continue to cooperate.

Disappointed with the results of the convention, Carey still clung to the hope of acquiring an industrial charter within the AFL. While at Atlantic City he spoke at length with John Brophy, CIO Director of Organization, and Lewis. They impressed upon him that the CIO was still an educational committee within the Federation rather than a dual movement.[66] He was advised to wait and he did. It was, however, becoming more and more difficult to hold to his course because of the pressures for independent action from his federal locals and the pressure for merger from the independents.

On December 9, 1935, Carey received another blow. The government called for joint conference of representatives of industry and labor concerning unemployment in Washington. Labor's representatives met prior to the conference and elected John P. Frey of the Metal Trades Department to represent the manufacturing and fabricating group. The radio workers fell into this classification. Carey demanded a delegate to represent the mass production industries. Outvoted and slighted, Carey and his supporters turned the meeting into a bickering session.[67] Aside from the organizational question of representation, the incident pointed up a side of James Carey's character that became increasingly evident as his power in the labor movement increased. Carey was a man who enjoyed the warm glow of the spotlight.

The question of amalgamation with the independents continued to occupy the minds of the leaders of the federal group. Torn between their hope for a change of heart by the AFL and their desire for one big union in electrical manufacturing, they continued to hold off the independents who were urging a merged union and a joint organizing drive in electrical and radio. Green's man, Lewis Hines, persistently warned against any collaboration. Block and Carey, however, were tiring of the AFL's stalling tactics. Since 1934, the AFL Executive Council had been saying that no charter could be considered unless the federal group stayed aloof from the independents. They had acceded to no avail. Now, said Carey, the National Radio and Allied Trades would cooperate with the independents no matter what the AFL said.[68]

With the concurrence of the delegates at the December conference of the NR & AT at Pittsburgh, Carey wired William Green requesting firm information as to whether the question of an industrial charter for the federal group would finally be discussed at the January Executive Council meeting.[69] Green agreed that it would.[70] After roaring their approval while Philip Murray of the United Mine Workers and John Brophy of the CIO castigated the AFL craft unions, the delegates also unanimously decided to form an independent national organization if the AFL refused to grant the charter. They also decided that another meeting would be held two weeks after the AFL Executive Council meeting to take action on that group's decision.[71]

Green directed James Carey to plead the case of the electrical workers before the council in Miami. Carey had little hope for success. Indeed, he fully expected the vote to be 15 to 2 against the issuance of the industrial charter with only John Lewis and David Dubinsky supporting the request. He was wrong. Only Lewis voted for the charter.[72] Dubinsky had already begun his trek back to the good graces of the AFL. In a terse wire, Green informed Carey that "the Executive Council decided that best interests of radio workers, including those you represent, would be served through . . . affiliation with IBEW."[73]

The decision was fully expected. Yet, although it is hard to believe that the craft unions thought that the radio workers would docilely accept the mandate, it appears as if they did. Arthur Wharton of the Machinists, for example, had his eyes on the electrical independents.[74] He apparently assumed that the NR & AT would accept the IBEW proposal, and that the independents, cut off from any hope of merging with an industrial union within the AFL, would then be absorbed into one of the other craft unions. Wharton intended it to be the Machinists.

Immediately following the Executive Council's decision, Green asked Carey to meet with President Daniel Tracy of the International Brotherhood of Electrical Workers to discuss merger terms. Carey agreed, but asked Green if the federal locals could maintain their present status if they rejected the IBEW proposal.[75]

Carey knew that there was no hope for merger with the craft union. The IBEW offered the NR & AT class B membership. The radio group was to have no special department in the IBEW, nor could they participate in the benefit program. Each industrial local was to have one vote as opposed to one vote per member in the craft locals.[76] When the NR & AT met in Washington in February to discuss the proposal, the mood of the meeting was hostile. IBEW president Tracy appeared at Carey's invitation, but after long, often acrimonious discussion, the proposal failed by a large vote.[77]

Carey, in the meantime, had received an ambiguous telegram from Green in response to his inquiry concerning the status of the federal locals should the meeting turn down the IBEW proposal. Green wrote that the federal locals would exist until they were transferred to the IBEW.[78] He was apparently prepared to disregard the decision of the federal locals in the matter and simply assign them to the IBEW. His lack of understanding of the temper of the NR & AT members was striking.

With Green's ultimatum in hand, the NR & AT met in Washington and took several significant actions. One more attempt at an industrial charter in the AFL would be made. In the likely event of failure, plans were drawn up for the establishment of a new national industrial union.[79] John Brophy and Katherine Pollock, both CIO officials, observed the proceedings.

After the Washington meeting, Green's agent, Lewis Hines, notified Carey that the federal charters would be lifted and the group expelled by the AFL.[80] He made it clear that the Executive Council had spoken its last word on the matter.

With this warning from Hines, Carey and representatives of the independent Electrical and Radio Workers lost no time in arranging for a joint convention of the two groups. A committee of four federal delegates and four independents met at Buffalo on February 22 and 23, and projected plans for the creation of one industrial union with jurisdiction in the electrical manufacturing industry. They sent out a call for a founding convention in Buffalo.[81]

An exhilarated group of 50 delegates assembled in Buffalo on

March 21 to form a new industrial union, the United Electrical and Radio Workers of America (UE).[82] Still reluctant to believe that they were permanently outside the house of labor, the delegates announced as one of their purposes the application for a national charter within the AFL. They did this knowing they had the full support of the CIO.[83] John Brophy's telegram to the convention branded the AFL action as "arbitrary," and the convention urged the Committee for Industrial Organization to give them assistance and support.[84]

As one of its final acts, the convention, according to a pre-arranged deal, elected James Carey President, and Julius Emspak, a young and virtually unknown independent from Schenectady General Electric, Secretary-Treasurer. The two men had youth in common. In 1937, James Carey was 26 years old, and Emspak only 33. Carey, born in Philadelphia in 1911, had little direct trade union influence while he was growing up. His parents were staunch liberal Democrats and Catholics. His first exposure to organized labor came as a teenager when he participated in a strike of movie projectionists in a New Jersey theater where Carey worked part-time as a projectionist's helper. He attended night school at Drexel and the University of Pennsylvania, but his true education in trade unionism came largely from two sources, an upbringing in an atmosphere of liberal Catholic social thought compatible with the papal encyclicals on labor, *Rerum Novarum and Quadregisimo Anno,* and advice from socialist, and strongly anticommunist, hosiery workers in Philadelphia who gave him counsel during his days as a young labor leader at Philco. His career in the labor movement began with the group at Philco which formed the first radio local in 1933. From there he went on the staff of the AFL and kept that post until the formation of the UE in March 1936.[85] He went from obscurity to being the "boy wonder" of the labor movement in three years. It was an auspicious debut, and Carey was in time to become fond of the spotlight, a trait that would prove to be his Achilles heel.[86]

In contrast, Julius Emspak preferred to work behind the scenes. Carey later claimed that Emspak's election marked the beginning of Communist influence in the union. Although he never admitted to party membership, over the years Emspak was repeatedly branded as a Communist. The obscure young man from Schenectady lived to see the day when he was labeled as one of the most influential American members of an international Communist conspiracy.

Like Carey, Emspak's background fit the profile of the educated, progressive young workers whom the Depression had directed into the shops where they used their education to help organize the mass production industries. He was born in Schenectady in 1904, of Hungarian immigrant parents. His father, a General Electric worker, was a socialist, although his death in a railroad accident when Julius was only nine limited any political influence he might have had. After his father's death his mother worked for General Electric as a cleaning woman and his two older brothers left school at fourteen to go into the plant. The family, although nominally Catholic, had a tradition of radicalism and anti-clericalism. Emspak too began work at the age of fourteen in the shop at General Electric, but he returned to high school after finishing his apprenticeship in tool and die making. With help from a loan fund created by Gerald Swope, GE president, he graduated Phi Beta Kappa from Union College and began graduate study at Brown University. After one year at Brown, Emspak left to look for a job. Disillusioned by the seeming irrelevancy of his graduate studies and hard pressed for funds, he first tried for work on a newspaper, but the Depression closed off that avenue. Desperate and in debt, he took a job in the shop at RCA in Camden, New Jersey, where he took part in a major strike. Six months later when he returned to Schenectady to work for General Electric, interest in the labor movement precluded his taking a white collar job when offered one by the company. He chose, instead, to return to the factory where he became an activist in the local and, according to later testimony by a close friend of those days, a Communist. He had also developed, by this time, along with so many others during those Depression years, into what James Matles later called a true "worker intellectual."[87]

In the Schenectady plant, Emspak became the protege of William Turnbull, president of the Schenectady local and later president of the Electrical and Radio Workers. Turnbull, a dedicated union organizer, was also a socialist.[88] He gave Emspak his first practical trade union education. When the time came to choose a secretary-treasurer for the newly formed United Electrical Workers (UE), the likely choice among the independents was Albert Coulthard from Lynn, Massachusetts, who had long experience in the labor movement and who had been the driving force in the organization of the local at Lynn General Electric. Coulthard, however, refused the office because of a reluctance to leave his home local and move to New York.[89] Instead, he, along with Turnbull, the most respected and powerful independents, supported young Julius Emspak. Coulthard pushed hard for the appointment because he believed that Emspak's education uniquely fitted him for the complex job of secretary-treasurer.[90]

Before the caucus of the independents at the founding convention settled on Emspak, a delegate from Lynn asked him directly whether he was a Communist. Emspak replied that he was not and never had been.[91]

And so two of the nation's youngest labor leaders set out to lead what was to become the third largest affiliate of the Congress of Industrial Organizations. Both bachelors at the time, they immediately made plans to establish the national office in a rented room at 1133 Broadway in New York City. With $99 from the union's meager treasury, they furnished the office with clothes racks, chairs, and roll top desks.[92] The two young men shared a room and, in between trips exploring New York, they began to run the UE. The first organizer hired, at a salary of $10 a week, was Ernest DeMaio, a young radical who had been active in the unemployed councils movement of the 1930s and who had gained his union experience as an organizer for the TUUL's Machine, Tool, and Foundry Workers.[93]

Carey's first official act as president was to send a letter to William Green informing him of the convention's instructions to persist in seeking an AFL charter.[94] Green replied, telling Carey, whom he pointedly refused to acknowledge as president of anything, that since his local had been expelled from the Federation for dual unionism and lack of payment of the per capita tax, there could be no further discussions with the AFL.[95] The UE was on its own.

2

BUILDING THE UNION IN THE CIO

There are no reliable figures on the UE's membership for the earliest period. Carey claimed 30,000 members when he appeared before the AFL Executive Council in January 1936.[1] When the UE joined the CIO in November 1936, it was credited with having 33,000 members.[2]

As the infant union turned its attention from the struggle for an AFL charter to the problems of growth and survival, its leaders realized that the first order of business had to be the organization of the huge corporations in the radio and electrical industry. In electrical manufacturing this meant General Electric and Westinghouse; in radio, the Radio Company of America.

Philco had already been organized. In order to protect their contract with that company, the UE leaders realized that RCA would have to be cracked. An independent union had organized RCA's Camden, New Jersey, plant in 1933, with the aid of the Philco federal local. In order to counter the new local, the company created a company union. The two groups remained relatively equal until the spring of 1936 when the independent group affiliated with the UE as Local 103. On May 20, the union requested a signed agreement. Company refusal led to a walkout on June 23, 1936.[3] The new union was about to be tested on the picket lines.

The spectacular strike lasted four weeks. It involved injunctions, the courts, the governor, the arrest of Carey and other UE officials, and violence. The phrase "Jersey Justice" became a byword in the labor movement. As the struggle at Camden held the attention of the press, John L. Lewis quietly negotiated with the company in New York. On July 21, an agreement was reached.[4]

33

According to Julius Emspak, the strike truly established the union in the eyes of the industry.[5] While the final settlement did not take place until October 1936, the July agreement marked an auspicious debut for the young organization. Not only had it met and bested one of the nation's largest companies, but it had done so under the most difficult circumstances. It had been bloodied, but it had won. The first crucial hurdle for any union had been crossed.

Progress during 1936 continued at a steady but unspectacular pace. Membership had increased by approximately 40 percent between April and September.[6] The first five months also produced three strikes and two lockouts.[7] By July, cash on hand amounted to only $3,226. This was hardly impressive for an organization that was feared by some of the industrial giants of America.[8]

The UE met in its first regular convention in September 1936. The group that gathered in Fort Wayne came full of hope for the future and proud of its accomplishments. It was an overwhelmingly young assemblage which heard Adolph Germer, CIO representative, liken industrial unionism to the class struggle.[9] The convention unanimously endorsed Labor's Non-Partisan League and the re-election of Franklin Roosevelt. A strongly worded resolution supported the Spanish Republicans and pledged financial aid to their cause.[10] While the convention was in session the AFL suspended the CIO unions from the Federation. Upon hearing the news, the UE convention passed a resolution directing its officers to apply for affiliation with the CIO.[11] The two organizations had worked together since the 1935 AFL convention in Atlantic City. During the RCA strike, CIO representative Powers Hapgood helped to direct the walkout, and John L. Lewis took the major responsibility for negotiating with the company.

The UE's officers met with the CIO's leaders in Pittsburgh during the first week in November 1936. Even though the CIO unions had been suspended by the Federation, they were not yet expelled. Their decision as to what to do with the UE's application was a crucial one for the trade union movement. Acceptance would lead inevitably to the charge of dual unionism and would indicate the desire of the CIO to establish itself as an independent and rival labor body. Lewis unhesitatingly signaled his desire to go it alone by accepting the UE and the Shipyard Workers as the first new affiliates of the CIO.[12]

CIO affiliation seemed to bring good luck to the new union. In December, after a sit-down strike, the UE won an unexpected NLRB election victory at the Schenectady plant of General Electric. More than 95 percent of the eligible workers cast their ballots, giving the UE more than a 1,000-thousand vote majority over the company union.[13] The election established the UE as the sole collective bargaining agent for the Schenectady employees. The company union quickly disbanded. This was especially important because the General Electric Workers Council had been one of the strongest of the nation's company unions.

A month after that victory, the delegates of seven General Electric locals met to work out a comprehensive, long-range labor policy that they hoped would be adopted for all the company's plants. UE had not had great success signing up members after the labor board elections, and the numbers declined even more when layoffs followed the slide in the economy in 1937. Thus, although UE had informal bargaining rights at the big GE plants in Schenectady and Lynn, and a presence in five others, most of the company's facilities remained effectively unorganized. In order to overcome this problem, the conference decided to push for national contracts.[14] The strategy produced definite results. By March 8, 1937, General Electric announced its willingness to bargain collectively on a national basis with UE, and workers in a number of plants began to organize as a result of the announcement. The UE chartered 29 new General Electric locals almost overnight.[15] While recognition came rather easily, it required over a year to negotiate an agreement with the company. On March 15, the first meeting took place between the union's negotiating committee and the company representatives. The union understood its weakness. James Matles told the union's GE Conference Board that "the issue here is that we have to be able to organize, to complete the organization of this company. We're nowhere, not even in the middle yet, we need a contract, that's what we need to establish the union as a recognized agent. . . . "[16]

In a surprise move, the company offered a contract based on the existing General Electric employees handbook, GEQ-105A. The booklet had resulted from the electrical industry NIRA code, which specified minimum employment standards for the industry. The UE's national officers, eager to get a contract, however minimal, urged the GE Conference Board locals to accept. But they rejected the offer, hoping to do better.

The officers had been correct; no appreciably better offer came and nearly a year later, chastened, the conference board agreed to sign. This was an early example of the independence of the locals that marked the UE throughout its history. During the additional year of bargaining, the UE managed to add a grievance procedure and, of utmost importance, the agreement included a provision that the contract would automatically cover all plants at which the UE won bargaining rights in the future.[17] GE chairman Swope thought it a "novel idea," and the agreement took effect on April Fools' Day, 1938.[18] Although the agreement was largely procedural and included no real wage concessions, it did provide the mechanism for a national contract and companywide bargaining. Given the depressed economy in 1938, with 60,000 UE members unemployed, the agreement was a considerable victory. Had the company been in a combative mood, it might have broken the union.

Seeds of the later discord among the general officers were sown during the first General Electric talks. At the beginning of the negotiations, Carey called a press conference to announce what had transpired in the closed sessions. The young president told the press that GE was about to crack. The breach of confidentiality shocked both union and company negotiators and disrupted the negotiations.[19] The union's General Electric Conference Board voted to bar Carey from the General Electric negotiations and from meetings of the conference board.[20] Albert Fitzgerald, later the UE's president but then a conference board member, claimed that Carey's style of "popping off" angered the delegates.[21] Matles speculated that Carey wanted to compete for headlines with negotiations then in progress in the steel and auto industries, in particular with John L. Lewis's public statements in those disputes.[22] Carey's behavior had risked offending Albert Coulthard, a powerful union pioneer from Lynn, and William Turnbull, his counterpart from Schenectady. The young general officers still held these "founding fathers" in awe and their disfavor could be disastrous.[23]

On June 9, the National Labor Relations Board supervised an election at the Bridgeport, Connecticut, plant of General Electric. The eight-month-old local received a sizeable majority and the UE's share of General Electric jumped to six plants. Later events were to show that the UE had won a local that would be a perennial thorn in its side.

Meanwhile, a group of young Communists and other militants were making significant gains in St. Louis with little or no help from the UE national organization. There, the grassroots nature of the left-wing presence in the creation of the UE was also evident. William Sentner, a young Marxist, had become a trade union militant as a result of the upsurge of organizing that followed the passage of the National Industrial Recovery Act. Sentner came by his radicalism naturally. His father, a Russian Jewish immigrant cloakmaker, had helped to organize the ILGWU in St. Louis as far back as 1909. Sentner remembered breaking windows in strikes "for two bits apiece" when he was a child. Following the American immigrant pattern of upward mobility through education, Sentner tried a university course in architecture, but soon found that Marxism interested him more. Two years on the road and four years as a merchant seaman reinforced his radicalism and concern for the working class. Back in St. Louis, he joined the John Reed Club of the Communist Party in 1934 and along with other members of the small St. Louis branch of the Communist Trade Union Unity League took the lead in a number of organizing drives. One such struggle involved several thousand black women in St. Louis's nutshelling shops, and Sentner, in his role as a TUUL organizer, played a major role and gained valuable experience for the CIO drive that followed. While on the payroll as an organizer for the Steel Workers' Organizing Committee, Sentner, at the request of Young Communist League members who worked at Emerson Electric, became the guiding force behind the organization of the UE in that plant. By March 1937, after repeated requests from the workers, Sentner went on the UE payroll and under his leadership the pro-UE workers captured the company union and carried out a successful sit-down strike.[24] The Emerson strike lasted 53 days, the second longest sit-down in American history, and launched the CIO drive in St. Louis. By the end, there were 6,000 UE members in St. Louis, and by the fall of 1937, the number in District 8 had soared to 16,500. To one Emerson worker who had tried and failed to organize a union before, Sentner and the Communist Party were "the light at the end of the tunnel, come to show you the way out."[25]

Sentner and the other Communist militants in St. Louis were unlike most of the other party members in the union in that they openly declared their party membership from the beginning. Not surprisingly, the anticommunist campaign in District 8 began earlier than in other districts. At Emerson, for example, anti-Communist workers organized in 1937 to drive party members out of leadership positions. To head off the argument that the presence of Communists in leadership positions would hurt relations with the company, Sentner asked that the President of District 8 be elected by referendum in each local, instead of at the district convention. Using this method, the UE members in District 8 directly elected Sentner to the presidency from 1937 until his resignation in 1948.[26]

Westinghouse remained the glaring omission in national organizing. The company had no intention of signing any agreements with the union. The East Pittsburgh plant and five smaller Pittsburgh area plants constituted the hub of the giant Westinghouse system. Early attempts at unionization reached back to the early 1900s, but all had failed until the advent of an independent local in 1935. Using the tactic of boring from within, the local captured the company union and petitioned for an NLRB election in April 1937. The campaign for members proved to be outstandingly successful, and the NLRB certified the UE as the sole collective bargaining agency for the 11,800 employees at East Pittsburgh without an election. The 7,200 employees who had signed UE cards more than satisfied the requirements for certification.[27]

Even though it had won a decisive victory, UE faced four long years of negotiations before Westinghouse agreed to sign a written contract. The company contended that collective bargaining was simply an opportunity for representatives of the employees to raise and discuss problems affecting the working force, with the final decision reserved to the company. It rejected the notion of a signed agreement as "not in the best interest of all concerned."[28] The union vigorously argued the point but took no action. By the fall of 1937, business conditions were again on the decline and the workforce began to shrink. The Union had missed its opportunity. Perhaps this cautious attitude can be attributed to the fact that the average age of Local 601 negotiators was over 40, and the average term of service of employees in the East Pittsburgh plant came to 17 years.[29] It was the oldest of the UE groups and the most settled. In addition, the fact that few other Westinghouse shops were organized made a strike a very risky venture.

By the time of the UE's General Executive Board meeting in New York in June 1937, the union's membership had reached 75,000, five times the previous year's total. In May 1937, alone, 11,000 new members came in. The members belonged to some 220 locals, 170 of which had been charted during the preceding three-month period.[30]

The General Executive Board meeting in June 1937 indicated the ambiguous ideological stance of the leadership. The Board urged participation in the left-wing American Youth Congress if it did not entail too much expense. The decision was unanimous. Carey, in fact, would later rise to be vice-chairman of the organization. Curiously, on the other hand, a request from the Friends of the Abraham Lincoln Brigade to Carey asking for use of his name as a supporter and for a contribution from the UE was tabled because the Board felt it too controversial.[31]

The 1937 UE convention that convened in Philadelphia heard Carey denounce AFL leaders as "palsied traitors" to the cause of labor.[32] If the AFL was palsied, membership figures showed that the UE was not. Julius Emspak informed the delegates that the convention marked a high point in the union's success. Seventy thousand and seventy-three dues paying members were on the rolls.[33]

Generally the 1937 convention proved to be a harmonious gathering, but there were already undercurrents of the left-right split which was to plague the organization. It must have rankled some of the conservative delegates when Carey announced that William Higley, Chairman of the Communist-front American Youth Congress, would speak to the delegates on a matter "of great importance to the welfare of organized labor." Higley praised Carey for taking one of the leading roles in building the Youth Congress in his position as vice-chairman.[34] When a resolution came up urging the UE to affiliate with the Congress, Matt Campbell asked Carey to explain what the organization was. Carey replied that he had attended its convention, the General Executive Board had investigated the organization, and its affiliates included both the boy and girl scouts. The convention adopted the resolution.[35]

A slightly deeper rift occurred on the resolution calling for the UE to endorse the Communist-front American League Against War and Fascism. Again Campbell opposed the resolution, although he declined to elaborate on his objections. Leo Jandreau from Local 301 in Schenectady led the fight for the resolution, pointing out that the United Mine Workers had endorsed the League. Nevertheless Carey's own Local 101, as well as several others, remained opposed. The brief flare-up ended when the sponsors permitted the issue to be referred to the General Executive Board.[36] In other business the delegates re-elected Emspak and Carey. Campbell nominated Carey for re-election "with all his faults," perhaps a reference to the young president's difficulties in negotiations with both General Electric and Westinghouse.[37]

The convention also witnessed the formal alliance between the UE and James Matles's group of machinists which had defected from the AFL and entered the union in June. In accordance with the decision of the General Executive Board, Matles became the occupant of the newly created post of Director of Organization.[38] Matles had originally taken his Machine, Tool and Foundry Workers into the International Association of Machinists (IAM) in March 1935, the same month that UE was formed.[39] That move followed directly on the decision of the Comintern in December 1934, to order the independent TUUL unions into the AFL. By 1935 Matles's Machine, Tool, and Foundry Workers, the Fur Workers led by Mike Gold, and the fledgling Transport Workers Union, were the only viable organizations left in the TUUL. The League dissolved the same month that Matles took his machinists into the IAM.[40] Matles demonstrated his central role in the TUUL not only by taking his machinists into the IAM, but by negotiating the merger of the TWU with the Machinists as well.[41]

Matles claimed that by merging his union with the Machinists, he would ease the chances of an industrial charter in the AFL for the electrical and radio workers. He agreed that the jurisdictional argument could be made for an independent union in the electrical manufacturing industry, but that a separate charter for his machinists could never be had in the AFL.[42]

While he had no idea that the AFL would expel the CIO unions, he believed that the AFL could not long deny industrial unionism in the mass production industries. The strategy at the time, in line with the Communist Party line of boring from within, was to merge with the IAM with the stipulation that new shops would be organized along industrial lines and to convert the IAM into an industrial union.[43]

But it is more likely that Communist Party confusion at the time of the dissolution of the TUUL played a greater role than Matles's prescience. The sudden surge of independent unions that followed the passage of the NIRA had caught the party flatfooted. By the end of 1933 the independents enrolled far more members than the TUUL. This led to a short-lived policy of merging the TUUL with the independents to create a new independent federation of labor.[44] During this period Matles began his discussion with the independent locals in electrical manufacturing and the radio locals.

No sooner had Matles successfully arranged the merger of his Machine, Tool, and Foundry workers with the AFL's machinists, than the AFL expelled the CIO unions in August 1936. This left Matles and his machinists even farther from the industrial union movement. Given these events, Matles must have wanted out of the merger with the Machinists almost as soon as he got in. His short stay with the IAM proved to be rocky. He and his group locked horns with the IAM at the 1936 convention when they challenged the craft union's secret initiation ritual which barred blacks from membership. The heated discussion almost turned the closed-door session into a brawl.[45]

Shortly after the convention, IAM president Wharton asked Matles to go to Philadelphia and meet with two industry representatives. John P. Frey, head of the AFL's Metal Trades Department, had arranged the meeting. The two businessmen turned out to be the president of Baldwin Locomotive Company and his counterpart from General Steel Casting. They told Matles that they had discussed the matter with Frey and had come to the conclusion that, in the face of an organizing drive by the CIO's Steel Workers Organizing Committee, they would be better off organized by an AFL union and that they were willing to cooperate in any way.[46]

Matles reported his repulsion at the idea to Wharton who wrote him a fatherly reply about the ultimate impossibility of industrial unionism.[47] Disgusted with the IAM and anxious to get into the CIO and the industrial union drive, Matles notified John L. Lewis of his Philadelphia meeting and then called the leadership of his locals together to take stock.

While these preliminary talks were in progress, Matles received a letter from Wharton stating that since the Supreme Court had upheld the Wagner Act, employers had expressed a preference to deal with the AFL rather than "Lewis, Hillman, Dubinsky, Howard and their gang of sluggers, Communists, radicals and soapbox artists, professional bums, expelled members of labor unions, outright scabs and the Jewish organizations with all their red affiliates."

"We have conferred," continued Wharton, "with several such employers and arranged for conferences later when we get the plants organized."[48] Under these circumstances, there was no hesitation when Matles received the word from the Communist Party to leave the IAM and join the newly-formed UE.[49]

Matles claimed that he took 14 IAM lodges and approximately 15,000 members with him when he pulled out. While those numbers are probably inflated, his old group of machine, tool and foundry workers came with him without a defection as did the new shops he had organized along industrial lines while in the IAM.[50]

In September 1937, 6,000 more machinists in three big IAM locals in electrical and machine plants in Minneapolis voted to apply for UE charters.[51] While not TUUL locals, the three locals were led by Communists and their decision to pull out of the IAM and enter the UE resulted from the same change of direction by Communist Party officials that had brought Matles into the UE. As the three largest local unions in Minnesota, they gave the left-wing control of the CIO Council in Minnesota until after the War.[52]

James Matles, who had come to the United States as a young man from Romania in 1929, and who learned his trade as an organizer in the machine shops for the Communist-led Trade Union Unity League, had joined with Carey and Emspak to complete the troika that would lead the union in its infancy.

The early years were trying ones. In late 1937 and 1938, the inventory depression hit the country, creating a difficult period for the union. In September 1938, the General Officers wrote that the UE had held its own in the face of adverse economic conditions. Sales in the industry were off some 35 percent.[53] With an estimated 60,000 members unemployed, the union could do little but hold on and maintain the organization.

The victory of the GE settlement in 1938 was offset by two strikes—one of which occurred in an unlikely place. Philco had always been considered as the ideal when UE discussed company relations. Nevertheless in early 1938, with the work force reduced by three-quarters, the company served notice that its workers would have to take a wage cut and return to the 40-hour week if the company were to remain competitive. The union refused and walked out on May 1.[54] The bitter strike that followed lasted four months and ended with the UE conceding most of the company's demands, but the union shop was salvaged. While hardly a victory, the young union had held on in the face of determined opposition from a major company during a period of severely adverse economic conditions.[55]

Another challenge in 1938 occurred at the Maytag plant in Newton, Iowa. There all of the forces of the company and the community were arrayed against the union. James Carey and District 8 president William Sentner were arrested on charges of criminal syndicalism and sedition. The charge of "bolshevism" was hurled against the union. Isolated from the mainstream of union activity, the workers gave in to the pressure from state, local, and company authorities.[56]

These two strikes, coupled with the decision of the CIO to establish a Utility Workers Organizing Committee, to which all UE locals in the utility field were transferred, had a chastening effect on the national convention in St. Louis in September 1938. The UE's strength had declined slightly. The officers put the best face on a bad situation by characterizing these serious losses as a "moving forward," considering conditions.[57] In reality, the situation was precarious. General Electric remained less than 50 percent organized as did Westinghouse, where no written contract had been won. The General Motors Electrical Division, the last of the "big three," remained almost entirely unorganized.[58]

Following the 1938 convention, a sequence of events took place which in time would contribute to Carey's downfall as President of the UE. According to Julius Emspak, he, Matles and Carey were returning home from the St. Louis convention when they decided that the success and importance of the UE entitled it to a spot among the CIO's officers. They decided to ask Lewis for the Secretary-Treasurer's spot for Carey.[59] Carey, on the other hand, claimed that he went to the 1938 CIO convention supporting John Brophy for the spot, and that only during the convention, at the request of John L. Lewis, did he agree to take the post.[60] Brophy supported the Carey version.[61] Whatever the case, Carey, strongly backed by Lewis, was chosen Secretary-Treasurer. Lewis's biographers saw Carey's selection as logical. Carey represented the new unionists from the mass-production industries. He was young, not identified with the left wing, and not from one of the nine original CIO unions. One observer believed that Lewis had picked Carey because he recognized him as a potential foil to the Communists.[62] Interestingly, even at this early stage, left-wing leaders like Reid Robinson of the Mine, Mill and Smelter Workers and Harry Bridges of the International Longshore Workers Union opposed him.[63]

Challenges continued in 1939. President Dan Tracy of IBEW, angered by a crushing defeat at the hands of UE in the RCA Camden NLRB election, used the report of the House Committee on Un-American Activities to charge the UE with being "nothing more nor less than a branch of the secret service of Joseph Stalin, Russian dictator. . . . One of the Communist fronts signified to the Congress of the United States as deeply tinged with Communism is the United Radio and Electrical Workers Union, so called," Tracy went on. "This puppet of the Communists executive board is but a branch of the so-called Communist Party. . . . "[64] The report to Congress alluded to by Tracy was the Dies Committee report, which listed the UE as having doubtful loyalty to the United States.

During this period, critics of the UE included James Carey among the Communist leaders of the union. This included the FBI, which, as late as September of 1941, suspected that Carey was a Communist Party member or at the very least a sympathizer.[65] Much of the suspicion came from Carey's activities with various Communist-front organizations. Carey played high-profile roles in the American Youth Congress and the American League Against War and Fascism, and lent his name to several others from time to time. The FBI's most damning information came from an informer prominent in the CIO in Washington State who reported that Harold Pritchett, a Communist official of the Timber Workers Union, claimed that he and Carey met with members of the central committee of the Communist Party of the United States and received instructions from them on the Party's trade union program.[66]

At this time, Julius Emspak estimated that one Communist party member sat on the General Executive Board of the UE and five or six party members were organizers in the field.[67] Emspak might technically have been correct, if open party membership was the criterion. William Sentner, president of District 8, who along with Carey had been arrested on charges of criminal syndicalism during the Maytag strike, had always openly proclaimed his party membership.[68] But if adherence to Communist Party policy was the criterion, Emspak's numbers are certainly misleading. Emspak and Matles themselves probably belong in this group. It is straining credibility to think that someone as influential in the old TUUL as Matles had been was not, in the party's argot, a "submarine."

Board member James MacLeish, president of District 4, also fell into this category, as did Ernest DeMaio, president of District 8. The number of open Communists on the staff, such as David Davis, business agent for Local 155 in Philadelphia, Nat Cohen, executive board member of local 475, and James Lustig, was also small. Far more numerous were the loyalists who lived in political limbo and did not participate in party matters except on a semiclandestine level, but openly supported the line.[69]

By 1938 and 1939, that line was strongly anti-fascist. At its 1938 convention, several resolutions condemning Hitler were considered and an anti-fascist peace resolution passed overwhelmingly.[70] This put UE in step with the garment unions and the other left-wing unions in the CIO, but not with John L. Lewis who remained isolationist during this period.

Throughout 1939, the *UE News* took a strong anti-Nazi stand. Roosevelt's condemnation of the rape of Czechoslovakia received warm support from the paper.[71] "Appeasers" were blasted and Hitler's step-by-step conquest of Europe received copious and hostile treatment.[72] Tentative resolutions for the 1939 convention called for ending the Neutrality Act because it favored the Nazis.[73]

But when the delegates gathered in Springfield, Massachusetts, in September 1939 for the union's fifth annual convention, the international situation had changed drastically. Russia and Germany had signed a nonaggression pact on August 23, clearing the way for the German-Soviet partition of Poland and the Soviet occupation of the Baltic states. Confusion reigned among American Communists as among Communists everywhere outside of the Soviet Union. As late as September 11, Earl Browder and William Z. Foster sent a letter to Roosevelt pledging their support for his preparedness campaign. Yet that same day Communist Party chairman Browder signaled the change in direction in a Madison Square

Garden speech. On September 19, *The Daily Worker* announced the new position of the Political Committee of the Communist Party under the headline, "Keep America Out of the Imperialist War."[74]

With the shift, the Communists returned to the rhetoric of the pre-Popular Front period, calling for neutrality in the "imperialist" conflict between the western democracies and Hitler, blasting Roosevelt, and ridiculing the values of "bourgeois democracy." The about-face meant the scuttling of the Popular Front. Many liberals and radicals who couldn't swallow the requirement that continued cooperation with the Communists required a break with the New Deal and support for Stalin's new foreign policy broke with the party.[75]

Shifting the line from the Popular Front to neutrality in a mass organization like the UE took some time. The 1939 convention was in session as the tumultuous debates were taking place in the politburo of the American Communist Party. The news caused confusion at the convention. *UE News* used the tortured reasoning that the treaty would somehow strengthen the resistance of the rest of Europe to Hitler.[76] Nevertheless, the delegates strongly endorsed the re-election of Franklin Roosevelt and passed a decidedly anti-Nazi resolution calling for the amendment of neutrality legislation to permit all nations of the world to purchase arms on a cash-and-carry basis.[77]

The UE's official position shifted four days after the public announcement in *The Daily Worker*. On September 23, 1939, the first sign came in a *UE News* editorial that criticized "Wall Street's" attempt to lead the nation into war for excessive profits.[78] On September 30th, the paper strongly came out for neutrality, blaming the war on big business and protesting the use of the working man as "cannon fodder."[79] Both Carey and Emspak spoke out strongly against United States involvement during this period.[80] The flip-flop did not put UE or the other left-wing CIO unions out of step with the mainstream of the still basically isolationist labor movement. In their Labor Day messages that year, barely a week after the signing of the Pact, John L. Lewis and William Green called for America to stay out of the European war.[81] With the signing of the nonaggression pact, John L. Lewis was returned to his pedestal as a hero of the left wing and "the very embodiment of the organized will of the working people."[82]

At the end of 1939, the CIO congressional program, strongly supported by all UE officers, urged that the United States stay out of the European war.[83] Although James Carey later claimed that Emspak and Matles did want to change the Officers Report to the

1939 convention after the pact had been signed but he refused, this was highly unlikely given Carey's own actions at the time.[84] As late as several months after the UE convention, Carey, speaking as both UE president and CIO secretary-treasurer, gave a "the Yanks are not coming" speech to a rally of Cuban trade unionists in Havana while sharing the platform with a high official of the Cuban Communist Party.[85]

Despite the dramatic events taking place on the world stage, there was satisfaction in the UE that the worst of the Depression seemed to be over. While the growth rate had not been dramatic, the union had managed to hold its own.[86] At the end of the thirties, the UE stood on the threshold of a period of both remarkable growth and disastrous internecine strife.

During 1940, Westinghouse, the last of the major producers to hold out against a written contract with UE, finally signed. On March 29, the NLRB ruled that the company was violating the legal responsibility to bargain. This decision, coupled with active organizational work by the union, succeeded by September in making the UE sole bargaining agent for 19 Westinghouse plants.[87]

Considerable progress across the industry added to the Westinghouse victory. By the end of 1940, the UE's membership showed a 65 percent gain over the previous year. Ten thousand new members joined the union in the first quarter of the year alone.[88] In August, Erie, Pennsylvania, the last big General Electric plant to be organized, entered the fold.[89]

As the union grew, so did the ideological conflict. By 1940, the *UE News* had adopted a stridently anti-war position. On January 6, a cartoon depicted Martin Dies, Chairman of the House Committee on Un-American Affairs, French prime minister Daladier, British prime minister Neville Chamberlain, and Wall Street as the fomenters of the War. Hitler and Mussolini did not appear.[90] Franklin Roosevelt, long a champion to the UE, came under bitter attack for his 1940 budget message which called for $1.8 billion for armaments.[91] Carey apparently still found nothing in this position that he could not accept. He continued to urge neutrality in his newspaper column in *UE News* and called for people to pay less attention to the Soviet Union and more to the domestic situation in the United States.[92] In reply to a question from the *New York Mirror*, Carey declared that "Labor's influence should and will be directed toward preventing our nation from being plunged into this war."[93] As late as December 7, 1940, Carey defended the *UE News* from criticism that it was an organ for the national officers and not for the entire union.[94]

Not surprisingly, Carey found himself lumped with Matles and Emspak when Communist charges flew. On August 13, 1938, the House Un-American Activities Committee, chaired by Martin Dies, had charged that the UE leadership was dominated by the Communist Party.[95] John P. Frey, an old nemesis of the UE, had testified before the committee and labeled the UE as a "red" union.[96] One year later, Joseph Zack, a former-Communist-turned-informer backed up Frey.[97]

In October 1939, Carey, Matles and Emspak replied to the Dies Committee charges. Matles denied party membership and stated that he did not intend to answer the charge again. In many future appearances before congressional committees, Matles was to hold firmly to that pledge. Carey and Emspak also denied any Communist Party membership and Emspak, who had come under particular fire from Zack, denied ever knowing the man.[98]

As a result of the Dies Committee charges, Carey wrote to the members of the committee asking them to make public any evidence they had that the UE was a Communist union. All he received in return were eight and one quarter pages containing the Frey and Zack testimonies.[99] On January 23, 1940, after an active campaign to clear the union's name, four members of the Dies Committee admitted that they did not have sufficient evidence to label the UE or its officers as Communists.[100]

Nevertheless, the officers realized the danger to the union of being tarred with the red brush. Matles wrote, on UE stationary, to William Sentner, Director of District 8, telling him that he, Emspak, and Carey had discussed the possible negative ramifications for the union of Sentner's open membership in the Party. "After due consideration," Matles asked him to "seriously consider . . . resigning from the Communist Party." He argued that "the interests of our organization and of the many thousands of its members would be better served by such action on your part." Although he later had second thoughts and renewed his Party membership, Sentner took the advice of the general officers in this case, resigning in order to give his undivided attention to serving the members of the union.[101] In the context of the debate over the degree of secret control of the UE by the Communist Party, this exchange of letters is remarkable. There was certainly nothing clandestine about it. Had Party control been as complete as the right-wing later charged, a polite request from Matles for Sentner to "seriously consider" the matter would hardly have been necessary. On the other hand, it might simply have been that Sentner was a special case, considering his strong belief that openness was always the better course.

The apparent unanimity of the officers did not last out the year. The strain began to show during the 1940 UE convention on the issues of conscription and endorsement of Franklin Roosevelt. The resolutions committee, in keeping with "the Yanks are not coming" position of the Communist Party after the signing of the German-Russian nonaggression pact, presented a report to the delegates condemning peacetime conscription. The right-wing forces, led by Matt Campbell, countered with a resolution opposing the Burke-Wadsworth Bill, the particular conscription measure then before Congress, but supporting conscription in principle as vital to the defense of the United States. Matles acted as chief spokesman for the administration resolution, which carried easily, 423 to 197. For the first time, Carey lined up with the opposition.[102] The question of conscription was closely connected to the endorsement of Roosevelt. In July, Carey had come out for the re-election of the President, who had lost much of his popularity with the left wing of the American labor movement because of his preparedness campaign. A compromise resolution emerged from committee instructing the general officers to investigate the question and make a final decision. This would almost certainly have resulted in support of the anti-Roosevelt position of John L. Lewis, at that time the hero of the left wing. A substitute motion from the floor called for outright endorsement. A compromise resolution finally won which authorized the general officers, after consulting with John L. Lewis and Philip Murray, to represent the interests of the UE with regard to an endorsement for Roosevelt.[103]

The ideological split also surfaced on other questions at the convention. Local 103 of Camden, New Jersey, submitted a resolution opposing all dictatorial forms of government, "be it German Nazism, Italian Fascism, or Russian Communism." A fight on the issue took place in the resolutions committee chaired by Matt Campbell. Finally, a substitute motion emerged condemning "all aggressions against the rights and territories of any people and any form of anti-democratic governments," and announcing that the convention stood "firmly for unionism, democracy and Americanism."[104]

An issue with much more significance for the future arose when the resolutions committee brought out a resolution on political minorities that specifically called for the right of all members of the union, regardless of political affiliation, to hold any office to which they were elected in the union. This was precisely the issue on which the 1941 convention would decide the future of James Carey. However, in 1940, Carey, along with Matt Campbell, supported a move to substitute the preamble of the UE constitution for the resolution because it covered, according to Carey, the same material as the resolution.[105] Thus Carey accepted in 1940 an interpretation of the constitution that he would diametrically oppose in 1941, and on which he would risk his career.

The 1940 convention ended in harmony on the surface, but there were plenty of signs of a deepening split among the union's leadership. Significantly, Matthew Campbell seconded Carey's nomination for the presidency with a ringing endorsement that he had never yet met the man or woman who could take Jim Carey's place.[106]

Events following the 1940 convention indicated the depth of the split. The outward manifestation took the form of two disputes; one concerning the issue of a private secretary for Carey, and the other concerning the amount of autonomy a local should have in deciding qualifications for its officers. Innocent as they seemed on the surface, the issues provoked the first open battles in the struggle for control of the union.

Carey first brought the subject of a private secretary out into the open in a letter to the vice-presidents in which he explained that the "increasing responsibility connected with the office of the general president" required him to secure a competent male secretary.[107] But the real issue was Carey's belief that he could not count on confidentiality if his secretary came from the left-wing United Office and Professional Workers (UOPWA). Carey said as much in a letter to the GEB members.[108] All secretarial help in UE, as in all CIO unions, belonged to the Communist-led UOPWA. Carey feared that any UOPWA secretary would be in collusion with the other general officers, particularly Julius Emspak.[109] In fact, Carey claimed that his present secretary was leaking confidential information to Matles and Emspak.[110] Apparently the charge had some substance. When a disgruntled member of Schenectady Local 301 wrote to Carey complaining about the "stranglehold of a small clique" on the Local, Emspak sent Local 301 business agent Leo Jandreau a copy of the letter and a copy of Carey's reply. Considering the deteriorating state of Carey's relationship with Emspak at the time, it is highly unlikely that this was done with Carey's knowledge.[111] Syndicated columnist Victor Riesel later claimed that Carey had warned his friends to be careful when they spoke to him on the phone at UE headquarters because he felt certain that Matles and Emspak were keeping close tabs on his activities. According to Riesel this happened as early as the fall of 1940.[112] In response to Carey's request, Julius Emspak notified the General

Executive Board members that hiring a secretary was a routine matter and did not require the attention of the board.[113] Emspak claimed that Reginald Kennedy, an activist in the anticommunist Association of Catholic Trade Unionists (ACTU) and a close friend of Carey, was the man Carey wanted for secretary. Turning the issue toward Carey's alleged neglect of his UE responsibilities, Emspak said the board wanted no part of an assistant president while Carey neglected his UE duties.[114] Matles pointed out that Carey had approved all appointments to the secretarial staff.[115] This may well have been so, but in fact, Carey's duties with the CIO probably made this function, like many others, a rubber stamping of decisions made by Emspak and Matles. The November meeting of the General Executive Board discussed the issue but reached no decision.[116]

Carey first took the split public in January 1941, in Pittsburgh, where he spoke of the "misapplication" of UE policy, stressing that the membership and only the membership should control the affairs of the union. He pointedly told his UE audience that his apparent disinterest in a takeover of UE by the Communists was the result of his confidence in the membership. In a clear reference to the left-wing, he stressed that only a power grab by a group out of touch with the true sentiments of the members would disturb UE principles of equality of membership and participation without regard to political affiliation.[117]

There were several factors that led Carey to bring the fight out into the open. One was certainly the secretary issue, on which he suffered defeat. The second, apparently, was his increasingly isolated position on the question of American involvement in the European war and on the more immediate question of preparedness. His Pittsburgh speech led to an immediate reaction. When Carey addressed a CIO meeting in Bridgeport, Connecticut ,the following week, several UE members charged him with "war mongering" and "red-baiting." The first charge came as a result of Carey's strong support of Roosevelt's preparedness program. The CIO's position had changed after the 1940 presidential elections when John L. Lewis had staked his CIO presidency on the election of isolationist Republican challenger Wendell Wilkie, and lost. Carey and Philip Murray, Lewis's successor, were now supporting Roosevelt's preparedness campaign and Auto Worker vice-president Walter Reuther's plan to use idle automobile plants to build assembly line airplanes at the rate of 500 per day.[118]

When the storm over the interpretation of the UE constitution broke, therefore, the leaders' split along ideological lines had already developed to a considerable degree. It has already been noted that at the 1940 convention Carey had accepted an interpretation of the preamble to the UE constitution that would allow any member to hold office if elected by the members, regardless of political affiliation. Even earlier, in his newspaper column, Carey stated that "We will discriminate against no worker for reasons of race, creed, color or political belief. . . . To deny any worker equality of participation would be a denial of democracy and the very life of unionism."[119] On February 15, 1941, Allis Chalmers Local 615 in Pittsburgh, led by a right-wing administration, inquired of Carey whether an amendment to its local bylaws barring Communists, Nazis, or Fascists from being representatives or officers of the local would be in conflict with the constitution of the international union.[120] Carey seized the opportunity to publicly challenge the left wing. He replied in a *UE News* column on March 22, 1941, taking the position that there was nothing in the national constitution which prohibited a local from barring Communists, Nazis, and Fascists from holding office.[121] The response angered Michael Fitzpatrick, District 6 vice-president, who criticized Carey for not first checking with him before responding. Carey wrote back claiming not to have changed his mind on the issue, but in truth, in six months he had done a complete about-face.[122]

In what columnist Victor Riesel called "unprecedented in labor journalism,"[123] Julius Emspak attached an editor's note to Carey's column. He explained that he had asked Carey to withhold this divisive column until after the General Electric, General Motors, and Westinghouse negotiations, or at least until the General Executive Board could meet to discuss the issue. According to Emspak, Carey first agreed and then changed his mind.[124] Carey knew that he would lose in the General Executive Board meeting, and he probably reasoned that it was to his advantage to take it to the rank and file where he sensed he could gain more support for an anticommunist campaign.

Carey was right about his chances with the General Executive Board. They listened as he explained that while he beleived the constitution prohibited barring anyone from membership because of political beliefs, a local could bar someone from holding office. Emspak countered with a lengthy statement which he proposed as the position of the General Executive Board. He held that any local bylaw curtailing the rights and privileges of any member on account of "skill, age, sex, nationality, color, religion, or political belief or affiliation" was inconsistent with and contrary to the international constitution of the UE, and against the welfare of the union. After a heated discussion, a motion adopting the Emspak statement carried. Only Harry Block, Matthew Campbell, and Carey opposed it.[125]

The stand of the executive board stated that "when a worker joins a union, he joins as a member having full and uncurtailed rights equal to those of any other member. We do not have 'class B' status for any of our members."[126] Cleverly, the officers wrapped themselves in the same rationale, which led a predecessor of the UE, the National Radio and Allied Trades, to reject, under Carey's leadership, the offer of a merger with the IBEW. Carey found himself on extremely shaky ground. He was on record during the 1940 convention supporting the current interpretation of the General Executive Board. The preamble in question read in part, "We . . . form an organization of all workers in our industry on an industrial basis, and rank and file control, regardless of craft, age, sex, nationality, race, creed or political beliefs. . . . "[127]

James Matles claimed that Carey invented the constitutional issue as an opportunistic move to save his office.[128] One of Carey's chief allies lent support to Matles's claim. Harry Block, one of the original drafters of the constitution, admitted that the local autonomy issue was a false one. He believed, in fact, that one of the weaknesses in the organization stemmed from the fact that the locals had too much autonomy. According to Block, however, the motivation was strictly anticommunism cloaked in local autonomy.[129]

The next crisis for Carey occurred because of his stand on preparedness. He was now firmly behind the Murray-Hillman position in the CIO. The UE General Executive Board had not taken an official position, but most, with the exception of Block and Campbell, were personally opposed. The issue came to a head in a dispute involving the National Defense Mediation Board. The UE was suspicious of the board, looking askance at any attempt to curtail the right to strike, particularly during their isolationist period. They reserved the right to reject any unfair recommendation by the board.[130] The case, which divided Carey from the majority of the UE board, concerned a strike at Phelps-Dodge. The National Defense Mediation Board had recommended a settlement unacceptable to the District 4 leadership. Carey had gone on record as agreeing with the decision. This enraged the officers of UE District 4 who requested a clarification from Carey. Carey made the request public in his column and agreed to meet with representatives from the disaffected district if a verbatim record of the meeting were kept.[131] Carey realized the difficulty of his position. He wanted the record to be absolutely clear in the event that he had to defend his actions.

By this time Carey knew that a move was under way to replace him. He said as much during a meeting with the UE staff representatives in Chicago in mid-June. Carey complained about the direction of the *UE News*, told the group that a fight was coming and they had better line up with him or else, and threatened to "knock a few heads together" if his opponents didn't straighten out.[132] The FBI had information to the effect that he was "no longer connected with the reds" and that he "was on the way out" as president.[133] In light of this, he did not hesitate to portray the issue of the Defense Mediation Board as part of his struggle with the left wing. The UE had two choices, according to Carey, to work through existing democratic institutions with the aid of progressive groups, as the union had always done; or reject and discredit the use of democratic institutions and obstruct their operation, await the collapse of progressive movements and hope, out of the ensuing chaos, to establish a new order.[134] He left no doubt into which category he placed his opponents.

The General Executive Board skillfully used the issue to isolate Carey. While advising the strikers to adhere to the NDMB order and return to work, the board members bitterly criticized the recommendation and reserved the right to reject future decisions.[135] The following issue of *UE News* fueled the fire by blasting the National Defense Mediation Board for what the *News* called its policy of imposing a war economy of scarcity on the country by holding up profits and holding down wages.[136] In open defiance of his fellow officers, Carey accepted an appointment as Murray's alternate on the board on June 16, 1941.[137] The case illustrated Carey's predicament. As CIO Secretary-Treasurer, he had little choice but to follow Murray's lead and support the Board's findings. Given his already precarious position in UE, his choice to stay close to Murray made eminent sense, but it widened the gulf with the General Executive Board and added a trade-union issue to the case being built against him by his opponents. As the dispute dragged on, the members of the General Executive Board kept a careful eye on developments elsewhere, which were adding another dimension to the struggle for control of the union.

The American Catholic Church's involvement in the labor movement went back to the Irish immigration of the second half of the 19th century. But massive church interest and activism on the labor front followed the millions of Irish, Italian, and Eastern European Catholics into the industrial unions of the CIO. Roman Catholicism's interest in labor flowed from several sources. It was grounded in *Rerum Novarum* and *Quadregesimo Anno*, the two papal encyclicals that propagated church teaching on the labor question. By the 1930s Catholic social thought envisioned a society based on Christ's teachings, a just wage, and harmony between the interests of labor and capital. As industrialization broke down traditional institutions and loosened the bonds between the Catholic working class and the Church, Catholic reformers recognized that the battle against secularization for men's souls would take place in the workplace. There the opponent that it feared most was communism. Not only was it the epitome of secularization, but also a utopian belief system that also offered workers an alternative version of salvation through sacrifice, solidarity, and struggle.[138]

The Church's main weapons in the battle for the hearts and minds of Catholic workers were activist priests whose mission was to carry the gospel of Christianity into the unions. These "labor priests" actively supported industrial unionism and fought against conservative anti-union influence in the Church. They founded labor schools to educate Catholic workers in the Church's social teaching and trained activists. Frequently Catholic activists and Communists found common ground in CIO organizing drives. Anticommunism, while always present, did not dominate the agenda during the thirties and through the war.[139]

Although the Church did not begin shifting its labor activity toward an almost exclusive emphasis on anticommunism until the end of World War II, one organization, the Association of Catholic Trade Unionists (ACTU), began to aid anticommunist factions in the UE in a much earlier period. ACTU had its beginnings in New York in 1937 as an offshoot of Dorothy Day's Catholic Worker Movement. In its desire to be a "real power for the Cause of Christ in the Labor Movement," while at the same time carrying "the message of trade unionism into every working-class home," the ACTU militantly espoused workers' rights to a voice in the determination of their working conditions and a just wage. Indeed in New York City the ACTU Chapter supported the Communist leadership of the Transport Workers Union against an attack by a right-wing, Coughlinite Catholic group, the American Association against Communism. But even at the height of the popular front, the ACTU never relaxed its distrust of Communists, nor did it waver in its determination to protect Catholic workers from contamination by Marxism.[140] According to ACTU principles, Catholic workers were compelled to leave Marxist-controlled or "nonchristian" unions, but not until they made every effort to rid them of the corrupting elements.[141]

By 1941 the ACTU claimed 10,000 members and had a network of labor schools and strong chapters in the key labor cities of

New York, Pittsburgh, and Detroit. In Pittsburgh, a fiery young priest named Charles Owen Rice led the organization. Rice was born in New York City to immigrant Irish parents who soon brought him to Pittsburgh where he was to gain fame as the most influential labor priest of the Cold War era. Rice grew up in a family of liberal Democrats who defected to Robert LaFollette's Progressive Party in 1924, but returned to the fold to become staunch Roosevelt New Dealers. After graduation from Duquesne University, Rice attended St. Vincent's seminary in Latrobe, Pennsylvania, where his liberal upbringing was reinforced by exposure to *Rerum Novarum* and *Quadregesimo Anno*.[142] In 1934, Rice became a priest in the diocese of Pittsburgh, a city ravaged by the Depression and the scene of mounting labor unrest. The young priest entered into the labor struggles of the city as one of the founders of the Catholic Radical Alliance. The Alliance, modeled to a degree on the Catholic Worker Movement, the pacifist social action group founded by Dorothy Day in New York City, had as its primary interest the propagation of progressive Catholic social doctrine among workers in their unions.[143] One significant difference between Dorothy Day and Charles Owen Rice was their attitude toward communism. Although Day rejected communism when she converted to Catholicism, she did not attack it or its adherents. Rice, on the other hand, was a committed and strident anticommunist from the beginning. In one of its first activities, the CRA demonstrated against American support for the Spanish loyalists. Rice went on the air as a radio priest in Pittsburgh as early as 1939 and effectively used that medium to attack Communist influence in the labor movement well into the 1950s. During his career he also wrote regularly for the ultra-conservative and extremely influential Catholic weekly, *Our Sunday Visitor*, which he later characterized as a "pact with the devil," informed for the FBI, founded the ACTU chapter in Pittsburgh, established and taught in labor schools, wrote pamphlets instructing local unions how to ride themselves of Communist influence, and established and maintained a nationwide anticommunist network. He boasted of having amassed "a dossier on every Communist in the U.S., a bigger anticommunist file than anybody else had."[144] Nowhere was his influence felt more than in the UE which, with its massive presence in Westinghouse in Pittsburgh, provided Rice with an arena worthy of his ambitions. James Matles later acknowledged that Rice "had few rivals in hostility toward the UE and few who could be said to have helped more to weaken and split the union."[145] There had always been considerable ACTU interest in James Carey because of his influence in the CIO, his Catholicism, and, of course, because of the Communist presence in the UE. As far back as Carey's election as Secretary of the CIO, the ACTU had sent a letter to John L. Lewis attacking Carey for speaking before Communist front groups. Carey answered the charge at that time by saying, "I seriously object to the labor movement used as a battleground for or against certain political philosophies. I am, therefore, very much opposed to any dictation from any sources outside the labor movement in regards to the policies of the labor movement. . . . "[146] By 1941, however, Carey needed allies, and ACTU, which had adherents inside UE locals in New York, New Jersey, Pittsburgh, and St. Louis was ready to seize the opportunity.

In March 1941, at the time when Carey was embroiled in the constitution controversy, Father Rice was leading an insurgent group in a struggle for control of the huge East Pittsburgh Westinghouse Local 601, the largest in the union. The organization of Local 601 had been led by experienced skilled workers, many of whom were Communists or Communist sympathizers. But the sprawling East Pittsburgh complex also employed thousands of younger, lower paid, and less-skilled workers. Divisions between the two groups plagued the local from its inception, with the less-skilled workers of the motor division forming the core of a right-wing challenge to the old radicals in the main tool room and generator division. These insurgents, in terms of age, skill, and income, had far more in common with the workers in the appliance plants than they had with the skilled workers who dominated their local leadership. Although in large measure the struggle was between groups with different needs and visions of trade unionism, the Communist issue, skillfully exploited by the ACTU, provided a convenient rallying point for the insurgents.[147]

Local 601's newspaper complained publicly about Rice's interference in local affairs early in 1941.[148] Julius Emspak wrote to Rice's bishop asking him to restrain the young priest from attacking the UE from the pulpit and in the press.[149] If nothing else, the exchange showed that Carey was not the only union officer with secretary problems. Rice received a copy of Emspak's letter almost as soon as the bishop. His source was the secretary in the office of Local 601 who informed Rice that she would keep him informed of any future developments.[150]

The chief target of the ACTU group was Charles Newell, Local 601 business agent. A skilled toolmaker, he had been one of the first four organizers hired by the international union in 1938, after gaining experience in James Matles's Communist-led Metal Workers Industrial Union. Claiming Carey as their source, the right-wing forces labeled Newell a Communist and cited as proof a statement supporting the Communist Party which carried Newell's signature and had appeared in the *Daily Worker*.[151] Carey denied telling Rice that Newell was a Communist, but the FBI office in Pittsburgh clearly believed that he had.[152]

The fight for the big Westinghouse local intensified through the spring and summer of 1941. Rice used the pulpit to denounce the current officeholders. In a letter read from Pittsburgh area pulpits in August 1941, he attacked Local 601 leaders Michael and Thomas Fitzpatrick as Communist supporters and called the local a sounding board for the Communist line. He urged members to vote for the anticommunist slate in the August elections for delegates to the District Council. He characterized the leadership of the local as men who were "for Communists who shot down the priests and sisters in Spain."[153] Michael Fitzpatrick, guilty by association of the murder of Spanish priests in August of 1941, would later be absolved of all his sins when he came over to the ACTU forces following World War II. In 1941, however, he was on the losing side as the insurgent slate, buoyed by the patriotic spirit that followed Pearl Harbor, carried the day.[154] In a preview of the bitter tactics that were to become commonplace on both sides of the left-right fight in UE after the War, the victors expelled Newell from the local, physically ejecting him from a union meeting at which he was defending himself. By 1942, with the United States and the Soviet Union fighting as allies against Hitler, the left wing recaptured the local. The victory had been "frittered away," according to Rice.[155]

Closely following events in the UE, the ACTU met in convention in Pittsburgh in September 1941 and passed a resolution calling upon the AFL and the CIO to instruct their affiliated unions to insert provisions in their constitutions to bar from union office members of the Communist Party or consistent followers of Communist policy.[156] This was the same issue that Carey had recently used to throw down a challenge to the left wing in UE. Considering that the initial request for a constitutional change barring Communists came from the ACTU-dominated Local 615 in Pittsburgh, it was not difficult to see the ACTU's hand in the orchestration of the entire matter.

On Sunday morning, June 1, 1941, Carey and his supporters received a serious blow. Matthew Campbell, General Executive Board member from District 2, died. In his tribute, Carey wrote, "We will miss you Matthew Campbell."[157] It was more than a tribute. Carey knew full well what the loss of Campbell would mean to his fortunes as leader of UE.

Albert Fitzgerald from the big Lynn, Massachusetts, General Electric Local 201 replaced Campbell. His first meeting with the General Executive Board was scheduled for June 20 and 21, 1941. Immediately following Campbell's death, Harry Block called Al Coulthard, Local 201's business agent, and asked him how Fitzgerald would vote. Coulthard supposedly told him that Fitzgerald would "do the same as Campbell."[158] Carey, anxious to line up Fitzgerald as a supporter, met him at Campbell's funeral and asked Fitzgerald to confer with Carey and Block in New York before the General Executive Board meeting.[159] Block, Carey and the new executive board member met for breakfast the morning of the meeting.[160] According to Block and Carey, Fitzgerald asked if Emspak and Matles were Communists. Carey replied, "Well, if they walk like a duck and quack like a duck, they must be ducks."[161] When the discussion turned to the fight for control of the union, Fitzgerald refused to commit himself, preferring to weigh the merits of each issue.[162]

The fact that Carey knew so little about Albert Fitzgerald indicates how much he had neglected his UE base. Fitzgerald was not an obscure rank and filer. He had been active in the union since its beginning, had helped to organize the Lynn plant, and successively served as shop steward, treasurer, and president of the important local union. He had also served as secretary of the Massachusetts CIO and became President of UE District 2 when Campbell died.[163] One arena where Carey could have gotten to know Fitzgerald was the vital GE Conference Board where Fitzgerald represented Lynn. However, since 1937, when he had been asked to remove himself from the negotiations by the Conference Board, Carey had not actively participated in the GE negotiations and had limited contact with the conference board. Matles and Emspak, on the other hand, did serve on the board and also took an active part in the GE negotiations. They impressed Fitzgerald as "hard and effective workers."[164]

Fitzgerald was thrust to the fore as a possible candidate for the union presidency almost immediately after his first General Executive Board meeting. According to Fitzgerald, the move began even before Campbell's death at the old leader's insistence. Fitzgerald claimed that Campbell called and asked to meet with him. Coulthard and Fitzgerald met in Springfield with Campbell. According to Fitzgerald, Campbell said he could no longer support Carey, that his patience had been tried with him, and would Fitzgerald consent to run for the UE presidency. Fitzgerald claimed to have hedged, but Campbell informed him that he was going to be nominated. Fitzgerald claimed the Carey-Campbell split had nothing to do with the political question. It resulted strictly from the fact that Carey had ceased to be an organization man, that he had been neglecting the UE and embarrassing it on many occasions, and Campbell believed that eventually someone would come along and defeat him. Campbell favored Fitzgerald because he had confidence in him and because he preferred someone he knew to an unknown.[165] There is some merit to this interpretation given the fact that Campbell, a UE pioneer, must have seen that the organization had become hopelessly split between Carey and the majority of the General Executive Board. He might have seen Carey's downfall as inevitable and was therefore of the opinion that Fitzgerald, a District 2 Irish Catholic from a large GE local with a spotless political past, was better than what the left wing might have decided to run against Carey. It might also have been true that Campbell was bothered by Carey's lack of attention to the UE. Carey admitted to having taken a risk when he decided to spend most of his time in Washington with the CIO at the request of Philip Murray. At the time, Murray had cautioned him that it might harm him in the UE.[166] Perhaps Carey should have taken a page from Murray's book. Although he served as President of the CIO, Murray never neglected to cultivate his power base, the United Steelworkers of America. He kept the reins of both organizations firmly in his own hands.

Ironically, June 21, 1941 had far greater significance than the fact that Albert Fitzgerald attended his first General Executive Board meeting. It was also the day that Adolph Hitler chose to unleash his legions against his erstwhile ally, the Soviet Union. The German invasion proved to be traumatic for the American left. On the day of the invasion *UE News* ran three anti-war articles and one cartoon.[167] Carey heard the news while driving home from the meeting. He felt vindicated.[168]

Unlike the Communist Party which turned almost immediately from "the Yanks are not coming" to the "people's program of struggle for the defeat of Hitler and Hitlerism," the UE kept silent immediately after the German invasion.[169] There was no immediate reversal of position. This was no doubt partially because Carey still controlled his column in *UE News*. In addition, while a change from an anti-war to a pro-war stance, and thus a return to anti-fascism, was actually a relief for Communists and fellow travelers, justifying such an abrupt switch to the overwhelmingly non-Communist rank and file required some groundwork. That began cautiously in the July 5 issue of *UE News* when several letters from locals urging military aid to Britain and the Soviet Union appeared. Carey reveled in the discomfort of his opponents. He used his column to mock the left wing for their reversal of position after the invasion:

> A back flip with a full twist and presto—Great Britain purged of all her sins—Hitler is to be hated even more than Roosevelt. The "imperialistic blood bath" becomes a peoples war for freedom; Sumner Welles becomes a progressive and Wheeler an enemy of the people.
>
> The performance of a trapeze artist in a circus is entertainment, but political acrobats in pink tights posing as labor leaders are a disgrace to the union and insult the intelligence of the membership.[170]

In the next issue of the paper Carey wondered why pro-Soviet letters to the editor were so prominent. He also claimed to have been told that he would be re-elected only if he changed his position on local autonomy.[171] In the first official indication of a reversal of policy, the *UE News* ran a three column, anti-German cartoon on August 9.

Awkwardly, just as the popular front was in the process of being resurrected, knowledge of the severe split among the general officers spread throughout the union. On August 3, the first pro-Carey organization surfaced. The statement of a group calling itself the Inter-Local Committee for Progressive Trade Unionism called for an end to Communist influence in the union and the re-election of James Carey. *UE News* gave the statement prominent play, calling it "historical" because it constituted the first formal statement of an organized faction in the union's history.[172] Another hint of trouble came from St. Louis. A group of delegates to the District 8 convention nominated a candidate to run against William Sentner. The challenge took Sentner by surprise. He attributed it to forces outside of the UE, in particular individuals connected to the Catholic Church and the Socialist Party.[173]

When the delegates assembled for the seventh UE convention in Camden, New Jersey, in September 1941, they could look back on the previous year with mixed emotions. They must have known that the 1941 convention signaled the end of the era of innocence for the union. On the one hand, the preceding 12 months had been phenomenally successful in terms of organizing activities. No union grew faster than the UE. From August 1940, to August 1941, the union gained 116,123 new members.[174] After capitalizing on the tremendous growth of defense production in the electrical industry, the UE announced its paid membership at a level of 255 percent of the 1937 level.[175] There had also been memorable highlights. A written agreement with Westinghouse finally became a reality. Twenty-six thousand employees of the General Electric Division of General Motors came into the UE under a national contract with the auto giant.

But the tremendous growth took place at a time when the union was splitting over the ideological question. Whether or not the charges by Carey and his allies that the union served as an arm of the Communist Party were true, it was probably true that with the exception of Carey and Block, official UE positions taken on lend-lease, preparedness, and Roosevelt's candidacy during the nearly two years since the signing of the Nazi-Soviet pact were not the positions of the average rank and file member of the union. But these were not trade union issues. No matter the foreign policy issues that preoccupied the leaders, as Harry Block explained, the rank and file were only interested in two things, "how much do I get in my pay envelope and don't increase the dues."[176] The members could hardly fault the leadership on bread-and-butter issues. No union could look down on the UE in terms of its service to its members. Another factor of considerable importance was that union members who had been through the struggles of the thirties had good reason to question the motives of those who called others Communists. The term had been so over used by labor's opponents that it had lost all precision.

There was also a conspicuous lack of evidence of any UE action detrimental to the defense effort in the period between the Molotov pact and the German invasion of Russia. While the leaders were attacking preparedness and conscription, James Matles urged 475 workers in a Brooklyn torpedo plant to delay a strike because of the importance of the plant to the defense effort. He asked that the United States Conciliation Service be given an opportunity to try to effect a settlement.[177] Of all strikes called against industries holding War Department contracts in the period from January 1 to June 12, 1941, not one involved UE. Of the 2,370,716 workdays lost in labor disputes in war industry, UE members were credited with none of them.[178] The UE's leaders clearly had no intention of allowing their support for the Communist Party's foreign policy to interfere with their prudent judgment on trade union activities.

James Carey traveled to the 1941 convention in Camden alone, leaving his wife in Garfield Hospital in Washington expecting a baby. Upon his arrival, a delegate informed him that a committee wanted to meet him. Emspak, Albert Coulthard and Albert Fitzgerald from Lynn, Mike Fitzpatrick from Pittsburgh, and Leo Jandreau from Schenectady came to Carey's room that evening at the Walt Whitman Hotel. They told him they wanted him to continue as president, but only if he would stop his anticommunist campaign and give in on the constitutional issue. Albert Fitzgerald agreed to drop out of the race if Carey would agree. Emspak, however, knew Carey well, and he whispered to Fitzgerald, "Sit down, sit down, don't be so eager to run out . . . this guy isn't going to give on this stuff."[179] Emspak knew his man. Carey refused. The group tried again the following night with similar results.[180]

The Officers' Report to the convention contained no hint of the split. No mention of the local autonomy issue could be found, and Carey joined his two fellow officers in condemning the Canadian government for interning Canadian vice-president Clarence Jackson for "Communistic activities."[181] Emspak demanded that the union take "every step necessary to crush Hitlerism," and announced that the disagreement within the union on foreign policy had now all disappeared.[182] The first resolution blasting Hitler passed by acclamation. Only after this show of sentiment on the part of the convention did *UE News* come out solidly in support of aid to the Allies.[183] Whatever their own feelings, the UE officers realized that it would be prudent to wait and cloak their actions with the sanction of the convention.

The real order of business before the convention, however, was the election of the officers. Significantly, before the voting on the presidency took place, Albert Fitzgerald felt compelled to tell the assembly, "I am not a Communist; I am not dominated by Communists; and as a citizen of the United States of America, I despise the philosophy of the Communist Party. But as a member and present officer and coming officer of this union, I will not let that issue tear this union apart."[184] Fitzgerald defeated Carey by the thin margin of 635 to 539. In a sense the closeness of the vote was a tribute to Carey's appeal and demonstrated a reluctance on the part of many delegates to turn out one of the founders of the union. This is indicated by the fact that the anti-Carey leadership's resolution on local autonomy with regard to local constitutions carried by a much larger margin, 792 to 373.[185] In other words, Carey's stand on the constitutional question met a solid defeat, but Carey the man fared a good deal better.

The generally accepted interpretation of Carey's defeat is that he had become too dangerous to the Communists and they had decided to destroy him. While there may be some truth to this, it is much too simplistic to attribute the defeat of a fairly popular young president entirely to Communist displeasure. There was, in addition, the charge that Carey had neglected the union. It was widely felt that he had ceased to be president of UE when he took the CIO position. Carey, himself, acknowledged that this may have been so, but countered with the claim that his position with the CIO gave the UE considerable prestige.[186] Block agreed, contending that no president of an international union ran the day-by-day operations of the organization.[187] Nevertheless, even the ACTU paper which later termed Carey's defeat a "liquidation" by the Communists, admitted that Carey faced the opposition of the leftists and "those rightists who could not forgive him for his past conduct."[188] James Weschler, writing in *The Nation*, explained the defeat as a Communist purge, but also admitted that there was right-wing opposition to Carey centering around the Lynn local.[189] This would seem to be borne out by the involvement of the conservative Lynn people in the Fitzgerald candidacy and Carey's surprise at seeing Al Coulthard, Lynn business agent, at the pre-convention meetings in Carey's room. Even more puzzling is why the Communist Party, three months into the popular front period after the German invasion of the Soviet Union, would want Carey defeated? In fact, it did not. Orders from the Party were to support Carey, but on this issue, one that had to do with control of the union, the left-wing leadership rejected Party orders.[190]

In a show of unanimity after the presidential election, Carey nominated Julius Emspak for re-election and Matles proposed that the UE support Carey for re-election as Secretary-Treasurer of the CIO. Carey claimed that he did this in spite of what he termed the treacherous activity of Matles and Emspak, because he wanted to hold to a pre-convention agreement.[191] Astonishingly, Matles claimed that Carey's actions could be explained by the fact that he realized his two fellow officers had nothing to do with his defeat.[192] The UE officers' support for Carey's return to the CIO can probably be best understood as a sop to the Communist Party's desire for popular front unity at all costs, as well as perhaps a conciliatory gesture within the UE.[193]

The formal show of unity did nothing to reduce the determination of the right-wing locals. After hearing convention delegate George Berry's blistering report on the convention, the general membership meeting of Local 105 in Philadelphia voted all but unanimously to ban Communists from holding office in the local.[194]

In a public statement immediately following his defeat, Carey stated that he was not "impressed by the sudden anxiety of the AFL and the public press over my welfare. Both have consistently maligned me and slandered me and all other leaders of our union. I am sorry, but not surprised, that the same attack is now falling on our president-elect, Albert Fitzgerald. I wish to declare publicly and unequivocally that the charges of Communism against him are as false as past charges against me."[195]

In his statement, Carey uttered one of the few compliments that Albert Fitzgerald would receive. He was to become one of the most maligned figures of the unfolding drama. On the morning following his election, Albert Fitzgerald, a registered Republican, a Roman Catholic, and a valued citizen of Lynn, Massachusetts, awoke to find that he had been transformed into a puppet of the Communist Party by the press.[196]

Harry Block and James Carey later claimed that the leftwing picked Fitzgerald because as a Catholic he would be an ideal front man. They claimed Fitzgerald agreed to be the tool of the Communists in return for the prestige of the presidency. Right-wing critics later referred to him commonly as a "stooge."[197] A UE member turned government witness testified that he heard James McLeish, left-wing president of UE District 4, say, "He (Fitzgerald) is dumb and will leave us alone."[198]

On the other hand, Harry Block sought to support his view that Fitzgerald was put forth as a front man by claiming that the new president was not even full time for this local, or the District, and that he had never negotiated a contract in his life.[199] Such an appalling lack of knowledge about the man who replaced Carey brings into serious question the charges made by the right wing against Fitzgerald. On the eve of another historic convention eight years later, the *New Republic* was to note that while the ruddy-faced, heavy-jowled UE president was known as a stooge for the Communists, actually "he is a thoroughly competent leader."[200]

Carey's defeat also dramatically altered the leadership of the right wing inside UE. Although he would remain titular head of the movement, Carey became practically an outsider in the UE ranks, three-quarters of whom entered the union after 1941.[201] Effective leadership passed to Harry Block, Carey's old colleague from Philadelphia, the only remaining right-winger on the general executive board, and to important local leaders such as James Click in St. Louis, as well as to the diligent Catholic priests whose determination to rid the UE of Communists never wavered.

3

THE POPULAR FRONT

Nineteen forty was the year that John L. Lewis, keeping the promise he made when he supported Wendell Willkie in 1940, declined to run again for the presidency of the CIO. Philip Murray, a United Mine Worker vice-president and head of the CIO's Steel Workers Organizing Committee, assumed the presidency of the CIO. Murray's decision to keep Carey as secretary-treasurer placed the young, ex-president of the UE in a rather unique position. The CIO had only two national officers, Murray and Carey. Murray's salary came from the United Steelworkers of America of which he was still president.[1] Carey's, on the other hand, came from the CIO. He was, in effect, completely dependent upon Murray for his position in the labor movement. Whatever Carey would do in the future, it was obvious that it would be done with at least the sufferance of Murray.

It is interesting to speculate on the reasons behind Murray's decision to keep Carey as secretary-treasurer. The personal styles of the two men were completely different. Murray, a quiet, deliberate leader, came out of the authoritarian school of the United Mine Workers. He instinctively knew that his power rested on his firm control of the huge steel union. Carey, on the other hand, favored the wide open style. He was flamboyant and his fate with the UE indicated that he had no love of the day-to-day drudgery of running a union. Perhaps Murray simply desired continuity. Another possibility was that Carey's style made him attractive to the methodical and self-effacing Murray. Of some significance, no doubt, was the rise of two distinct camps within the CIO as early as 1941. Murray's closest adviser, general counsel Lee Pressman, lined up on the left as did *CIO News* editor Len DeCaux. Perhaps Murray realized the need to establish a balance between the two factions. Maintenance of Carey as secretary-treasurer served this purpose. He was an irritant to the left wing, and this helped both to counter right-wing attacks on the CIO from outside enemies and to balance the influence of the left-wingers within. Murray kept Carey under wraps for the duration of the popular front period.

The period from Fitzgerald's election to the attack on Pearl Harbor proved uneventful. The union had been through a traumatic change of leadership and was given only a few short months' respite before the Japanese forced the United States into the war. This did not mean that the wounds created by the struggle for power had healed. They definitely had not.

One of the first skirmishes occurred over the establishment of a UE legislative office in Washington. The 1941 convention, in a resolution on priorities and curtailment, had instructed the general officers to establish a Washington office.[2] Carrying out this mandate led to a sharp reaction on the part of Block and his supporters. At the November meeting of the General Executive Board, Fitzgerald's first as president, Emspak announced the opening of a capital office and the appointment of Russ Nixon as the UE's Washington representative. Block voted against the approval of Nixon.[3]

Block claimed that it was the consensus of opinion in District 1 that when the UE needed anyone for a position, that position should be filled from within the union.[4] In a letter dated October 15, 1941, Block stated that "it was never my understanding at either the UE convention or the Executive Board meeting which followed that we would go outside the UE to engage anyone for the position." According to Block, Nixon was unknown to him and, he believed, to most of the other board members. He stated his opinion that a matter so important should have been decided by the entire General Executive Board.[5] While Block argued against Nixon at on the grounds that he was an outsider, his real reason was that he believed him to be a Communist.[6]

In replying to Block, Emspak stressed that the engagement of Nixon was entirely consistent with the motion passed by the General Executive Board in its meeting on September 6 and with the general policy pursued by the UE at all times in exhausting all possible means to obtain the proper person for a specific job.[7] The reply failed to satisfy Block who returned to his district and continued to voice his dissatisfaction with the choice.[8] Nixon took office on December 1, 1941, as UE legislative representative. He had previously been chief national legislative representative for Labor's Non-

Partisan League, was a Harvard Ph.D., and had taught both at Harvard and M.I.T.[9] There was little doubt that he was a Communist.

There were several other matters of urgent concern to the General Executive Board when it convened for its November meeting in Detroit. The issue over which the 1941 convention had split, local autonomy in writing constitutions, still plagued the organization. The Board set out to establish a procedure for the approval of local constitutions. The general officers were charged with reviewing local constitutions and making whatever recommendations were necessary to the local unions. At each quarterly meeting of the General Executive Board, the general officers were to report their activities in this area.[10] Ostensibly this was to bring all local constitutions into conformity with the international constitution. In fact, however, the only real area of disagreement concerned barring members from holding office because of political beliefs.

Communications from a number of locals concerning restrictive clauses came to the Board. The GEB instructed Julius Emspak to inform those locals that the interpretation given by the international convention on this question was the democratic decision of the organization, and that if any member was affected by the action of any local on the basis of amendments to their constitution, he or she could appeal. The motion carried with Harry Block voting against it. A secondary motion designed to keep the controversy out of the *UE News* also passed over Block's opposition.[11] Despite all attempts to lay it to rest, however, the constitution issue continued to surface time and time again.

On this issue also, Block returned to his district dissatisfied but not defeated. Determined to keep the controversy alive, his district's constitution committee brought forth a slightly modified resolution for submission to the general officers. It banned anyone "who by act or deed supports any kind of an association that advocates the overthrow of our government by force, violence, or other unconstitutional means."[12] It carried easily.

On December 7, 1941, the news of the Japanese attack on Pearl Harbor shocked the leaders of all factions within the UE, as it did the rest of the nation. The entry of the United States into the war as an ally of the Soviet Union cemented the popular front. The reaction among rank-and-file union members mirrored that of other segments of society. At the Hatfield Wire and Cable Company in Hillsdale, New Jersey, one extreme manifestation of patriotism occurred when two UE members refused, for religious reasons, to salute the flag at a ceremony held just four days after Pearl Harbor.

Other employees refused to work if the company retained them. The UE local approved the company's dismissal action, and the international union, to its discredit, made no attempt to have them reinstated. Apparently for the leadership of UE, everyone was welcome in the union but conscientious objectors.[13]

The union moved rapidly to offer its full support to the war effort. The UE quickly accepted the CIO's no-strike pledge.[14] On the day following the attack, the three general officers urged all UE members to forego premium pay for weekend work and to increase production by 15 percent. This was to be accomplished by an increased effort by the workers, over and above such increases as would be effected through improved methods or techniques.[15] Only in the heat of great crisis would the leaders of a trade union suggest such a speed-up. In its emergency meeting on December 15, the General Executive Board approved the statement of the general officers. Harry Block voted with the majority.[16] Franklin Roosevelt quickly appointed Julius Emspak to the National War Labor Board.[17]

Although the excitement of the attack on Pearl Harbor had completely overshadowed the split in the union, the popular front rhetoric could not obscure the fact that it still existed. On December 17th, the right-wing forces, with the aid of Father Charles Owen Rice, defeated the pro-administration leadership of Westinghouse Local 601 in Pittsburgh. It was the largest Westinghouse local and the first big right-wing victory.[18]

Almost immediately after Pearl Harbor the *UE News* began to agitate for an all-out war effort in the "people's war against fascism."[19] The demand for a second front to relieve pressure on the Soviet Union began shortly after the United States entered the hostilities. A steady stream of second front resolutions poured in from locals across the country. "Win the war in 1942" became the motto. In March the General Executive Board passed its first resolution calling for an invasion of Western Europe. A telegram to Roosevelt commended him for demanding an allied invasion.[20] Even right-wing controlled District 1 passed a resolution calling for the rapid opening of a second front.[21] In 1942, everyone was a friend of the Soviet Union. At almost every General Executive Board meeting the second front resolution became part of the agenda. It is interesting to note in this respect that in the pages of *UE News* the war was primarily against Germany. There was little mention of Japan, which had not declared war on the Soviet Union.

A number of officials of the UE served on the Citizens Committee to Free Earl Browder, the Communist Party chairman who had been jailed for passport fraud during the neutrality period.[22]

While numerous UE personalities and locals took an active role in the campaign, the general officers, cautious as always, stayed in the background, and the union never took an official position on the matter. In May 1942, President Roosevelt commuted Browder's sentence.[23] Four months later, Attorney General Biddle, a bitter foe of the Communist Party, cited the Citizens Committee to Free Earl Browder as a Communist organization.[24] However, at a time when American and Soviet troops were fighting a common enemy, the revelation caused hardly a ripple.

While he may not have been in the majority, Biddle was certainly persistent. On May 28th, having lost the Browder fight, he ordered Harry Bridges, president of the West Coast Longshoremen, deported as a Communist.[25] On this issue there was an immediate reaction from the labor movement. Philip Murray denounced the deportation order as a "blow not only to all concepts of American justice but even more a blow at national unity and morale necessary for victory in the war against the Axis." Charging that Biddle had relied on "heresay evidence . . . ," Murray pledged CIO support to "the elected leader of thousands of American workers."[26]

In support of Murray, UE fired a telegram to Biddle protesting the deportation order.[27] While the UE's action was hardly surprising, the rationale behind it was peculiarly indicative of the kind of popular front thinking practiced by the pro-Soviet left during the war. In its resolution on the matter, Biddle's action was called a surrender to "appeasers" who were particularly anxious to drive Bridges out of the United States. Their motive was supposedly to eradicate the acknowledged leader of popular support on the West Coast for the war effort. The UE denounced Biddle's action as directly injurious to the "people's war effort against Fascism."[28] In other words to be anticommunist in 1942 was to be pro-Nazi. The popular front had not co-opted everyone, however. Father Rice, and probably most of the ACTU, supported deportation of Bridges.[29] The UE right wing, however, remained silent on the Bridges matter. It was but one of several instances where it distanced himself from the more extreme positions championed by its clerical allies.

While the frenzied events of 1942 obscured the split within UE, both sides probably looked forward to the September convention with some trepidation. It was important for the union to present a united front, but it was surely known by the general officers that the split would surface in some manner during the convention.

A strident "win-the-war" group convened in Cleveland. They cheered as Robert Patterson, Assistant Secretary of Defense, spoke of the superiority of American tanks and planes.[30] The apparent unanimity broke down, however, when the delegates got down to the business of the convention. In the spirit of war-time unity, the Carey-Block forces did not run a slate of candidates in opposition to the general officers. Nevertheless, the split surfaced on a number of other issues. On the issue of a second front in Europe, the right wing submitted a minority report. Reluctant to oppose an invasion, they urged that the timing be left to the military.[31] But for the UE leadership, the priority was relief for the beleaguered Soviet Union. At the UE convention, however, the issue was never in doubt. The majority resolution carried 1,417 to 623.[32]

Nor did the controversy over autonomy in the writing of local constitutions disappear during the war. Two locals from Harry Block's district submitted resolutions that would have barred Communists, Nazis and Fascists from holding office in UE. Both were soundly defeated, but the issue had been kept alive.[33]

While the constitution issue remained the touchstone of the right-wing group, they injected another issue at the 1942 convention. On June 4, District 1's executive council passed a resolution which prohibited all paid international and district staff men from being elected to office, being executive board members, trustees, or auditors. Significantly, it called for their exclusion from the constitution committees of a district.[34] The right-wing forces believed that James Matles, from his position as Director of Organization, had loaded the UE staff with Communist organizers.[35] They had in mind men like Charles Newell in Pittsburgh, William Sentner in St. Louis, and Ernest DeMaio in Ohio. These three, and others like them, had originally been sent by the international to organize in the Midwest.

Sentner and DeMaio had risen from their staff positions to be district vice presidents and General Executive Board members. Others, like Newell, who remained on the staff, held elected office in local unions they had helped to organize. To the right wing, this constituted a method by which the incumbents could continue to dominate locals in which the majority of the members were anti-communist. In some locals, staff men became targets of insurgent right-wing groups who usually removed them from office and any participation in the local if they gained control. This was true, for example, of Westinghouse Local 601 in Pittsburgh, the big Frigidaire Local 801 in Dayton, Ohio, and the tumultuous Emerson Electric Local 1102 in St. Louis.[36] District 1's resolution was a deliberate move to bring the issue out into the open. As early as May, the district had asked the General Executive Board for an interpretation of the constitution concerning the ability of staff members to hold office in local unions. Fitzgerald and Emspak replied at the time that "the mere fact that an individual is being paid by the international union is in itself no bar to holding any office to which the member has been properly elected by his local, whether it be an officer in the local union or a delegate or officer in an affiliated body of the international union."[37] Emspak delivered the opinion of the general officers that District 1's decision on the status of organizers as delegates to district councils had no constitutional basis.[38] This exchange set the stage for the 1942 convention debate. The convention floor fight began when Block's Philco Local 101 and two other right-wing locals proposed barring organizers or representatives on the payroll of the international union from being delegates to the UE convention unless they had been working members of the organizations they represented for at least one year.[39] Speaking for the proposal, Block claimed that "no organizer, no representative who never worked in a plant of the UE can get on the floor of this convention and state that he voices the opinions of the people back in the shop, because he doesn't know their problems." He asked the delegates to decide whether policy for the UE was to be decided by people who were workers and members of the UE or by individuals who came into the union as staff representatives.[40] Block couched his argument in trade union terms, but the delegates knew that at the heart of the problem lay the Communist issue.

Matles realized the true nature of the attack and replied to the central issue. He pointed out that in the 12-month period before the 1941 convention, 17 representatives had been added to the organizing staff. All were approved by the General Executive Board, and all 17 had been approved by Carey. The evidence seems clear that this was the case. If large numbers of left-wing staff were put on the payroll, then Carey approved them. Either he was complicit or not paying attention. In one notable case, Ernest DeMaio pressured Matles to put his brother Tony, a veteran of the Abraham Lincoln Brigade and a Communist, on the UE staff. Matles was sympathetic, but told DeMaio in no uncertain terms that he would have to clear it with Carey. Shortly thereafter, reacting to requests from DeMaio for more outside staff appointments, Matles told him firmly that the UE had "reached a point . . . where it is almost impossible to put anyone on our payroll not coming from our own shops. He instructed him to "look around for some men to be put on our staff from our own shops and locals."[41]

In countering the charge that some 40 percent of the convention delegates were organizers or paid representatives, Matles pointed out that only 24 of the 600 delegates were organizers or paid representatives, and four of them had been unable to attend the convention. In the previous year, he argued, 21 paid representatives had delegates' credentials, two of whom did not attend. After offering these statistics in his defense, he attacked the right wing. He spoke of "questions that are raised by way of whisper, the questions that have been raised during the past 12 months in the dark corners, the poison that has been spread quietly in a few local offices."[42] Following his speech, a delegate from Local 1202 rose to ask how many votes the 24 paid delegates represented. Julius Emspak calculated that the staff men represented some 81 votes out of a total of 2,058. The minority resolutions were overwhelmingly defeated.[43]

Shortly after the convention, to the certain displeasure of the General Executive Board, District 1 re-elected Harry Block.[44] However, the opposition had been spirited, and it was no secret that the administration was out to unseat him. In its frustration, the General Executive Board took an unprecedented action and censured Block for his activities in supporting a group of candidates in the New Jersey CIO elections who were opposed to the UE administration.[45] As 1942 drew to a close, gaping cracks were evident in the "win-the-war" unity of UE.

Agitation for a second front continued, and at times the UE's rhetoric, if not its practices, went beyond sound trade union considerations. Julius Emspak became a member of the President's Labor Victory Committee and spoke in support of the proposition that, for the duration of the fighting, wage demands and other "normal" trade union activities were to be suspended. Even the general cost of living increase provided for in the Little Steel Formula was to be forgotten.[46] *UE News* pointed out that the Soviet Union continued to do the lion's share of the fighting and hinted that there were those who would have been happy to see Germany crush Russia.[47] Placed in that number was John L. Lewis. The miners' leader, hero of the left during the neutrality period of the Russo-German Pact, now became the chief appeaser.[48]

At a UE "win-the-war" rally in Brooklyn, Joseph Curran, then the left-wing leader of the National Maritime Union, blasted Lewis as the "Champion of forces at home attempting to create a fifth column in the United States."[49] Lewis had committed the unpardonable sin of refusing to support the no-strike pledge. Nothing, however, could match the fury of both the left and right in the United States when Lewis called a general strike in the bituminous fields on May 1, 1943. Julius Emspak telegraphed Franklin Roosevelt on behalf of the UE urging that he direct Lewis to call off the coal strike. If he failed to get a favorable response, Roosevelt was urged to move for a showdown with the UMW leader on his right to "organize disruption of the war effort."[50] There was no mention of the responsibility of the coal operators. On June 12, the General Executive Board went on record as supporting Roosevelt in his dispute with Lewis.[51] Their zeal hit a new high when the *UE News* put strikes on a par with race hatred and the anti-labor Smith-Connally bill as part of an American version of Hitlerism.[52] While nearly all of the labor movement in June 1943, voiced similar views of Lewis, there were some predictable UE exceptions. Harry Block personally refrained from entering the controversy, but two of his right-wing District 1 locals passed resolutions calling John L. Lewis the only man fighting for the interests of labor and saying that instead of condemning Lewis, the UE national officers should have followed his lead and helped him along.[53]

When the delegates convened in New York for the 1943 convention they were treated to a "win-the-war" rally sponsored by the UE in Madison Square Garden replete with representatives of labor, industry, and the theater. The officers' reports called again for a second front, reaffirmed the no-strike policy, and once more attacked Lewis.[54] In the area of political action the convention endorsed Franklin Roosevelt for a fourth term. It was the first official UE endorsement of a presidential candidate, and it would be the last until 1964.[55] Resolutions calling for international labor cooperation, including the Russian unions, and assailing criticism of the Soviet Union, were passed overwhelmingly. To top off the meeting on just the right patriotic note, Matles was inducted into the army in full view of the assembled delegates.[56] The one obvious omission in what appeared to be a harmonious convention was the refusal of UE openly to endorse James Carey for secretary-treasurer of the CIO.[57] There was no longer any pretense of UE support for Carey. It made little difference. Murray had come out from beneath the shadow of Lewis and had established himself firmly in control of the CIO. If he wanted Carey, and he did, there was nothing anyone could do about it.

Minor squabbles arose between the right wing and left wing during the remainder of 1943. Once again a pro-administration slate challenged Block in District 1, and once again he beat back the effort, this time with some 55 percent of the vote. His opponent, a supporter of the administration and president of Local 155—an old machinist group—was Carl Bersing.[58] The question of hiring organizers flared again in the case of Peter Umholtz from District 1. Umholtz had applied for a job on the UE staff. He came out of the pro-Carey Lykens, Pennsylvania, local. The general officers took no action, and Block queried Emspak as to the reason.[59] Emspak shot back that it would be foolish for the international Union to hire Umholtz because his right-wing local opposed the policies of the international union in a basic way. Emspak claimed that it hardly made sense to place someone on the staff who would not carry out the convention decisions of the organization.[60] Block certainly expected this result, but he now had another example of the attitude of the general officers toward views differing from their own. The persistent scrutiny by the right wing of the hiring of staff members caused some concern on the part of the general officers. Early in 1944, Carl Bersing cautioned Emspak about hiring a prospective organizer because her appointment would be challenged in District 1. The reasons, he said, were her inexperience and "the affiliation and the type of work activity she is presently connected with."[61]

Despite the apparent hostility between Carey and his supporters and the UE leadership, the relationship between Philip Murray and the UE remained good on the surface. Murray appointed Fitzgerald as one of the CIO delegates to the Allied Labor Conference scheduled for London in June 1944.[62] Later in the year Murray spoke at the UE convention and praised the officers and members of the electrical union.[63]

But the dispute between Block and the other board members continued to simmer over a number of issues. President Fitzpatrick of District 6 accused him of meddling in the affairs of his district.[64] There was continued agitation from District 1 over the alleged appointment of left-wing organizers.[65] The question of local constitutions refused to die. The board found it necessary to take a new tack with regard to the matter. Over the objection of Block, a motion passed which recommended a constitutional amendment strengthening the present provision governing approval of local constitutions. It stated that the national constitution took precedence if the local document had not been approved, but controversial constitutions continued to come in from right-wing locals.[66]

The union continued to espouse a firm "win-the-war" philosophy until the long awaited invasion of the European continent. On June 10th, *UE News* ran a special D-Day issue that accurately reflected the joy at the beginning of the attack in the West.[67] Vasily Kuznetzov, president of the Central Council of Trade Unions of the Soviet Union, praised UE for its strong support of international trade union unity.[68]

Going into its tenth annual convention, the spirits of the UE along with those of the nation were high. The war had finally turned around in Europe and the Pacific, and victory appeared certain. The popular front in the United States never proved stronger than when the Red armies in the East and the Americans and British in the West began to tighten the noose on Nazi Germany. This spirit permeated the convention. The delegates re-affirmed the no-strike pledge by a vote of 743 to 4.[69] Sidney Hillman, who had been one of the chief villains of the left during the neutrality period, addressed the delegates and blasted "Jew-baiting and red-baiting" as "two sides of the same coin."[70] The National War Fund presented an award for "gallantry in giving" to the UE for contributing more than $3 million for war relief needs.[71] Yet even in the face of this patriotic and self-congratulatory assemblage, the right wing doggedly continued its agitation. A right-wing slate challenged the general officers and suffered a solid defeat. Fitzgerald won easily over Martin Hogan of Hartford, Connecticut, a product of the Catholic labor schools established in that state by the anticommunist labor priest, Joseph Donnelly. In another test case, the administration forces soundly defeated a Carey-Block supported amendment that would have changed the method of electing officers to a membership referendum.[72] An observer at the tenth UE convention could surely have gotten the mistaken impression that the right-wing forces within the union were near extinction.

Just one month after the convention the right wing won a significant victory in District 8. Twenty-five locals in Missouri, Iowa, Illinois, and Indiana comprised this district. The largest were in St. Louis, including Wagner Electric, Century Electric, and Emerson Electric. Unlike left-wing strongholds such as Districts 2 and 3, District 8 consisted primarily of appliance and small motor plants in which the workers tended to be young, often female, and semiskilled or unskilled.[73] Trouble in District 8 reached back at least to 1941 when a right-wing group in Local 1102 at Emerson Electric first challenged District Vice President William Sentner. James Click, whose father had been a Socialist Party activist, led the insurgents.[74] While not a Socialist Party member himself, Click was close to party members in St. Louis where Socialists forged a good relationship with the ACTU chapter and played a major role in the right wing in the appliance plants.[75]

The District 8 constitution provided that only one officer of the district could be nominated or elected from any one local. This meant that as long as Sentner, District 8 President, held his position, no other member from Local 1102 could be elected to any district office. A fight developed over this at the district convention in

St. Louis. James Click was nominated for recording secretary. He ran as a right-wing candidate. A motion carried to convene the Resolutions Committee to consider the question of the article of the District constitution. By a 6 to 2 vote, the committee ruled that Click could not run. A motion calling for the approval of the committee's report was moved and seconded. Click then called for a roll call vote, and the right-wing forces defeated the committee report 141 to 113. An amendment allowing two officers from any one local carried by a narrow margin. Click was then elected as were two other right-wing candidates, splitting the Board in half. The extraordinary victory effectively brought Sentner's own local into the Carey-Block camp.[76]

Soon after the victory in District 8, the right-wing group in Pittsburgh caused a flurry. Harry Sherman, a former part-time business agent and lawyer for Local 615 instituted a suit against the international union, including all the national officers and all the executive board members except Harry Block. Sherman charged the defendants with being engaged in a "general Communistic conspiracy" to seize control of the CIO. Their aim, he charged, was "to destroy the American system of free enterprise and private property and to set up by means of a general strike, accompanied by force and violence, a Communistic dictatorship." Sherman claimed he had been threatened with death and forced out of the union by those who opposed him. The story received national press coverage.[77]

According to the UE national office, Sherman had been expelled the previous winter by District 6 because he organized a group calling itself the "committee of eight" to fight UE in two NLRB elections at the plant of the American Radiator and Standard Sanitary Company in Pittsburgh.[78] In the fall of 1943, left-wing forces in Local 615, the local which had first raised the question of excluding Communists from membership, brought charges against Sherman. The right-wing leadership refused to act on the charges. The local's failure to act was appealed to the left-wing district executive board by whom, after failing to appear for the hearing, Sherman was expelled. Local 615 ignored the District's action and continued to employ him.[79] The Allegheny County Court subsequently threw Sherman's suit out.

There were also ominous rumblings from the big General Electric Local 203 in Bridgeport, Connecticut. Anticommunists had been active in the local since at least 1942. UE staff representative Charles Rivers called the Connecticut Valley "Carey's second headquarters." By late 1943 the left and right wing forces had begun a six-year war for control of the local. In December 1943, a right-wing insurgency under the tutelage of Father Donnelly swept into power.[80] To top the year off, in what was becoming an annual irritation, District 1 re-elected Harry Block.[81]

In spite of what must have seemed a perpetual state of siege to the general officers, the UE's internal problems did not paralyze its trade union operations. During World War II, three major factors affected collective bargaining: the no-strike pledge, the Little Steel Formula, and the establishment of the War Labor Board as the chief arbiter of labor-management disputes that might interrupt defense production.[82]

UE faced this set of circumstances with a five-pronged program including:

1. Industry-wide stabilization
2. Opposition to wage freezing
3. Collective bargaining for all matters affecting wages
4. Effective control over prices, profits and rationing
5. Correction of inequalities and substandard wage rates.

The union fought for economic stabilization throughout the war. It, like all unions, reacted negatively to the inability of the government to stabilize prices during the long wage freeze.[83]

In spite of its zealous rhetoric about worker sacrifices for the war effort, at no time did the UE fail to push vigorously for economic improvement within the bounds of wage stabilization. Although negotiating in an atmosphere of considerable restriction, during 1942 and 1943 the union managed some wage gains as well as considerable improvement in the area of night bonuses, paid holidays, job classification, and time values.[84]

In its dealings with Westinghouse, the union demanded a 17 cent wage increase to compensate for the rise in living costs, a cost of living escalator clause, and a 40-hour work week guarantee for the duration of the contract. In deciding the case, the War Labor Board refused the wage increase and the escalator clause because they were not permissible under the Little Steel Formula.[85] The union argued that while Westinghouse employees' wages had remained the same since May 1942, increased living costs had reduced the real earnings of the workers.[86]

Some critics have charged that UE's enthusiasm for production during the war led to a deterioration of working conditions, including the speed up, as a result of the proliferation of piecerate incentive systems. The right wing, of course, made this same argument at the time. Much of the criticism springs from UE's Production for Victory Plan, better known as the "Pull-Out Plan," which was more or less a carbon copy of the Communist Party's Production for Victory Plan articulated by Earl Browder in December 1942. In fact, the party worked out its win the war production policy in a series of meetings with Communist CIO leaders during 1942. But Browder also attributed much of what he included in his influential pamphlet, "Production for Victory," to discussions with UE delegates during the union's 1942 convention in New York City.[87]

The UE proposed a voluntary increase in output of 15 percent and cooperation with management. In addition, vacations were more or less given up during the war, and although it never happened, the UE's national officers recommended that overtime pay be sacrificed, if corporations would agree to do the same with "excess" war profits, with the money going either to the government or to buy war bonds. Of course, there is little doubt that the offer to give up overtime was rhetorical. Certainly no one at UE headquarters expected industry to sign on to their half of the bargain. Finally, UE's leaders discouraged "unreasonable" wage demands and called for cost-of-living increases only.[88]

There is no doubt about the UE's enthusiasm for the war effort, but there is considerable doubt as to whether this led to abuses of workers under piecerate or other incentive systems. While the historical response of skilled workers had been to resist pay systems tied to unit of output, by World War II this battle had largely been lost in the UE. Incentive pay systems were commonplace in the electrical industry, particularly in the appliance factories. As an organizing tactic, the UE had often incorporated existing piecework systems into its contracts. There were two basic reasons for this. First of all, it led to earlier agreement from the companies, and second, it ratified existing piecerates and procedures that workers had been able to establish by using shortcuts and other means to beat the system. At no time was this easier to do than during the war when piecerate prices were never higher nor management supervision more lax. According to Harry Block, "Management had cost plus ten. . . . They didn't give a damn." In addition, with basic wages held steady by the Little Steel Formula, along with overtime, piecerate systems provided workers with a way to increase their earnings.

Perhaps the best proof of the lack of worker discontent with incentive systems in electrical manufacturing is the fact that, unlike in the auto industry where incentive systems were new to the workers and led to wildcat strikes and a right-wing victory, the right wing in the UE failed to turn the issue to its advantage.[89] When criticism did surface, it usually came from skilled workers. In Schenectady, craftsmen asked Communist Party organizer Max Gordon how they would go back to a normal work pace if they quadrupled production during the war.[90] Nor was there evidence that UE did not work hard to protect those workers, such as janitors and repair men, who could not take part in individual incentive plans. Workers were also protected against the reduction of piecerates in UE contracts, and workers idled because of a shortage of materials continued to receive their normal base pay.

In this regard the UE's wartime performance differed little from that of the other left-wing unions. Whatever the pressure from the Communist Party and the rhetoric of the Communist labor leaders, wartime contracts in the UE and other left-wing unions did not cede increased prerogatives to management, nor did they weaken workers' protection in the grievance procedure. This was apparently another case of the unwillingness of the Communist labor leaders to submit themselves to Party discipline when it meant giving up hard-won union gains and threatening their leadership positions.[91] Clifford McAvoy, the UE's Washington representative, reacted "with astonishment" to Louis Budenz, the *Daily Worker* editor, when the paper supported a compulsory labor bill that had been introduced in Congress. While the party was supporting the bill, the UE was not.[92] And although Communist UE activists in the shops did meet to discuss how to implement the party's wartime plans and enforce the no-strike pledge, they did not shed their responsibilities to the members. When workers at the Babcock and Wilcox plant in Bayonne, New Jersey, unexpectedly struck, their Communist officers and stewards backed them up.[93]

The UE also used the wartime regulatory machinery effectively. In the 1,843 labor dispute cases involving the UE before the regional War Labor Boards, the union won numerous contract improvements outside of the wage area, including 10 percent shift differential premiums, and graduated vacation plans. In the New York region, six paid holidays became the established rule in all UE shops. For Westinghouse salaried workers, the union obtained the Board's approval for merit increases as well as automatic 10 percent increases after six months. At General Electric a new step rate plan for salaried workers came into being.[94]

During the war years organizational activity went on at full clip. The UE made extraordinary organizing gains, along with most of the mass production unions. Eight hundred and thirty-one NLRB elections were won covering some 335,692 workers. At the beginning of the War UE had 316,000 members in 578 plants. By VJ-Day, 750,000 workers in 1,137 plants belonged to the union.[95]

Many who entered the union during the war were women. By 1945, the UE represented more than 260,000 female workers, some 40 percent of the membership. In spite of the dramatic wartime increase in the number of women in the union, a large female membership was nothing new to the UE. Women had always constituted a significant portion of the workforce in electrical manufacturing, especially in the appliance shops. Because of this, the union had a history of struggles over the issue of substitution of women workers for men. Thus the implications of the war mobilization for the wage structure were obvious to the leadership. As early as May 1941, District 6's executive council warned that the wage differential between men and women could pose a serious danger for wage standards in the industry should war come.[96]

Equal pay for equal work had been on the UE's bargaining agenda before the war, and no matter its zeal for sacrifices during the conflict, the union did not back off of its demands after Pearl Harbor. As a result of agitation initiated by women at the East Pittsburgh Westinghouse plant, the issue was included in national bargaining in 1942 and resulted in an agreement by Westinghouse to narrow sex differentials by two cents an hour throughout the company. By the end of the war, 68 percent of the UE's members worked under equal pay clauses.[97]

But the longstanding industry practice of classifying work as "women's jobs" and "men's jobs" undercut the effectiveness of equal pay for equal work because it did nothing to raise the rates of women employed on traditionally female jobs. The UE feared that industry would use the flood of women coming into the industry to reclassify traditional men's jobs by making minor alterations and reducing the pay rate. This threatened the entire wage structure, and could, the UE's leaders feared, result in the undermining of men's job rates in the postwar period. To forestall this, the UE frequently challenged managerial designation of new jobs as women's jobs, and argued that all new jobs should be classified as men's jobs, no matter who performed them.[98]

The UE's 1945 War Labor Board case against General Electric and Westinghouse was a pathbreaking challenge to the classification of certain jobs as women's work. Far ahead of its time, the union put forward the comparable worth argument that jobs customarily performed by women were paid less, on a comparative job content basis, than those customarily performed by men. The UE attacked the widespread practice of making minor changes in men's jobs, reclassifying them as women's work, and reducing the rate of pay. The Board found for the union in November 1945 and ordered the companies to raise women's pay and to set aside so much per hour for an equity fund to be distributed to women according to collective bargaining agreements.[99] Unfortunately, by the time the decision came down, the war had ended, and the companies ignored the order. The UE did not let the matter die, however. The union made pay equity a major issue in bargaining with General Electric, Westinghouse, and General Motors in 1946, and used the War Labor Board order as the basis of its argument. After striking all three companies, the UE won settlements reducing the differential in men and women's pay.[100]

Women also made great strides inside the UE during the war. By the end of the war there was one woman on the general executive board, Ruth Young, and more than a third of the full-time organizers were women. The 18 female local union presidents and 33 vice-presidents also demonstrated the opening up of the union's elected offices to women.[101]

The UE's concern for women made sense on sheer numbers alone. By the same token, the relative neglect of issues relating to black workers reflected their small numbers in the industry and the union. The UE consistently supported organizations such as the Committee to Abolish the Poll Tax, the National Association for the Advancement of Colored People, and the Committee for a Permanent Fair Employment Practices Commission. But there were relatively few black members, only 5 percent by the war's end. This resulted from several factors. Most electrical manufacturing took place in the Northeast and Midwest, often in small towns and small cities without large black populations. The union's overwhelmingly white membership reflected this. When the UE did push at the local level for equal opportunity for blacks, it was in cities such as New York and St. Louis with heavy concentrations of black workers. The *St. Louis American*, the city's black newspaper, commended the UE for being in the "forefront of racial issues" there.[102]

Because most blacks and women in the electrical industry had been hired during the war, they tended to rank low on seniority ladders. In addition, management, often with the compliance of the local unions, frequently kept women and blacks in segregated, low-skill and low-pay departments, thus making the seniority they did accrue largely meaningless. After the war, when industries reduced their workforces and/or made room for returning servicemen, women and blacks experienced a layoff rate much higher than that of white workers.[103]

The UE had a distinguished war record. Some 200,000 members served in the armed forces.[104] UE shops turned out more than $17 billion worth of war material. Not surprisingly, adherence to the no-strike pledge was above average. During the war, the national average was one-tenth of 1 percent of available time lost through strikes. UE lost only one-thousandth of 1 percent.[105]

As the war neared its end, strife within the union seemed to lessen. During February 1945, President Fitzgerald, along with James Carey, was in London as a participant in the World Trade Union Conference. Clarence Jackson, Communist UE vice president from District 5, went as a Canadian delegate. Although relations between Carey and Fitzgerald remained cool during the conference, the actions there had little real effect on the UE. Fitzgerald along with left-wingers Joe Curran and Reid Robinson, President of the Mine, Mill and Smelter Workers, did favor a less suspicious attitude toward the Soviet trade unions than did Carey and the chief British delegate, Sir Walter Citrine.[106] However, all of the decisions of the London Conference were reached by unanimous vote. Wartime unity still prevailed.

The group met again in Paris in September. At this conference they approved the actions of the London Conference and elected Louis Saillant, a French Communist, general secretary of the newly formed World Federation of Trade Unions. The ideological split between Fitzgerald and Carey surfaced more clearly in Paris on the issue of whether the WFTU should concern itself with trade union matters only and stay away from political action. Carey and Citrine favored the narrow trade union orientation, while Fitzgerald sided with the Soviet desire for a politically active organization.[107] Although this issue had partially divided along ideological lines in the CIO delegation, the division was not yet total. Sidney Hillman, chairman of the CIO delegation, also supported the Soviet stand.[108] There was also no objection from Philip Murray, who was probably anxious to increase the prestige of the CIO in the field of international labor.[109] A few years later when the CIO withdrew from the WFTU and any cooperation with Communist labor federations, the role played by Hillman and Murray in its founding was conveniently overlooked. At the conclusion of the Paris meeting the CIO delegation, including Carey, visited the Soviet Union.[110] The aura of cooperation and brotherhood fostered by the wartime unity had not yet cracked completely on the rocks of the Cold War. In all the *UE News* reporting of the WFTU meetings in Paris, no mention was made of Carey's contribution. He had become a nonperson.

The war with Japan officially ended on August 14, 1945, and barely one month later, on September 11, the General Executive Board signaled the end of the wartime honeymoon between labor and management. The UE, after consultation with the United Steelworkers and the United Auto Workers, announced a demand for a two dollar a day wage increase.[111]

At approximately the same time *UE News* began its agitation to bring the soldiers home.[112] By December the cry became more specific. A District 8 resolution given prominent space in the paper called for an "immediate end to our unwarranted intervention in China, Korea, Indochina, and Java." The paper strongly urged the removal of all United States troops from China and the desertion of Chiang Kai-Shek.[113]

By this time the officers of the UE, along with many other left-of-center factions in the United States, saw the drift of United States policy into a confrontation with the Soviet Union. Although there were great hopes for the success of the United Nations, the UE had by this time become sharply critical of the Truman Administration and its stance toward the post-war world. American troops were still in China and stirrings were evident in Greece. On December 3, Truman gave them a trade union issue from which to mount an attack. He requested, in the midst of the auto strike and threatened strikes in steel and electrical, legislation similar to the Railway Labor Act that would allow him to appoint a fact-finding board and to establish, in effect, a 30-day, no-strike period in labor disputes that were vital to the public interest.[114]

UE reacted immediately. The General Executive Board condemned the Truman proposal as "robbing labor of its freedom to bargain collectively and the right to strike. . . . "[115] In spite of their developing differences on foreign policy, in this attack UE was in the mainstream of the labor movement. William Green called the proposal "unacceptable."[116] Philip Murray reacted even more vigorously and charged Truman with yielding in "abject cowardice" to industry's refusal to engage in collective bargaining.[117] There was a significant addition, however, in what UE said. The left-wing leaders could not resist burdening the trade union justification with their foreign policy agenda. Included in their statement was the accusation that the Truman Administration lent encouragement and sometimes direct aid to antidemocratic forces in nations throughout the world; a clear reference to China and Greece.[118]

Though Murray did not comment publicly on the UE's position, later events made it clear that there were fundamental differences of opinion on the proper role of the labor movement of the

United States in the Cold War confrontation with the Soviet Union. As the ideological polarization of the world continued to widen, so too did the split between Murray and the UE. It would not be trade union issues which would lead to civil war in American labor. Up to the end of World War II, the UE's penchant for speaking out on foreign policy issues had, because of the flow of circumstances, never brought it across Murray's path. Now, however, the tide had changed. UE's consistent left-wing positions had outlived their era. The United States in 1945 was moving decidedly to the right and this tide was destined to catch many Communists, fellow travelers, and liberals who were unwilling to make the fundamental switch to anticommunism that the times demanded for survival.

Nevertheless, as 1945 drew to a close, the depth of these fissures was not yet apparent. With the United Auto Workers already on strike and the steelworkers about to go out, 84 percent of UE members in GE, Westinghouse and General Motors voted to strike if their demand for a $2.00 a day increase was not met.[119]

— 4 —

THE END OF THE POPULAR FRONT

At the end of World War II, Communists led or were dominant partners in the leadership of the UE and 17 smaller CIO affiliates. These unions represented about one third of the CIO's membership. In addition, Communists were partners, although not dominant ones, in the CIO's largest affiliate, the United Auto Workers. State and city CIO councils in New York City, Minnesota, Wisconsin, and Washington were effectively controlled by Communists. It was undoubtedly the high water mark of Communist influence in America, although because of the need to lead masses of non-Communist, even anticommunist workers, the control was fragile and had to be carried out in secrecy and with particular care to maintaining alliances with the CIO's centrists, above all with Philip Murray.[1]

Throughout 1946, while the strength of the anticommunist opposition grew in the CIO and in society at large, this fragile alliance held. In spite of their growing differences with Truman's foreign policy, American Communist Party Chairman Eugene Dennis urged continued support for the united front with noncommunists. "Unfortunately," Dennis told a CP National Committee meeting, some Communists had a "cavalier attitude" about relations between the Murray-Hillman centrists and the left-wing unions in the CIO. He charged the recalcitrants with misjudging and distorting Murray's "generally progressive" positions and turning disagreements into major conflicts with Murray and the "non-left forces in the CIO." Dennis emphatically rejected such tendencies. According to the Communist Party Chairman, the basic policies of the of the CIO were progressive and vital to the struggle for economic justice, democracy, and peace.[2]

85

Following the victory over Japan, the nation turned to the task of demobilizing its huge military establishment and converting from wartime to peacetime production. The war had resulted in a huge growth in the labor force. Labor leaders looked with considerable alarm at the possibility of loss of income from the end of overtime work, downgrading, and the reappearance of large-scale unemployment. These fears, added to the firm stand by business against wage increases without government relaxation of price controls, led to a 12-month series of labor-management conflicts unmatched for their scope and intensity in any comparable period of American history. Between August 14, 1945, and August 14, 1946, 4,630 work stoppages took place. They involved 4.9 million workers who lost 119.8 million man-days of work, or 1.62 percent of all work time in the period.[3]

Although the strike wave involved virtually all major industries, three of the most significant conflicts took place in the automobile, electrical manufacturing, and steel industries. The relationship of two of the participants in the 1946 strike, the UE and the UAW, was to have considerable effect on the future of the electrical union and the CIO. Soon after VJ Day, the UAW Executive Board selected General Motors as the company against which to test the union's demands for a 30 percent wage increase with no accompanying increase in prices.[4] The company's refusal to meet the demands led to a strike of 180,000 auto workers in more than 90 plants on November 21st. The strike and negotiations with General Motors fell under the direction of the young UAW vice-president who headed the General Motors Division, Walter Reuther. Reuther, a young Socialist whose rise to power within the UAW had been meteoric, had become the darling of the union's right wing in its attempt to unseat R. J. Thomas, who had Communist support, as president of the union. The dispute between the two men heated up when Thomas called the General Motors strike premature and criticized the injection of the price issue into the negotiations. Before the General Motors strike ended, Reuther was obviously a candidate for the presidency of the UAW.[5]

In the meantime, considerable activity was taking place in the electrical and steel industries. Whatever action the 30,000 UE members in the General Motors Electrical Division took would obviously affect the Auto Workers. In December, a national delegates conference of the striking General Motors workers urged the UE to call out its members in the electrical appliance division.[6] Nearly one month later, on January 6, 1946, some 200,000 UE members set up mass picket lines around 78 plants of GE, Westinghouse, and the General Motors Electrical Division. UE asked for 25 cents an hour.[7] One week later, on January 21, 800,000 steelworkers, encompassing practically the entire basic steel and steel fabricating industries, walked off their jobs. Labor had effectively, for the first time, closed down the heart of America's industrial might.

UE's actions in the 1946 strike have often been cited as proof that the electrical union would sacrifice the interests of the workers so that it could carry out its ideological stratagems from a firm base.[8] It is important to follow the chronology of the 1946 strikes in order to examine the validity of this proposition.

In the last days of January 1946, while still on strike with General Motors, the United Auto Workers signed with the two other major automobile companies, Ford and Chrysler. The union accepted a raise of 18 cents per hour from Ford and 18.5 cents from the Chrysler Corporation. Instead of the 30 percent demanded from General Motors, these raises equalled 15.1 percent and 16.7 percent respectively.[9] Prior to the settlement, Philip Murray, negotiating with the United States Steel Corporation, had accepted President Truman's suggested 18.5 cents per hour formula as fair. It was the steel industry which had refused the Truman figure. Thus, even before the steelworkers went on strike, their leader, the president of the CIO, had accepted the 18.5 cents formula.

On February 12th, after striking for five weeks, UE announced a settlement with General Motors for an 18.5 cents wage package.[10] By that time Reuther had reduced his demands to 19.5 cents. The settlement drew a quick reaction from the United Auto Workers. The February 11th meeting of the Auto Workers city-wide strike committee in Detroit adopted a resolution that emphatically condemned this "double-crossing" of the striking General Motors workers by the UE leadership.[11]

Just three days later, on February 15th, Philip Murray accepted an identical 18.5 cents settlement from United States Steel.[12] On March 13th, after 113 days, the United Auto Workers finally settled with General Motors for the 18.5 cents package that they had long ago accepted from Ford and Chrysler and which Murray had signified his willingness to accept as early as January.[13] One day later General Electric and the UE agreed to the same settlement and on May 10th, Westinghouse did the same. In light of the fact that it was Philip Murray who originally accepted the 18.5 cents formula, and of the fact that the UAW had also accepted it with Ford and Chrysler, it seems somewhat questionable to accuse UE of selling out a brother union by accepting the established pattern from General Motors. This is especially true in light of the fact that by the time of the UE settlement the UAW's hourly demand had been reduced from 30 cents to 19.5 cents, and the company and the union were locked in a struggle for the one cent an hour above the Steelworker and UE settlements—one cent that Reuther needed to save face and the company had vowed not to give under any circumstances.

At the conclusion of this long siege of 1946 strikes, several important conditions had been created which were to be crucial to the future of the CIO. First of all, by signing with General Motors while the UAW remained on strike, the UE incurred the lasting enmity of the rising star of industrial unionism, Walter Reuther. Although Murray, not the UE officers, set the wage pattern for 1946, he remained above attack. UE, on the other hand, had given Reuther a tailor-made issue to use in his civil war with the left wing in the Auto Workers. UE's action had immeasurably strengthened the Reuther forces in their attempt to unseat R. J. Thomas. It was Thomas who signed with Ford and Chrysler, leading to the subsequent UE agreement with General Motors.[14] Whether or not the settlement was honorable, it is difficult to lay the blame at UE's door in light of the actions of Murray and Thomas. Nevertheless, the events of 1946 catapulted Reuther to leadership and placed within the councils of the CIO a powerful leader of a huge union to whom Murray, no matter how reluctantly, would have to pay considerable attention.[15] His victory in 1946, however, was not yet complete. The left-wing faction backing Thomas captured the remaining three posts on the executive board. Reuther's onslaught against the left-wing unions would have to wait at least one more year.

The developing split between the UE officers and the leadership of the CIO and the Democratic Party also threatened the UE's alliance with the CIO centrists. In the midst of the 1946 strike, Winston Churchill gave his famous "Iron Curtain" speech in Missouri. His call for a binding and perpetual military alliance between the United States and Great Britain against the Soviet Union met with derision in *UE News*, which attacked the idea of an alliance as an attempt to preserve Britain's tottering empire.[16] Lining up in support of Henry Wallace, whose position in Truman's cabinet was fast becoming untenable because of his opposition to the administration's Cold War policy, the UE's leadership charged that the United States foreign policy was being shaped by "monopolists" and "imperialists" seeking to provoke another war.[17]

This attitude signaled a break with Murray on the issue of containment of the Soviet Union, and was quite significant. While it may have been obvious to many observers that Murray and the UE officers had fundamentally differing views on foreign policy, the circumstances of world events had always left them supporting roughly the same positions, even if for different reasons. During the long period from 1937 to 1947 Julius Emspak served as a member of the CIO Resolutions Committee and without exception participated in the formulation of CIO foreign policy and supported those formulations. According to the UE, not once during those years, either publicly or in CIO Executive Board meetings, did problems or differences surface between UE and CIO on foreign policy.[18]

The significance of the obviously widening split within the CIO was not lost on Murray. Reuther's victory in the 1946 UAW convention left the two largest CIO unions, the UAW and the USWA, in the right-wing camp. Differences also began to become apparent in the strategy for "Operation Dixie," the CIO's massive, and ultimately unsuccessful, Southern organizing drive. The UE contributed $500,000, but UE organizers were not asked to participate, nor were organized shops that fell under the UE's jurisdiction turned over to the union.[19] One of the first manifestations of Murray's mood occurred in the steel union at the May 1946, convention. Murray authorized a "statement of policy" which read, "this union will not tolerate efforts by outsiders . . . whether they be Communists, Socialists or any other group, to infiltrate, dictate or meddle in our affairs."[20] Although the statement also disavowed any intention of purging anyone for their "thoughts or beliefs," the weeding out of left-wing influence had begun. It was characteristic of the thorough and deliberate Murray to clean out his own union completely of left-wing influence before the showdown with the left-wing forces in the CIO.

While the statement spoke of outsiders meddling in the affairs of the United Steel Workers of America, nobody was under the misapprehension that the warning was also meant for the Catholic labor activists carrying on anticommunist struggles in various CIO unions. Their activities had diminished somewhat during the last years of the war, but they returned to the fray with renewed vigor in 1946, and the UE remained their main target. In a revealing exchange of letters, two labor priests indicated the extent of their activities. In a letter to the Rev. Thomas Darby in Hartford, Connecticut, Father Rice spoke of the need for concerted action with the UE right-wing at the 1946 UE convention. "Incidentally," he wrote, "I am in favor of putting Jim Carey back there as President but over the years I have found him of damn little assistance."[21] In reply, Darby explained his promptness as an effort to get Rice to "back off on Jim Carey for a while. He'll probably be glad to run for it (President) if we must call on him. However, (Reverend) Donnelly in Hartford and Leo Brown, S. J. in St. Louis have rank and filers we might find have the right caliber. Jim C. is a little bit too much of a chameleon."[22] This exchange calls into question Harry Block's claim that Catholic influence in the UE right-wing movement was minimal.[23] It is also revealing to learn that an important segment of right-wing leadership shared somewhat Matles's and Emspak's opinion of Carey.

Right-wing activity in the UE was obviously on the upswing. The left-wing executive board of Local 801, the big Frigidaire local in Dayton, Ohio, suspended two right-wingers for assisting an attempt by the International Brotherhood of Electrical Workers (AFL) to raid a UE shop using the Communist issue as its selling point. While the officers of UE lauded the local for repudiating AFL efforts to disrupt the organization, they most certainly recognized the threat that this new factor posed to the organization. The IBEW raid proved to be the first of a long list of raids on UE shops by a variety of unions.[24] Events in Local 801 had been plaguing the international leadership since 1942 when a right-wing faction began to challenge for leadership with the covert support of James Click from the big right-wing Emerson Electric local in St. Louis.[25] Charges of embezzlement, the beatings of left wingers, and other disruptions created a situation so tense that a state of permanent war existed in the local as the two sides traded victories during the war.[26]

An even larger challenge confronted the left-wing leadership of UE in Connecticut when Bridgeport Local 203 went on record advocating that "any member who acts in the interest of Communism or any other ism be enjoined from becoming an office holder in Local 203."[27] One month later the local announced changes in its bylaws establishing penalties for anyone convicted of "introducing Communist political doctrine into the business of the union."[28] While the international had repeatedly attempted to put a stop to such changes, it had little effect. Local 203 defiantly disregarded directives of the UE convention.

District 2 in New England, particularly Connecticut with its large Catholic working class, had been fertile ground for the insurgents since early 1940 when a group of dissidents in Hartford warned the general officers that UE staff were more interested in building the Communist Party than "strong, clean unions," and that unless "more correct and American ways" were adopted, they would bring the issue out into the open. By 1941, the right-wing forces, dubbed the "Christian Front" by the incumbents, had mounted a spirited, if unsuccessful challenge for control of the district. The right-wing managed to win control of at least ten locals by 1946, including the important Springfield General Electric plant.[29]

There were several reasons for the right-wing success in Connecticut. One was the Catholic Church's influence in the labor movement, fashioned out of excellent organization and the presence of the Diocesan Labor Institute, founded by the Reverend Joseph Donnelly. Many of the most dedicated right wingers honed their skills in institute classes. When they graduated to the intra-union battles, they returned to share their first-hand experiences with new recruits. Often those instructors came from the Mine, Mill, and Smelter Workers and were part of the right-wing insurgency in that left-wing union in Connecticut's "Brass Valley." The UE insurgents benefited from their experience. In cities where both groups had strength, such as Bridgeport, they also became a potent conservative political force, often supporting Republican candidates and attacking CIO-PAC.[30]

While these local battles were widely scattered, their intensity and the similarity of tactics employed by the insurgents left no doubt in the minds of the general officers that the right wing, no longer restrained by the wartime spirit of cooperation with the Soviet Union, was about to mount a concerted drive to capture the UE. District Council 2 fired the first salvo in counter attack on August 3rd, blasting the right wing for "red-baiting" and calling it an ally of the enemies of labor.[31] The attack was well timed. Just eight days later, representatives of ten locals met in Pittsburgh and formed an organization calling itself the UE Members for Democratic Action (UEMDA). Harry Block, after his election as chairman, called on the rank and file to oust officers with Communist "leanings." The UE could either return to the ranks of CIO unions with "sound objectives" or continue as a front for the Communist Party.[32]

UEMDA drew its strength from several quarters. One, of course, was Catholic anticommunism, which had particularly important influence in District 6 in Western Pennsylvania, District 8 in St. Louis, District 2 in New England, and District 4 in New York. Less significant, but important, were the Socialists. Prior to the United States entry into World War II, Socialists and Communists fought each other bitterly in a variety of unions such as the International Ladies Garment Workers, the Auto Workers, the American Federation of Teachers, and the Southern Tenant Farmers Union.[33] Although the Socialist Party did not have many members in the UE, most were activists and militant anticommunists.

In cities where the party had some presence, Socialists provided the often inexperienced right-wing leaders with valuable expertise and commitment. As early as 1940 one Socialist UE member wrote that he had "made real progress in rounding up honest, progressive workers" in the New York locals who were opposed to Communist Party control of UE.[34] By 1946, Socialist Party labor secretary William Becker boasted of "orchestrating an anticommie movement" among Socialist Party members in UE. Becker identified a strong Socialist Party presence in key locals in New York, Lynn, Massachusetts, and Pittsburgh. Another factor of importance for the Socialists was their strength in the Auto Workers where they played key roles in supporting Walter Reuther for the presidency. After the UAW and the UE had their falling out over the 1946 General Motors strikes, the Socialist Party and Reuther cooperated in the anticommunist drive in UE.[35]

The Socialists in UEMDA also helped to tone down the confessional character of the organization, and made it a viable alternative for left-wing opponents of the Communist party who would have rejected serving in an army commanded by Roman Catholic priests. In fact, relations between the Socialists and Catholics varied from location to location. They were difficult in New York and good in Michigan, but the two groups did provide much of the leadership of the UE insurgency.[36]

Albert Fitzgerald reacted immediately to the founding of UEMDA blasting Harry Block and James Click and charging them with fronting for individuals outside of the union who were trying to meddle in its affairs.[37] He undoubtedly meant ACTU. He was on firm ground since the ACTU met concurrently in the same hotel with the founding meeting of UEMDA in Pittsburgh. The ACTU provided by far the largest and best organized group for the UE insurgents. The organization had been fighting the UE leadership since 1939. These successes had led to the formation of the "UE Committee for Rank-and-File Democracy," the group that issued the call for the Pittsburgh meeting that led to the formation of UEMDA.[38]

Father Rice more or less choreographed both meetings as participants moved back and forth. This was not surprising because ACTU's expressed purpose was to plan strategy for the upcoming 1946 UE convention in Milwaukee, including the selection of a candidate to run for president against Albert Fitzgerald.[39]

Hard on the heels of the UEMDA-ACTU meetings, the IBEW won the first NLRB election against UE which could be traced to the Communist issue. The AFL union used the UEMDA press release condemning the UE leadership effectively at the last minute to clinch the victory at the Farnsworth Company plant in Huntington, Indiana. John Gojack, president of UE District 9, blamed the loss directly on Block and Click.[40] Just prior to the UE convention, the General Executive Board formally condemned Harry Block and all who attended the Pittsburgh meeting for the "disruptive" activities against the union.[41] The depth of UE's concern became evident when for the first time James Matles took notice of the effect on organization when he blamed losses at two plants on copies of the Pittsburgh UEMDA press release which were distributed on the morning of the NLRB elections. At Sangamon Electric in Illinois, the UE lost 800 to 650, although a majority of the workers had signed UE cards before the election.[42]

Thus was the stage set for the 1946 UE convention. The right-wingers had decided to make their most serious challenge in Milwaukee. A huge news buildup preceded the meetings. The drama was heightened by the action of John Metcalfe, president of Local 601, the largest UE local, who resigned charging that Communists controlled the union. He claimed the enormous majority of "Catholics, Republicans, Democrats, and all good labor men" deeply resented the activities of the small number of Communists who had seized control.[43] The largest contingent of newsmen ever to attend a UE convention observed the proceedings. The battle started almost immediately after President Fitzgerald welcomed the delegates. The officers report, which blasted the United States and Britain for their European and China policies, was immediately challenged by the UEMDA contingent.[44] They were overwhelmed.

The UEMDA, however, had decided to do battle on a variety of fronts, and their organization and discipline revealed the contribution of the more experienced floor leaders from the ACTU. The UEMDA ran a slate of challengers headed by Harry Block against the general officers. Carey had decided not to run.[45] For the first time the right wing issued minority reports from each committee where they had representation. Key floor fights took place on the foreign policy resolution and on the belabored constitutional issue of whether a local union could set ideological requirements for its officer.[46] In an attempt to seize a popular issue, UEMDA opposed an increase in per capita payments from the locals to the international union.[47] The administration forces easily turned back each challenge.

Ironically, the fact that Philip Murray addressed the convention compounded the difficulties of the right wing. Prior to the meetings the press had speculated that the surfacing of UEMDA, along with similar moves within the left-wing Mine, Mill and Smelter Workers, would force Murray away from his hands-off policy.[48] They were mistaken. Murray was obviously not ready to come out into the open with the anti-left-wing fight. His speech gave little comfort to the right wing. He praised the UE administration for its splendid support of the CIO and of him personally. Somewhat obscurely he told the delegates that the CIO was not going to be bothered by "ideological mumblings of groups that are hell bent upon destroying it." He warned that the organization was "fundamentally American."[49] When asked whether the "reds" in the CIO would come under attack, he responded by saying that he wasn't "a very good hunter."[50] The delegates gave the CIO president a tremendous ovation and immediately passed a resolution supporting him.[51] Then, apparently seeing no contradiction in their actions, they re-elected their left-wing general officers by a 6 to 1 margin over their challengers.[52] The irony of the situation lay in the fact that while Murray spoke, many of his men were actively engaged in purging left-wingers in CIO councils around the country. In fact, James Carey, his secretary-treasurer, was engaged in similar work on the floor of the UE convention.

The victory of the UE leadership appeared so complete that the victors could not help rubbing it in a bit. A resolution condemning "red-baiting" passed by a vote of 2,818 to 687.[53] With obvious relish the delegates condemned the newspapers for their attacks on the union before and during the conventions. They took great satisfaction in the fact that the press had been disappointed in what happened at the convention, and that Block and Carey had been "figures with feet of printers ink."[54] In his closing remarks, Fitzgerald urged the delegates to return to their local unions prepared to stamp out factionalism wherever they found it.[55] The members from District 1 took him quite literally. On October 7, they voted Harry Block out of office by a narrow margin and replaced him with James Price, business agent for the pro-administration Local 107 in Essington, Pennsylvania, and a one-time member of the Industrial Workers of the World.[56]

But even as their control over the union seemed more secure than ever, the left wing was contemplating a step that would contribute mightily to the disaster that would eventually befall the union. One other discussion that took place behind closed doors at the convention was the possibility of UE's support for independent political action. In fact, the convention passed a resolution calling for the establishment of a "People's Party" in 1948 if the two major parties "refused to heed the will of the American people." A few weeks after the convention, not long after Henry Wallace had resigned from the Truman cabinet because of foreign policy differences, *UE News* urged him to take his fight to the people.[57] Emspak telegraphed Wallace indicating UE's shock at Truman's action. He pledged support to Wallace's criticism of Truman's foreign policy and urged him to continue his fight for a policy of peaceful cooperation among the great powers.[58] A good indication of the way in which the administration's policy was developing could be seen in District 4 in New York and New Jersey, often the most closely aligned to the general officers, and firmly under Communist control. At a meeting the District Council pointed out that more and more the foreign policy of the nation was being "dictated" by the most reactionary elements in the Democratic and Republican parties and by the business interests. The resolution commended Wallace for bringing to the people the issue of whether the country was to be drawn into another war or to continue the fight for peace.[59]

It is certain that these actions did not please Murray, who only in July had appointed Julius Emspak as one of a five-man board to control the activities of the CIO Political Action Committee following the death of Sidney Hillman.[60] The divergent path taken by UE and the other left-wing unions on the foreign policy issue was making it difficult for Murray to suppress an open break. Only a few weeks before the national CIO convention in 1946, a committee of 34 members calling itself the "CIO Committee for Democratic Trade Unionism" had formed to fight left-wing influence in the CIO. Murray directed it to disband and "cease those activities which properly belong to the CIO and its affiliates."[61] One wonders if the left wing noted the irony implicit in the order. Whatever his intent, circumstances were making it impossible for Murray to ignore the matter when the delegates assembled in Atlantic City.

Murray came to the convention well armed for handling the growing split within the organization. Meeting on November 15, 1946, his executive board gave Murray the authority to take over funds and property of local and state industrial union councils which failed to conform to CIO policy. These central bodies were directly chartered by the CIO and were not autonomous.[62] Murray also brought the issue of communism before the CIO Executive Board, but lack of agreement there led to the appointment of a committee of six, equally balanced between right and left wings, to draw up a statement on the question.[63] What Murray wanted was clear; an anticommunist statement that would be acceptable to the left wing.[64] The strategy obviously required the left wing to give up something in order to forestall more drastic action by Murray.

The policy had three objectives: to reduce the influence of the left wing, to soften the blow by hamstringing the right-wing opposition, and to convince the public that the whole issue existed largely in the press.[65] Central to this strategy was the statement of policy on communism which emerged from the committee of six with unanimous approval. It rejected "the efforts of the Communist Party or other political parties and their adherents to interfere in the affairs of the CIO."[66] Only two delegates at the convention, both from the left-wing National Maritime Union, voted against it. Apparently they had not gotten the word from the Communist caucus since they later reversed their vote.[67] Subsequent events were to prove their first instincts correct. Solid left-wing support for this statement can only be explained by the fact that Murray must have made it known that the statement was a sop to public opinion in lieu of action. The CIO president declared that the statement set up "guideposts that necessarily must be followed by each of our international unions and all of our subsidiary affiliates."[68] Or it can be seen as a recognition by the party of the necessity to allow the trade union Communists the independence necessary to maintain their influence in increasingly perilous times. Nevertheless, the 1946 statement provided the justification for the right-wing, rank-and-file movements of the next few years.

There were other indications of the changing mood of the CIO at the Atlantic City convention. Murray had Carey renominated for secretary-treasurer by his steelworker vice-president, Van Bittner, the significance of which must have been obvious to the left wing.[69] The convention adopted new rules for industrial union councils which prohibited them from making pronouncements on national and international issues unless the national CIO had already ruled on such questions, barred them from sending delegates to organizations not recognized by the CIO, and rearranged the voting rules.[70] Finally, Murray replaced Reid Robinson, president of the left-wing Mine, Mill and Smelter Workers, as a CIO vice-president with the new leader of the CIO anticommunists, Walter Reuther. Robinson had solicited a $5,000 loan from an employer with whom the union had a contract, giving Murray a perfect trade union issue on which to act without having to raise the ideological split.[71]

Whatever Murray's intention in asking for the anticommunist resolution at the 1947 convention, it did not take long for its impact to be felt. Immediately following the convention, a rash of UEMDA activity struck UE. The right wing even ventured onto the floor of the solidly left-wing District 4 convention where a small determined anti-administration group waged a floor fight.[72] The UEMDA won control of six locals in New York, Pennsylvania, and Connecticut.[73] In a close and disputed election an anticommunist slate managed to elect one of its members for the first time as vice-president of the huge General Electric Local 301 in Schenectady.[74] In Pittsburgh, under the careful guidance of Father Rice, UEMDA swept the annual election of Westinghouse Local 601.[75] In Fitzgerald's own Lynn GE local, a committee to drive the Communists out of office had formed.[76] *Labor Leader*, the publication of the ACTU, reported that in the month of December, UEMDA groups had won control of five UE locals with a total of 22,000 members.[77] The losses continued into the new year. In January of 1947, four more locals shifted to the right wing, including General Electric Local 901 and Magnavox Local 910 in Fort Wayne, Indiana, and General Electric Local 419 in Mt. Vernon, New York. But the big loss was the big Frigidaire Local 801 in Dayton, Ohio, which had been the scene of a bitter struggle for several years.[78]

The full implications of the CIO resolution on communism soon became apparent in Connecticut and Minnesota. In neither place was UEMDA a factor. Right-wing forces had gained control of Bridgeport Local 203 in 1946. The local, which had been troubling the general officers almost from its inception, and which left-wing staff representative Charles Rivers called a "perennial nightmare," exploded into national prominence on February 4.[79] Though out of power, the left-wing forces in the local had continued to fight. On February 2, some 1,300 members out of 6,000 met and instructed the officers to proceed with action against members who were "Communists, fellow travelers, Ku-Kluxers, or Columbians."[80] Two days later, the officers met and expelled 26 members of the local for being Communists or Communist sympathizers, justifying the action as in line with "national CIO policy." Almost all of the 26 who received notification of expulsion from Joseph Julianelle, right-wing business agent, were former officers or stewards of the union. Some, such as Josephine Willard, Jake Goldring, and Frank Fazekas openly professed Communist Party membership, but others, such as Oliver Arsenault, were local Democratic Party activists. The Local 203 board directed Julius Emspak to remove the expelled members from the international union's mailing list.[81]

UE reacted immediately. Fitzgerald fired off a telegram to local president, Michael Berescik and business agent Julianelle ordering them to cease "the unconstitutional expulsion of members of Local 203 and to withdraw and revoke immediately all expulsions."[82] On February 10th, the General Executive Board revoked the charter of the local in response to a petition from the ousted members and sympathizers.[83]

The action taken by the officers in expelling the 26 was a bit too strong even for other elements of the right wing. Although Berescik and Julianelle were UEMDA members, the ACTU called their action "a clear violation of the UE constitution" and "wrong in itself." The tone of the criticism was that the Bridgeport group, which ACTU's paper, *Labor Leader*, claimed was never part of UEMDA or ACTU, "lost its head" and "went off the deep end."[84] There was good reason why even the most militant anti-administration supporters took pause at the actions of the Bridgeport group. Under the maintenance of membership clause which the union had with the company, expulsion from the local also meant loss of jobs. As for the ACTU's disclaimer, it is significant that when the District 2 Council met in Boston and voted overwhelmingly to reinstate the expelled members, the UEMDA faction at the meeting voted against it.

There were several significant factors discernible in the Bridgeport confrontation. First, the tactic of expulsion proved to be fairly ineffective, perhaps even counterproductive. However, it was significant that while the administration used every weapon at its command to whip the local back into line, it failed. Importantly, the Connecticut courts sided with the insurgents in ruling the UE's revocation of the charter invalid because no charges were filed against the local and no hearing was held before the charter was revoked.[85] In addition an attempt to get an injunction restraining the officers of Local 203 from performing their duties failed.[86]

The insurgency in Bridgeport also demonstrated the diversity of the anticommunist forces. Many of the prominent Bridgeport right-wingers were active in the Republican Party. One of their major goals, indeed the basis of their platform as early as 1943, was the removal of the local from partisan politics, or, in the context of CIO labor politics of the time, from Democratic Party politics. As soon as they took office at the beginning of 1944, the new officers of the local ended all support for PAC, which they, like the ACTU and conservative forces everywhere, considered a Trojan horse of Communist power in the United States. This suited Republican congressional candidate Claire Booth Luce, a Roman Catholic and a bitter critic of CIO-PAC and Sidney Hillman, who enjoyed considerable support among the right-wing forces in Local 203. In nominating her for congress in 1944, UE steward Joseph Napolitano declared that "working men in this country will not consent to being used by Sidney Hillman and the Political Action Committee as poker chips in a political gamble for power." After the Republican surge in the congressional elections of 1946, which was even greater in Connecticut than elsewhere, the political influence of the Catholic Church and the right-wing officers of Local 203 grew considerably.[87]

The situation in Minnesota appeared even more ominous, constituting as it did almost a microcosm of the developing political forces that were threatening the left's place in the CIO in general. Since its inception the Minnesota CIO Council had been controlled by Communists and their allies through UE locals that held a majority of CIO members in the state. This dominance increased in 1941 when an organizing drive under the leadership of an open Communist, William Mauseth, succeeded in organizing Honeywell, a manufacturer of electrical equipment. The Honeywell UE Local 1145 grew dramatically during the war and emerged as the largest local union in the state. Because of anticommunist attacks on him, Mauseth withdrew into the background and turned the leadership of the local over to his protege, Robert Wishart, who became president of the state CIO council and a power in Minnesota's leading liberal political force, the Farmer Labor Party. Wishart began his rise to the top of CIO politics in Minnesota as a leader of the Communist-led secession of Minneapolis locals of the Machinist Union into the UE in 1937. Always identified closely with the left, Wishart never admitted to Communist Party membership, although he had been a mainstay of the Communist-led Workers Alliance and his name appeared in an advertisement lauding the *Daily Worker* on its twentieth anniversary.[88] But by 1946, the labor and political environment in Minnesota had changed dramatically. The growth in the state of the anticommunist United Steelworkers and the United Packinghouse Workers had given them considerable power in the state CIO. Equally threatening was the rise of Hubert Humphrey, the young mayor of Minneapolis, who had organized anticommunist liberals in the state to do battle for control of the Democratic Farmer Labor Party. Humphrey's attack was particularly galling because he had largely been selected by the Minneapolis labor movement, dominated by the left-wing UE, and elected because of labor support.[89] The pressure led Wishart to abandon his UE allies. In January he had resigned as a member of the UE Executive Board. On March 13, 1946, he suddenly, without warning, submitted his resignation as President of the state CIO council.[90] Wishart's defection led to the left-wing loss of control of the Minnesota CIO. The loss was a severe one for the UE administration and for the CIO's left wing. Clarence Hathaway (former editor of the *Daily Worker*) and William Mauseth, both UE business agents, had hitherto exercised great influence in labor councils in the state. The president of UE District 11, which included Minnesota, was

Ernest DeMaio. DeMaio, the first paid organizer on the UE staff, had a long list of Communist affiliations including incorporation of the left-wing *Chicago Star*, directorship in the Abraham Lincoln School in Chicago, and membership in the Joint Anti-Fascist Refugee Committee.[91] His brother, Anthony DeMaio, a UE staff representative for the district was a former officer in the Abraham Lincoln Brigade in the Spanish Civil War.[92] The trouble in Minnesota was especially significant because, rather than a narrow intra-union struggle, it resulted from the efforts of a coalition of liberal political and union groups that had previously been the key popular front allies of the Communists.[93]

The startling events in Bridgeport and Minnesota were by no means the only problems the UE administration faced early in 1947. The first manifestation of the CIO's swing to the right came in January when Joseph Curran pulled the National Maritime Union out of the left-wing orbit and began a purge of his old allies in the union.[94] Closer to home, UE District 4 issued a warning to all locals to beware of the outside connections of adherents of the UEMDA. The occasion for the warning was the activity of a UEMDA group in Local 411, Rahway, New Jersey. There the local leadership sought a charter from either the UAW or the United Steelworkers. George Addes, UAW secretary-treasurer and a foe of Reuther, wrote Albert Fitzgerald of his deep regret over the situation. He also wrote of the UAW policy against raiding other CIO unions.[95] A year later with Addes gone and Reuther in complete control, any hint of solidarity disappeared.

The UE blamed UEMDA for the trouble in Rahway. An article in *UE News* accused Block of encouraging Local 411 to secede. Block denied any such complicity and issued the following statement: "The UEMDA are opposed to any group leaving the UE and feel that the only way the situation can be corrected is within the UE-CIO. To that end we will remain in the UE, and we will use our energies for the benefits of the membership of the UE."[96] An investigative committee in District 1 absolved Block of any wrongdoing in the Rahway situation. The finding displeased *UE News*, which felt the committee missed the point.[97] In fact, the report of the committee was probably accurate. The goal of UEMDA was to capture control of UE. One of the great problems it would increasingly face was the tendency for right-wing locals to secede because they thought capture of their own international to be impossible. This belief and raids by other CIO unions cut severely into right-wing strength, a strength which was growing rapidly. By February 1947, James Carey claimed the support of locals with over 55,000 members.[98] In the last two months of 1946 alone, according to ACTU, some 40,000 had come under right-wing control by election.[99]

To make matters even worse for the administration, opposition forces within UE, capitalizing on the growing anticommunist feeling in the nation, continued to pick up powerful allies. The long round of congressional loyalty hearings that would climax in the McCarthy era was beginning. Before the House Committee on Un-American Activities, Louis Budenz, ex-editor of the *Daily Worker* who had turned government informer, testified that both Emspak and Matles were members of the Communist Party and that, in fact, Emspak was the mysterious "Comrade Juniper," a secret trade union leader who sat on the party's highest councils.[100] Aid also came from another quarter. In its issues of February 27 and March 1, the widely read *Saturday Evening Post* ran an article by Joseph and Stewart Alsop entitled, "Will the CIO Shake the Communists Loose?" It dealt at length with UE affairs and depicted Carey and the UEMDA as heroes.[101]

Fitzgerald fought back. At a meeting of the CIO vice-presidents in February 1947, he charged Carey with giving aid and comfort to insurgents within the union. Murray, however, remained neutral on the surface and took no action.[102] At the semi-annual convention of UE District 9 held at Richmond, Indiana, in March, Fitzgerald, in replying to questions concerning the loyalty of his fellow officers, disclaimed any knowledge of Communist affiliation and cautioned the delegates to pay more attention to wages, hours and working conditions. He blasted Budenz for charging Emspak with being an active Communist for 20 years by pointing out that the secretary-treasurer was still in high school 20 years before. Obviously in reference to the *Saturday Evening Post* article, he joked that maybe "someday the UE would have a movie about James Carey which would be called, "The Charles McCarthy of James Matles." He ended by announcing a booklet published by UE and written by Matles which answered the *Post* article.[103] UE had published the reply in booklet form after the magazine refused to publish it.

While the attack in the magazine obviously rankled, the pressure coming from the government proved even more serious. UE officials were being challenged on the loyalty question at every turn. At a hearing of the Senate Committee on Labor and Public Welfare, Fitzgerald, Emspak and Matles hotly denied that they were Communists. Ostensibly called to hear testimony on pending labor legislation, the hearing degenerated into a discussion of the political affiliation of the UE officers. Senator Robert Taft first injected the issue.[104] Several weeks later at the hearings of the

House Labor Committee for the same purpose, Representative John F. Kennedy grilled his old Harvard economics instructor, Russ Nixon, on the extent of Communist influence in the UE. Nixon answered the persistent young Massachusetts Congressman that some Communists were members of the union, and he defended their right to believe in communism.[105] Another questioner of the UE Washington representative was Congressman Richard Nixon of California who proved much more interested in how Russ Nixon and UE stood on military aid to Greece than he was in what he had to say about the labor legislation before the committee.[106]

The UE's problems with the government were just beginning. On June 16, 1947, a House Committee on Un-American Activities (HUAC) spokesman announced that the committee had uncovered a group of UE members willing to testify, and that it was opening hearings on the UE in Washington.[107] No one was surprised that the mysterious witnesses were from the Bridgeport local. The Bridgeport story had gotten national exposure and in his questioning of Fitzgerald during the previous hearings, Senator Taft had inquired about the situation. On July 19, 1947, Michael Berescik and Joseph Julianelle were announced as the first witnesses.[108] In a whirlwind, two-day hearing on the extent of Communist influence in the union, the HUAC first heard the recounting of the Bridgeport episode from Julianelle and Berescik. Julianelle assured the committee that he had "good reason" to believe that Matles and Emspak were Communists, but he had no "proof."[109] His colleague, Berescik, however, was not quite so positive. His testimony is interesting as an example of the tone of the hearings.

> **Mr. Stripling:** (Chief Investigator—HUAC) "Do you consider Mr. Matles or Mr. Emspak to be Communists?"
>
> **Mr. Berescik:** "Well sir, Mr. Emspak, frankly, from what I have heard him say—he is quite evasive—a very able speaker—on the basis of what I read in the paper I would call him a Communist, but on the basis of conversation with the man, I couldn't say, I couldn't call him a Communist."
>
> **Mr. Stripling:** "Do you think that he and other officials of the international union conducted the affairs of the international union in such a way as to conform to the Communist Party line?"
>
> **Mr. Berescik:** "So far as Jim Matles is concerned—he is the director of organization—I will say that if I was to give credit

to any one man in the UE for building up the UE to its present position, I would give it to him. He is second to none in any group in this country when it comes to organizational matters. However, in the last few years Mr. Matles has deviated from his original program and I think, and have every reason to believe, the international ranks—that is, in District 2—interested in doing a job on local 203 and any other so-called dissident forces within the UE. But from the organizational standpoint, Jim built the UE where it is."[110]

On such testimony the committee went about building its case against UE. Also based on such "expert" opinion, the names of the 26 expelled members of Local 203 were placed in the record.[111]

On the second day of the hearings, two UE members who claimed to have once been members of the Communist Party testified. One, Salvatore Vottis, a former UE member from General Electric Local 301 in Schenectady, testified that the Communists controlled the local from its inception and that they held secret meetings during UE conventions to outline strategy. According to Vottis, Matles and Emspak ran these meetings. He also claimed that Matles and Emspak had attended Party meetings in the Vottis home.[112] This was more to the committee's liking. However, James Conroy, another former party member and sympathetic witness, categorically stated that while James McLeish, District 4 president, Michael Fitzpatrick, District 6 president, John Gojack, president of District 9, and William Sentner, District 8 president, were Communists, to the best of his knowledge Emspak, Matles, Fitzgerald, and Russell Nixon were not.[113] This was an interesting admission from a self-proclaimed former party member from New York City where Matles and Emspak could have been expected to have been known had they been party members. On this inconclusive note the hearings ended. Nothing had really been accomplished, but the press had linked the UE name with communism across the country. The hearings, and their timing, had established a pattern. Three times in the next four years congressional committees would investigate UE on the Communist issue. Each time the results would be inconclusive but the attendant publicity would damage the image of the administration and have the effect of aiding the insurgents. The timing of congressional hearings to coincide with crucial events in the left-right fight in the UE was no coincidence. Clearly the government had become the ally of the UEMDA.

UE News gave the hearings copious coverage, hoping that the sight of UE members aiding a "labor-baiting" government commit-

tee would backfire against the UEMDA.[114] But much of the publicity value was lost when Harry Block, head of UEMDA, refused to
testify. He had been invited to testify,[115] but declined on the grounds
that "he and his associates" felt that the affair was not the business
of the committee which had entered into an intra-union matter.[116]
Block never changed his position, even though Carey testified at a
later date. Aside from wanting to keep the fight within the union,
he later indicated the he knew that HUAC was no friend of his or of
the labor movement.[117]

Spurred on by their successes, the right wing continued to
work from within to capture local unions. In June the movement hit
close to home as Local 1237 in New York, an 800 member group,
charged UE general officers with misusing union funds by contributing $1,000 to the Civil Rights Congress, "a well known Com-
munist front organization,"[118] By August the local, of which James
Conroy, ex-Communist turned ACTU activist, was business agent,
had openly moved into the UEMDA camp.[119] The Catholic connection could be just as effective in the small towns of the Midwest. In
a right-wing attempt to capture a local in Tell City, Indiana,
Catholic priests supplied the names of contacts, saw that UEMDA
leaflets were distributed inside the plant, and arranged for news
stories hostile to the UE to appear in the local newspaper. The
right-wing organizer of the attack did note that as soon as other
arrangements could be made, they "must quit using the Catholic
rectory" to forward their cause.[120]

In an attempt to stem the dissident tide, the General Executive Board took drastic action. The administration, long having
taken its stand in defense of the existing UE constitution, developed constitutional amendments for presentation to the September
convention. One of these gave the General Executive Board the
power to suspend any local in circumstances which "might have"
led to revocation of their charter. During the period of any such suspension, and before a hearing, a suspended local was not to be entitled to representation at any meeting or convention of the UE. A
second declared that any disbandment, dissolution, secession or
disaffiliation of any local union was to be null and void if seven or
more members indicated their desire to retain the local charter.[121]
These were signs of growing panic within the General Executive
Board. For the first time the Board had thought it necessary to take
extraordinary measures against the insurgents. It also indicated
their growing fear of raiding by other unions.

To add immeasurably to the complications facing the union,
the House of Representatives, on June 4, 1947, passed the Taft-

Hartley Act, the culmination of an anti-labor drive which had begun during World War II and was fueled by the spectacle of the steel, auto, and electrical unions simultaneously on strike in 1946.[122] Significantly, in terms of the UE leadership's future political role, the Democrats in Congress voted with the majority to a considerable degree. In the House the Democratic vote was 106 to 71 for the bill.[123]

The UE reacted quickly. At a special meeting of the General Executive Board in Washington immediately following passage of the act, the general officers unanimously agreed not to submit any issue to the determination of the new National Labor Relations Board, nor comply with the act in any way, including the required signing of affidavits swearing that they were not Communists.[124] The position put them in good company in those early days. Following a meeting of the CIO National Executive Board at the end of June, Philip Murray announced the CIO would "work unceasingly in the political field to ensure the political repudiation of those reactionaries who are responsible for the Taft-Hartley Bill"; a bill, according to the CIO leader, that would "condemn the great mass of the American people to Depression living standards." Murray himself spoke out in opposition to the compulsory "loyalty oath" in principle "and refused to comply with the Taft-Hartley law in this respect."[125] He added significantly, however, "I am not thinking in terms of a third party."[126]

Murray's stand was critical. As long as the national officers of a union failed to sign the noncommunist affidavits, it could not utilize the NLRB. This meant that it could not be on the ballot in an NLRB election while organizing a plant or defending against a raid. As long as no union signed, the bill would have made little difference; but if a competing union had signed the oath, the noncomplying organization would be put at a considerable disadvantage. At the beginning all CIO unions did not comply. However, in the UAW, where Walter Reuther continued his struggle for control against his executive board, rumor had it that he wanted compliance.[127] This was ominous for UE, and it was confirmed at the August 1947 meeting of the UAW Executive Board when Reuther pieced together a majority in favor of signing the affidavits.[128] The UAW's action led to a rapid breakdown of the CIO's united front against compliance. Soon after, the Rubber Workers, Textile Workers, and Shipyard Workers followed suit. By October, when the CIO convention convened in Boston, only the left-wing unions, Murray's Steelworkers, and a few others held out.[129]

The first crack in the UE's solid front against Taft-Hartley came from a likely source. An advertisement appeared in the Bridgeport paper congratulating the officers of Local 203 for announcing that they would accept Taft-Hartley. The General Electric Company paid for the ad.[130]

It was fortunate for the UE's leaders that they had found some temporary common ground with Murray over the issue of noncompliance, because events on other fronts continued to drive them even farther apart. Their differences on the question of American foreign policy especially dramatized the growing polarity. Looming even larger was the possibility of a third party in the 1948 election. As early as January 28th, the CIO Executive Board decided that "it was politically unwise to inject a third party into the political scene of 1948."[131] Six weeks later Truman announced his new doctrine for Europe when he asked Congress for authority to send military supplies and missions to Greece and Turkey to help defeat Communist-led insurgencies.[132] The UE General Executive Board reacted immediately and blasted the "Wall Street" policies of Truman.[133] *UE News* ran the usual spate of letters supporting the administration position and without comment ran a full-page reprint of the text of Henry Wallace's speech attacking the Truman foreign policy.[134]

Murray, however, continued to walk a tightrope. While he supported the Truman Doctrine, he attacked the activities of a right-wing group of New York CIO leaders who had formed the "CIO Committee for Democratic Unionism." Murray called it "dual unionism" and ordered it to disband.[135] He was obviously trying to hold his *prima donnas* together. Any right-wing activity within the CIO would have to be carried on with Murray's approval or not at all. In the highly charged atmosphere of labor management relations and international affairs in 1947, Murray realized the great danger to organized labor if a split developed within its own ranks. For the time being the lid would be kept on.[136]

Murray's continuing delay caused some concern among the right wing. Carey was quick to play down his boss's action to other members of UEMDA. He called a rumor that Murray was cracking down on the right wing a "vicious, unprincipled lie, made up of whole clothe deliberately, with malice aforethought."[137] Carey knew whereof he spoke. This was borne out on April 15, 1947, when ACTU held a re-organization meeting at the Fort Pitt Hotel in Pittsburgh. William Hart, District Director of Murray's steel union in the Allegheny Valley, became president of the Pittsburgh ACTU chapter.[138] From that point on Hart and his local union members took an active part in area UEMDA activities.[139] It is naive to think that this happened without Murray's imprimatur.

The relationship between Murray and ACTU has never been clarified. There is no question that Rice had Murray's ear. Murray, a devout Catholic, could hardly have remained unaffected by the Church's bitter hatred of communism. Rice, as his spiritual advisor, must have been influential. On the other hand, Murray was a strong trade union leader who probably arrived at some of the same conclusions as ACTU, although for what he considered trade union rather than ideological reasons. Rice claimed that he and Murray had often discussed UE and that Murray admitted it had fallen under Communist control. Rice claimed that Murray hated the Communists but could do little about them. Murray had told him, said Rice, that Matles was a dangerous man. These revelations, in a letter from Rice to his Bishop, included the vignette that Vince Sweeney, editor of *Steel Labor*, had told him. According to Sweeney, Fitzgerald got drunk one evening at a convention and "slobbered" all over him with a story that he was not really a "Communist bootlicker."[140] It is difficult to assess a letter like this, but there is no reason to doubt the sincerity of Rice in communication with his ecclesiastical superior. In any event, subsequent events were to bear out his assessment of Murray's mood. At the May meeting of the CIO Executive Council, Murray lashed out at the left wing over the internal struggle within the Mine, Mill and Smelter Workers. According to ACTU, Murray directed the CIO affiliates that "if Communism is an issue in any of your unions, throw it to hell out and throw its advocates out along with it."[141] Right-wing controlled CIO councils moved immediately. In Harrisburg, the Pennsylvania State CIO, largely controlled by Murray's Steelworkers, overwhelmingly passed a constitutional amendment barring "Fascists, Klansmen, and Communists" from holding office. At the national level, Murray also began to practice what he preached. In June, Len DeCaux, editor of the *CIO News* and long identified with the Communists, resigned. He was replaced by Allan Swim, a right-wing advocate who had been acting as publicity man for the CIO's ill-fated Southern Organizing Drive.[142] With DeCaux gone, only Lee Pressman, CIO General Counsel, remained as a left-winger in the inner councils of the CIO.

In the midst of this turmoil, the biggest UE convention in history convened on September 22 at the Bradford Hotel in Boston. More than 1,000 delegates and 2,000 alternates attended. It was to be the bitterest meeting in the history of the organization. Henry Wallace addressed the convention. He attacked the Truman Administration and blamed the Communist charges against UE on men who did not believe in collective bargaining or social progress—men who "cry communism," but whose real fear is democracy.[143] The UEMDA faction sat quietly as the majority of the delegates roared their approval.[144] The show of support for Wallace must have been heartening for the UE officers since they were most certainly eyeing him as a third party candidate for the presidency in 1948. In fact, the resolutions committee brought out a resolution on political action that called for the creation of an independent political force "answerable to no boss or machine and responsive only to the will and the rank and file."[145] The feeling of betrayal by the Democratic Party in the areas of foreign policy and labor legislation was unmistakable. The right wing, however, doggedly put forth a minority resolution that cautioned UE against endorsing a third party movement unless the CIO also did so.[146]

The UE's third-party resolution raises the question of how much the support for an independent party among the leadership anticipated, rather than followed, the decision of the Communist Party to move in that direction. Talk of a labor party had been around since 1946 when, as a response to Truman's seizure of the railroads during a strike that year, A. F. Whitney, the Railway Brotherhoods' chieftain, pledged his whole union treasury to defeat Truman in the 1948 election. A number of other unions that year adopted third party resolutions. Murray and other CIO leaders had also often praised Henry Wallace, but their early interest in him was more as someone who might challenge Truman for the Democratic nomination than as the leader of a third-party effort. The issue hardly came up at the Labor Day meeting of the left-wing state CIO Council in New York. Harry Bridges opposed the creation of a third party in California as late as November 23, 1947, and as late as October and November of 1947, both Wallace and the Communist Party were quite undecided about taking the route of independent political action.[147]

In fact, the UE's support for a third-party movement also predated the changes on the international scene that led the American Communist Party to its all-out support for and leading role in the creation of the Progressive Party. The event that pushed the American Communists into outright opposition to their centrist allies in the CIO on the issue of independent political action took place in early October in Poland where representatives of nine Communist parties, not including the Americans, created the Cominform. Ostensibly an information bureau for international communism, it was in fact a call for Communist parties to finally shed the popular front and take the offensive against American imperialism. Although Cominform policy was adopted in the context of postwar

Western European circumstances, in particular the Marshall Plan and the expulsion of Communists from coalition governments in Italy and France, the American Communist Party embraced it as its own. Yet it made little sense in the American context and was a fateful step which would lead to the rupture of the CIO left's already shaky alliance with Murray and expose it to all of the anti-communist forces that had been building since the end of the war.[148] Given that the UE convention met before the creation of the Cominform, it is difficult to attribute the union's endorsement of independent political action entirely to a rote response to orders from Communist Party headquarters.

After dispensing with political action, the convention set out on a bitter week-long attack on UEMDA. Some 70 resolutions from local unions and districts attacked UEMDA as self-seeking, unprincipled, and responsible for helping to enact Taft-Hartley. A convention resolution condemned UEMDA and called upon it to disband. Carey battled against the resolution for several hours but was overwhelmed in the end, 3,823 to 596.[149] The majority resolution called for the expulsion of right-wing insurgents if disruption continued. To be sure there were a number of right-wing resolutions submitted, but the administration conveniently listed them in the booklet of proposed resolutions prepared by the union for distribution to the delegates under the heading of "red-baiting."[150]

In the face of this onslaught, UEMDA proposed to continue what they called their "unswerving loyalties and adherence" to the policies of the CIO. "These policies," they continued, "permit no un-American manifesto; they permit no adherence to foreign policy designed in other countries and advanced by their self-appointed emissaries in this country. Our fight will be waged in an orderly way by UE members acting fearlessly and in good conscience and in accord with CIO trade union proposals under the protection guaranteed us by the American Democratic process and Constitution of the United States."[151] At no place in the manifesto was there a trade union reason mentioned. Nothing more clearly indicated the almost entirely ideological nature of the struggle. The UEMDA manifesto had little effect on the delegates present. In the election of officers, the incumbents won by huge margins, eight to one in the case of the Albert Fitzgerald-Harry Block race.[152]

The news that the United States government had once again entered the lists against the UE tempered the joy caused by the decisive defeat of the insurgents. The War and Navy Departments had barred Communists or persons "affiliated with Communists or Communist activities" from working in plants manufacturing secret military equipment. The policy had already been applied against officers and members of the UE in four plants. The president, vice-president, and shop steward of Local 103, RCA Camden, had been barred from departments doing classified work. No charges were lodged against the officers. The government's explanation simply was that they were not allowed in if they were Communists or affiliated with Communists or their activities. Other plants where dismissals and transfers occurred were Westinghouse, Baltimore; Sylvania, Kew Gardens, New York; and Sperry-Rand, Long Island City, New York. Time would prove that it was the beginning of a new blacklist of ordinary industrial workers.[153] With what must have been mixed feelings of victory and impending disaster, the officers of UE looked toward the coming CIO convention.

The ninth national CIO convention convened in Boston on October 3. It was a curious gathering with Murray still trying to restrain those who were in favor of immediately driving out the left-wing unions. There were indications, however, that while for the record Murray planned to keep hands off, his actions gave the green light to the anticommunists. For example, the potentially divisive question of the Marshall Plan was skillfully handled. The foreign policy resolution did not mention it, but supported the shipment of food and other aid to needy countries, provided it was not used "to coerce free peoples."[154] The cautious wording assured its unanimous approval by the Executive Council, including the left wing. Murray then made his feelings quite clear by turning the convention into a demonstration for Secretary of State George Marshall, the chief guest speaker, and the principle architect of the European Recovery Program.[155]

On the question of signing the noncommunist affidavits and complying with the Taft-Hartley Act, the drift to the right also became clear. Murray told the convention that while he had "personal convictions" against filing the affidavit, he urged the delegates to adopt a resolution permitting any CIO officer to sign.[156] While this bow to autonomy seemed admirable, it was considerably out of character considering how Murray normally ran the CIO. His decision on this matter can be ascribed to several factors. Murray had become increasingly sensitive to the growing anticommunist feeling in this country and realized the potential danger to the labor movement. Second, a recent NLRB ruling had eliminated the need for national CIO or AFL officers to file affidavits.[157] The officers of each individual organization were required to sign. This relieved Murray from having to speak for the entire CIO on the matter. Murray must have realized the danger of noncompliance to some unions that would be subject to raiding from AFL unions claiming similar jurisdictions. The AFL had already announced it willingness to sign. For Murray's union, the United Steelworkers, noncompliance posed little danger. It had little to fear from raiding.[158]

Matles warned the delegates that he did not believe the CIO could say that "on the one hand the Taft-Hartley Law is intended to cut our throats and that we intend to change the Congress and abolish the law, but in the meantime we will sneak in through the back door and be the first in line, then maybe a given employer will cut our throats just a little bit."[159]

Although the surface unity of CIO had been maintained, it had become a one-sided calm at best. Murray had begun to move, no matter how slowly and carefully, to remove the influence of the left wing from the CIO. One obvious indication of Murray's intentions came from the UAW. On October 31, 1947, Walter Reuther informed the NLRB that the UAW Executive Board had voted to comply with the Taft-Hartley provisions.[160] Shortly thereafter at the UAW convention, Reuther won full control of the union's executive board. Murray, who the previous year had remained neutral or even favored R. J. Thomas, addressed the 1947 UAW convention and praised Reuther for the "splendid support that little red-head has given Phil Murray since his incumbency."[161] The significance of events in UAW came through clearly to Father Rice who explained in his column in the *Pittsburgh Catholic* that "it should not be too hard for the Auto Workers to take over disputed . . . UE locals. . . . He (Reuther) should move in and take over. I'd like to see him do it."[162]

The right-wing forces in UE interpreted Murray's attitude on Taft-Hartley as an indication that he was giving the insurgents the green light without actually breaking personally with the left-wing unions. The UE immediately came under pressure from two locals over the question of compliance. In a completely unexpected move the Camden RCA local voted overwhelmingly to repudiate the administration policy and directed the members of their local executive board to file the affidavit even though the general officers would not.[163] The Camden local had up to this point been a staunch administration group. The officers of Local 1237, James Conroy's UEMDA local in New York City, also decided to sign. The NLRB soon ruled, however, that a local union could not qualify under the act, even if its officers signed. This meant the only solution for some of the right-wing locals was secession and affiliation with a union whose national officers had signed.[164]

The changing collective bargaining environment made the task of the general officers even more difficult. In the years between

1945 and 1947 profits in the electrical industry sagged dramatically and labor costs climbed substantially as a percentage of corporate sales. The companies, led by Westinghouse, responded by raising incentive standards and reducing piecerates. Westinghouse had always been difficult. It had initially resisted unionization more vigorously than its counterpart, General Electric, and during the 1946 strikes, it had also taken the most intransigent stance. Soon after that settlement, Westinghouse slashed piece rates throughout its plants and began transferring work to new, nonunion plants in the South. As a result of these and other factors, employment in plants represented by Local 601, which had been in constant turmoil because of the ideological conflict, fell from 22,000 in 1944 to some 13,000 in 1950.

These cutbacks hit hard at the new, younger labor force that had entered the factories during the war. Unlike their older, more skilled and higher paid predecessors who had stressed issues of job security and seniority, the new workers always lived in economic insecurity. Their need for higher pay to cope with postwar inflation came at a time when the companies had embarked on cost cutting strategies. Their frustrations made them likely recruits for right-wing, rank-and-file movements.

In addition, relations between the companies and the union in the electrical manufacturing plants rapidly worsened after the war. Fearful of the rise of the shopfloor power of workers during the war, General Electric and Westinghouse tightened up their labor relations policies. They succeeded in turning the tide during the 1946 round of strikes, and by the end of 1947 were well along in their strategy to roll back union power. Its internal dissension and the union's increasing vulnerability on the Communist issue made UE an easy target for the strategy. After the 1946 strike, General Electric appointed Lemuel Boulware to the position of vice president for labor and community relations to implement the strategy. It was a clear sign that the welfare capitalist, corporatist legacy of Gerard Swope was dead at GE.[165]

5

CIVIL WAR AND EXPULSION

The future looked bleak for the UE by early 1948. Murray had clearly moved to the right, and the left-wing unions could only stand by and hope that the CIO leader would go no farther. Only CIO counsel Lee Pressman remained as a left-wing influence in Murray's inner councils and he would soon leave. Walter Reuther, having gained the upper hand against his opponents in the Auto Workers, provided a frightening specter for UE. There were signs that "Red Mike" Quill, under attack from a joint ACTU-right-wing group in his own Transport Workers, would soon join Joe Curran as a defector to the right.

Tensions in the international trade union movement also added to the growing distance between Murray and the left. The CIO, along with the British Trade Union Congress (TUC) and the Soviet unions, had played a major role in the formation of the World Federation of Trade Unions (WFTU) in September 1945. The organization, which included the reconstructed union federations of most of the Western European countries, had as its goals the perpetuation of the anti-fascist alliance into the postwar years and the assurance of a powerful trade union voice in the construction of peace, prosperity, and justice. The CIO's role gave it a prestige on the world scene that its bitterly anticommunist rival, the AFL, had denied it up to then. The firm support of the left-wing unions for cooperation with the Soviet Union during the popular front euphoria at the end of the war gave them additional common ground with Murray, who sent Albert Fitzgerald and Joseph Curran along with James Carey as part of the CIO delegation to the founding meeting of the WFTU.

But as the shadow of East-West confrontation fell across the postwar world, allied unity began to crumble and the fate of European labor movements, then largely controlled by the left, became crucial to the American goal of keeping Western Europe out of the Soviet sphere of influence. With the inception of the Marshall Plan, a coherent strategy emerged. The first goal was the splitting of the unified, Communist dominated federations in France and Italy. The second was the removal of the CIO and the British TUC from the WFTU. The third was the creation of a new, anticommunist, pro-American international made up of the AFL, the CIO, the TUC, and other anticommunist unions in Europe and elsewhere.

The State Department lacked the labor contacts and expertise to carry this out on its own. Soon after the war it struck an alliance with the AFL to build anticommunist stability in Western Europe by undermining Communist influence in European labor movements. Central to this policy was the destruction of the WFTU. As the Cold War intensified, the pressure on Murray to bring the CIO into line increased and by 1947, the CIO had become an ally in this undertaking. As Murray's chief envoy on European labor matters, James Carey played a major role in the evolution of the CIO policy, thus helping to widen the growing gulf between Murray and the left-wing unions in the CIO.[1]

Against the background of the growing East-West confrontation in Europe and soon after the creation of the Cominform, the American Communist Party's national leadership held a series of meetings with key left-wing union leaders to discuss electoral strategy. At a tumultuous December 15, 1947, meeting they announced the decision to back a third party. As further support for the decision, party leaders pointed to the likelihood of revolutions in France and Italy—an exaggerated expectation that explains in part the rush of the American party to use the third party endorsement to find common ground with Cominform policy.

The significance of the decision for the future of Communist influence in the CIO did not escape one key labor leader. When Mike Quill pointed out that the decision would split the CIO, he was told that the central committee expected the Communist Party union leaders to bring their unions into line behind Wallace whatever the consequences. Quill reportedly responded, "to hell with you and your Central Committee." Shortly after he left the party and purged his Transport Workers of Communist influence.[2]

Two weeks after the Communist Party decision, on December 29, 1947, Henry Wallace announced his candidacy for the presidency as the standard-bearer of the new Progressive Party. *UE*

News reflected the sentiments of the general officers by giving full-page coverage to the announcement.[3] Murray responded swiftly. On January 22, the CIO Executive Board met in Washington and voted 33 to 11 that a third party in 1948 was "politically unwise." At the same time it maintained the fiction of nonpartisanship by announcing that the CIO had not decided on any candidate.[4] After the meeting Murray somewhat vaguely informed reporters that the statement laid "a moral obligation" upon CIO unions, but that there was no intention of forcing them to stay in line.[5] Both Fitzgerald and Emspak voted against the resolution, and Fitzgerald urged the Board to recognize the right of member international unions to decide policy matters for themselves when differences of opinion exist.[6] Before the vote the UE representatives asked for a postponement until they could consult with their members. Murray pointedly reminded them that they had not felt it necessary to consult with the membership when they voted for an anti-third party resolution during the 1944 CIO convention.[7]

The split over the third party issue widened rapidly. Murray obviously had decided that Labor's political salvation lay with the Democratic Party. It should be remembered that up to this point organized labor had not been completely satisfied with Truman. In fact, early in 1948 Carey and Reuther flirted with a movement to draft Dwight Eisenhower as the Democratic standard bearer. Less than a year before the election, AFL and CIO officials doubted that Truman could command any important section of the labor vote.[8] But the question of who the Democratic candidate would be was beside the point. The third party had no chance to win, but it could endanger the CIO by splitting the progressive vote and bringing the Republicans, the party of Taft-Hartley, to power. Truman's veto of Taft-Hartley had largely healed the rift with the labor movement. To Murray, nothing less than the survival of the labor movement that had been created during the New Deal was at stake.[9]

These truly must have been the worst of times for the left-wing leaders of CIO unions. On the one hand the Communist Party expected their loyalty and support for Wallace. The government pressed on with the demand that they sign the noncommunist oath in order to enjoy the protection of the National Labor Relations Act. Anticommunist insurrections from within and raids from right-wing unions from without occupied much of their time. It is not surprising that their response was far from monolithic. Some, like Quill, simply left the fold and returned to the good graces of Murray. Only five CIO unions actually endorsed Wallace. Many of the other leaders personally supported the Progressive Party, but refused to risk trying to win endorsements from the rank and file. The UE followed this middle road, knowing that the division in the UE ranks was too great to endorse Wallace.[10] Nevertheless UE left-wingers worked for Wallace across the country. In District 7 they called themselves the Voluntary Association of the UE Independent Political Committee of Ohio and Kentucky. Local 768 in Dayton, Ohio endorsed Wallace as early as February 1948 and sent 5 delegates to the Wallace for President State Convention in Cleveland. No doubt this pattern was duplicated elsewhere. On the other hand, right-wing locals also disregarded the official nonpartisan policy. Delco Local 755 in Ohio endorsed Truman and refused to allow the UE international staff representative to distribute a leaflet outlining the nonpartisan stance of the UE at the plant gates. Attempts by left-wing supporters of Wallace to distribute Progressive Party leaflets outside the plant gates at Frigidaire led to their suspension by Local 801 for actions contrary to the good and welfare of the local union.[11]

Julius Emspak and Albert Fitzgerald informed Murray that they were resigning from CIO-PAC because of its partisan activities against the third party.[12] They charged that the organization had become an "appendage of the Democratic machine."[13] The withdrawal meant a loss of some $100,000 to PAC. Shortly thereafter, Wallace named Fitzgerald co-chairman of the Wallace for President Committee.[14] The UE president stressed that with the permission of the UE General Executive Board, he was acting as an individual in backing Wallace. He emphasized that this did not constitute a UE endorsement of Wallace.[15] When asked how his action would affect UE's already shaky relationship with the CIO, Fitzgerald reminded reporters that Dan Tobin of the Teamsters and Bill Hutcheson of the Carpenters had long played major roles in different parties and the AFL had survived.[16] Whatever their rationalization, the left-wing union leaders had done what the anticommunists had said they would do: put the Communist Party's political goals ahead of the CIO's welfare.

While Murray and UE continued on a collision course over the crucial issue of political action, the CIO drive to the right accelerated. James Carey had become the CIO's chief spokesman for the Marshall Plan.[17] Murray's use of Carey on this critical issue indicated his continued support for the man who was actively leading the insurgents in UE.

Of more significance was the resignation of Lee Pressman as CIO general counsel. The brilliant Pressman, with Murray from the beginning and practically a son to him, left to run for Congress on the Progressive Party ticket.[18] This may have been the issue that Murray used to accomplish what must have been a very painful act for him, but Pressman's well-known, left-wing sympathies made it impossible for him to stay much longer under any circumstances. Ever since the CIO's move to the right in 1946, the anticommunists around Murray, especially his friend and confessor, Father Rice, had been pressing him to remove Pressman from the inner councils of the CIO. When Len DeCaux resigned as editor of *CIO News*, it was only a matter of time until Pressman followed. Almost immediately Murray moved against another left-wing luminary. Through Allen Haywood, Murray notified Harry Bridges, president of the West Coast longshoremen, that as regional director of northern California for the CIO, he must either carry out the CIO program or resign. Bridges refused to follow either course and was removed.[19]

Not everyone buckled under to the directive. When the Los Angeles CIO Council heard from John Brophy that the CIO would not be satisfied with expressions of neutrality on the Marshall Plan, a third-party movement, or Henry Wallace, it paid no heed. The CIO immediately revoked its charter.[20] Brophy then informed all the Industrial Union Councils that they were expected to toe the CIO line. When some refused, they too lost their charters.[21] Perhaps more significantly, in June 1948, Murray's United Steelworkers of America decided that Communists, Fascists, or members of other totalitarian organizations would be ineligible to hold membership in the union.[22]

Carey, in the meantime, looked like anything but a deposed union leader who had consistently been rejected by his union's rank and file since 1941. On June 25, President Truman named him to the Public Advisory Board set up by the Foreign Assistance Act.[23] Carey publicly claimed to have the "reds on the run" in the CIO, citing the removal of DeCaux and the cleaning up of the industrial union councils.[24] Carey's activities in UE also continued. Fitzgerald complained often to Murray, who, he said, seemed somewhat embarrassed by his secretary-treasurer's activities. Murray promised to "have a talk with Jim about it, he shouldn't be doing these things."[25]

Fitzgerald attributed Murray's lack of action to the influence of the ACTU. Whether the ACTU used Murray or he used the ACTU is difficult to determine, although the latter seems the more likely. Nevertheless, by late 1948 or early 1949, Murray's Steelworkers provided most of the financing for the ACTU in the Pittsburgh area. Cash payments of $1,000 per month passed from Murray to Father Rice to help.finance the fight for control of the UE.[26]

Aware of the many-sided alliance forming against them, the UE general officers set out on a one-month, 20-city tour to mend fences and to stiffen the resolve of their supporters. The tour began on January 8 and reached as far west as Minneapolis and the officers, while pounding away at Taft-Hartley, picked up valuable information as to the state of the union.[27] Much of what they heard was not good, nor, often, was their reception. At a number of stops they were met by right-wing forces who interrupted meetings. In one case things turned ugly. In District 6 in western Pennsylvania, both sides had been trading expulsions for months. Most right-wing locals in the district refused to allow the left-wing district staff and officers to attend local union meetings or to participate in bargaining or grievance handling. When the three general officers arrived to address local union officials and stewards at the Fort Pitt Hotel, a minor riot broke out. Matles condemned the right-wingers for "storm trooper" tactics, while the Pittsburgh newspapers blamed the disturbance on left-wing attempts to keep their adversaries out of the hall.[28]

When the weary officers returned home, more bad news awaited them. James Conroy's Local 1237 in New York City, long a thorn in the side of the administration, had announced its withdrawal from UE. The pretext was a threatened court action by Remington-Rand to void the contract on the grounds of the UE officers' refusal to sign the noncommunist affidavits. Conroy was both an ACTU and UEMDA member.[29] Shortly thereafter the big, right-wing controlled Westinghouse Local 601 in Pittsburgh demanded that the international officers sign the noncommunist affidavits.[30] Although these setbacks were serious, the touring officers probably heard even more ominous rumors concerning the designs of the UAW on dissident UE locals. For the UAW, whose officers had complied with Taft-Hartley, the frustrated and alienated right-wing UE locals were like fruit ripe for the picking. Father Rice described Reuther and the UAW as being "hungry for the carrion."[31]

Although AFL unions such as the IBEW and the IAM had been raiding UE locals since early 1947, the CIO onslaught did not begin until a year later. At its meeting in Chicago during the week of March 1, 1948, the UAW Executive Board perfected secret plans for a series of raids against UE locals.[32] The beginning of the unprecedented jurisdictional warfare between the two big CIO unions broke out on March 19th, with the disaffiliation of UE Local 251. With only two dissenting votes, the local decided to affiliate with the Auto Workers. Auto union leaders also announced that Local 265, with over 7,000 members at the Royal Typewriter Company in Hartford, Connecticut, would shortly take similar action. Soon the UAW had captured almost all of the UE's locals in the armament and typewriter industries in the Connecticut Valley.[33] When the predicted Hartford secession materialized, both Charles Kerrigan, New York UAW regional director, and a spokesman for Reuther in Detroit, announced that their union would not raise any objections to any local's entering UAW even though it was currently in another CIO international. They denied, however, that they had taken the initiative, explaining that they only decided on their policy because the dissident unions had threatened to leave the CIO if not taken in by UAW.[34] This became the UAW rationale up to the end of the civil war in the CIO.

Murray, pressed by the UE on the issue, mildly rebuked the UAW, telling other CIO union heads that he disapproved of raids and that the CIO did not condone them.[35] The UE denounced the raids as having been taken in collusion with employers and announced plans to distribute leaflets bearing Murray's letter to the employees.[36] In Washington, James Carey told reporters he had no comment on the UAW drive.[37] The response of Murray to the raids clearly demonstrated his guarded support of Reuther's actions. He had definitely not yet decided to drive the left-wing unions out of the CIO, but rather still had hopes of either aiding right-wing elements to capture control from within or persuading leaders of left-wing internationals to switch allegiance as had Joseph Curran. The strategy soon bore fruit when Michael Quill head of the Transport Workers Union defected to the right wing. Apparently the UAW interpreted Murray's waffling as a green light. Two days after Murray's mild letter to Reuther, Charles Kerrigan announced that UAW attempts to capture dissident UE locals would move from Hartford to the New York City, northern New Jersey area.[38] Kerrigan proved to be a man of his word. He told the press that rebel UE members had begun to distribute UAW membership cards among the 500 employees of the Metropolitan Device Corporation. By late afternoon that same day some 320 signed cards had been returned. The Auto union then announced they would file a petition for an NLRB election in the plant. Because of their officers' refusal to sign the noncommunist affidavits, UE would be unable to participate in the election. This left them in the ironic position of asking their supporters to mark the ballot "no union." This same strategy was to be used time and again in the next two years.[39]

The raiding of one union by another was a matter of great seriousness in the labor movement. Even many right-wing members took pause at such tactics. In April, UEMDA met in Pittsburgh and drafted a proposal asking that anticommunist locals continue their fight against the left wing rather than bolt to another union. Significantly, however, there was no criticism of the Auto Workers.[40] While the UE right wing found it difficult to criticize Reuther's actions, this was not the case within his own union. UAW Local 51 went on record condemning the parent organization for its raiding tactics against other CIO unions, particularly UE.[41] Cadillac Local 22 in Detroit also informed UE that it had gone on record condemning its own international's raiding tactics.[42]

At the insistence of the UE's General Executive Board, Murray asked Reuther and UE officers to meet with him to discuss the raids.[43] Reuther did not even bother to reply. In an uncharacteristically passive response, Murray had his spokesman announce that the CIO was unable to compose the "jurisdictional" warfare between UE and UAW. Allan Haywood of the CIO telegraphed Charles Douds, regional director of the NLRB, to decide what further action should be taken on petitions for elections from current UE members who had signed UAW cards. The plants in question were the Megenthaler Linotype Company with 2,150 employees, the Intertype Corporation with 450 workers, and the Metropolitan Device Corporation with 500 workers.[44] For Murray, who ruled the CIO with so strong a hand, to meekly accept Reuther's rebuff did not ring true. His decision to allow a vital internal problem of the CIO to be settled by an agency established under the hated Taft-Hartley Act indicated how much he wanted to avoid a confrontation, not only because Murray himself knew that UE could not use the services of the board but also because Murray's own union was in the same predicament since Murray too had refused to comply by filing the noncommunist affidavit.

All was not defeat for UE in these struggles, however. UAW raids were turned back in Orange, New Jersey, where ACTU played a leading role, at National Carbon in Ohio, and at Scharader Sons and the Spiral Binding Company in New York City.[45] Particularly satisfying were UE victories over the UAW at Detrola and at Vickers, both in Detroit, the home of the auto union.[46]

Win or lose, the UAW's actions opened the gates to raids on dissident UE locals by other unions. The International Association of Machinists raided the big Detrola local in Detroit; both IBEW and the Machinists raided the International Register Company local in Chicago; in Los Angeles, IBEW and the Teamsters made up the raiders; and at the White Plains, New York, plant of Lerick Incorporated, the AFL Jewelry Workers got into the act.[47] The list seemed endless. In Pittsburgh it was the Glass, Ceramic and Silica Union of the CIO, in Cleveland the AFL's Carpenters.[48] Between the passage of Taft-Hartley in the summer of 1947 and the withdrawal of UE from the CIO in the fall of 1949, rival unions conducted more than 500 raids on UE locals.[49]

The ideological struggle also affected UE strike situations. In a strike at the Univis Corporation in Dayton, Ohio, national guardsmen broke up the strike in a campaign marked with red-baiting. The strike provided another example of government collusion with the right wing. The House Labor Committee called five strike leaders to Washington to testify the day before the National Guard moved in.[50] At the Hoover Company in Canton, Ohio, the entire establishment of the community—press, police, and churches—blasted the UE strikers with an intensive anticommunist campaign. The company attacked UE's officers for not signing the affidavits, refused to bargain until they did, and chastised the workers for following Communist leadership.[51] The local paper proclaimed that "it is nothing short of a crime that the Hoover Company—of all companies—finds it necessary to deal with the United Electrical Workers Union—the largest labor organization in America dominated by the Communists."[52] At Local 124, RCA, in Lancaster, Pennsylvania, a barrage against UE strikers in the local papers included quotes of statements made by Harry Block.[53]

The effects of the charges against UE sometimes reached the absurd. In Essington, Pennsylvania, Local 107 undertook to sponsor radio broadcasts of the local high school football games. Only two or three schools on the schedule agreed to allow this. One even claimed that if UE remained as the sponsor, it would forfeit the game.[54] The constant harassment from many quarters took a toll on the pro-administration locals. The president of Local 768 in Dayton, Ohio, lamented to his executive board that dissident members, a hostile local press, and an IBEW raid had overwhelmed the staff of the local who found themselves unable to cope with the workload and apprehensive about the future.[55]

By this time Fitzgerald and the other general officers knew that other CIO unions were helping to finance the UEMDA and ACTU. Chief offenders were apparently the USWA, the UAW, and the Textile Workers led by the strongly right-wing Emil Reive.[56] Still reluctant to attack Murray directly, UE lashed out at the ACTU. The issue arose over the publication by Father Rice of a pamphlet entitled, *How to De-Control Your Union of Communists.* Heretofore the UE had hesitated to attack Rice and ACTU because of the union's heavy Catholic membership. The pamphlet, however, openly admitted the direct link between UEMDA and ACTU when Rice offered to put interested union members in touch with UEMDA.[57] Matles circulated the pamphlet and a letter Rice had sent out instructing rank-and-filers on how to elect right-wing convention delegates to the membership of the General Executive Board. According to Rice it was still good policy for the right wing to stay in the union and fight, but that circumstances might change at any time.[58]

The UE officers also confronted the United States Government, which had entered the fray the previous year, and was increasing its pressure. Harassment came in a variety of forms. In March, James Lustig, UE organizer in District 4, was arrested for refusing to turn over the records of the Joint Anti-Fascist Refugee Committee, of which he was a member, to HUAC. At its twelfth convention, UE had gone on record as supporting the committee as a voluntary charitable organization whose aim was to alleviate suffering among the victims of "Franco Fascism."[59] In scattered companies around the country, some UE members and officers continued to be denied access to certain departments for security reasons.[60] Fitzgerald protested in a letter to Truman.[61] Instead of satisfaction from the President, Fitzgerald received a letter from the Committee on Education and Labor of the House of Representatives requesting him to come to Washington on September 12, 1948, to answer charges that the UE had "failed to set its house in order concerning its ideological aspects."[62] The significance of scheduling the hearings to start only four days before the UE convention was not lost on the UE officers. Representative Charles Kersten, Wisconsin Republican and chairman of the subcommittee, and a Taft-Hartley supporter, claimed he was not trying to break the union, only to expose charges of Communist domination in the labor movement, a vital consideration in case of a crisis between the United States and the Soviet Union.[63] The timing of the hearings, however, suggested the possibility of collusion between UEMDA and the government, and Harry Block later admitted that UEMDA was trying all along to get the United States Government to lend its weight by implicating UE as a Communist-dominated organization.[64] In fact, the right-wing forces had been cooperating with the FBI for some time. By early 1942 much of the Bureau's suspicion of what Hoover called "Mr. Carey's communistic activities" had been allayed, and FBI field offices in New York and Washington were ordered to destroy their copies of Carey's custodial detention card which, during the war, marked one as a security risk in case of an emergency.[65] Shortly after, on July 3, 1943, Carey first enlisted the aid of the FBI in the UE fight by asking the Bureau to do background checks on certain left wingers. Hoover's staff had some qualms, believing that it was nothing more than a strategy to help Carey move to the top, but Hoover agreed, fearing as he did that communism's greatest threat to the United States lay in its influence in organized labor. By 1946 Carey saw Hoover regularly to discuss Communists in the CIO. On August 24, 1948, the FBI received a query on Carey's reliability as a friendly witness from an aide to Congressman Fred Hartley of New Jersey, who sat on the House Committee on Education and Labor that had summoned Fitzgerald to Washington. Hartley and congressmen John F. Kennedy of Massachusetts and Charles Kersten of Wisconsin met with Carey and an ACTU advisor, Father William Gordon of Long Island, to discuss Carey's testimony.[66]

Before his appearance at the hearings, Fitzgerald publicly blistered the committee and the investigation. He called Kersten a completely unprincipled publicity seeker, liar and slanderer. He attacked the 80th Congress for misusing the investigative power and for brazenly flouting every interest of the "common people" of the country. He called the scheduling date an obvious interference with pre-convention preparations and a form of blackmail against the convention delegates.[67]

On September 2, to the accompaniment of nationwide press coverage, Carey and Fitzgerald testified before the Kersten Committee. Carey's testimony, which included a brief survey of UE's history, also included the charge that Westinghouse and General Electric, in order to buy a measure of industrial peace, were firing anticommunists at the request of the UE officers.[68] In illustrating why GE would rather have a Communist-led union, Carey explained that a Communist shop steward could not be very aggressive in processing a grievance if the employer had evidence that he was a Communist, because of fear of exposure.[69] This was to be a recurring theme of the UEMDA attack. When asked for examples of anticommunists who had been fired, Carey pointed to two cases, that of Bart Enright who ran against Matles for Director of Organization in 1947, and Sam Basmajian, a UEMDA member from Camden. According to Carey, Enright lost his job at Westinghouse in Jersey City because he was a UEMDA member. Basmajian supposedly had the same misfortune at the Camden RCA plant.[70] Carey's unlikely picture of the paragons of American industry in collusion with the Communists must have greatly confused the committee. Matles later countered the testimony by claiming that Enright had been discharged by the company for recurrent absence and Basmajian had not been fired but was on a leave of absence.[71] No less a group of anticommunists than Lemuel Boulware, GE vice-president, William Barron, GE labor relations counsel, and George Pfeif, GE manager of union relations backed up Matles on the Enright case, claiming he had been fired after many warning notices and prior discipline for repeated absence. An RCA spokesman corroborated Matles's statement on Basmajian.[72]

Like previous hearings, these had little conclusive effect, but gave nationwide exposure to the charges against the union. Some 33 witnesses testified from both sides of the ideological split. Such old hands as Louis Budenz, James Conroy, and Salvatore Vottis were called on more or less to repeat the testimony they had already given to other government committees. The interrogation of the UE officers, with very few exceptions, consisted of vague questions relating to the Communist conspiracy and the Soviet Union. Trade union issues were largely ignored. The net result was to reinforce the image of the UE as the agent of the Soviet Union.

Against this backdrop, the thirteenth annual UE convention opened in New York on September 6, 1948. In the weeks preceding the meetings the left-right lines had been drawn even more clearly. The Progressive Party convention had met in Philadelphia in July with Albert Fitzgerald as permanent chairman.[73] At its September meeting, the CIO Executive Board formally endorsed Harry Truman for President by a vote of 35 to 12. The endorsement came in the form of recommendation from a meeting of Murray, Carey and the CIO vice-presidents. Only Albert Fitzgerald voted against the recommendation. In the executive board session the left-wing unions voted against it in a bloc.[74]

Fitzgerald opened the UE convention by warning the delegates that he would try to be fair and allow all shades of opinion to be expressed, but that there would be "no room in this convention for organized disruption."[75] He had good reason to suspect such disruption was coming. Prior to the convention Father Rice offered Fitzgerald the ACTU's support and membership in "the smallest club in the world" if he would go the way of fellow Irish-Catholic CIO labor leaders Mike Quill and Joseph Curran and split with Emspak and Matles. Fitzgerald refused the invitation.[76]

The general officers wasted no time in meeting the issue of the Wallace candidacy head on. In their report to the convention they indicated their opinion that both the Democratic and Republican leadership had demonstrated their hostility to the people and that they believed Henry Wallace offered the best program. Because of this they had requested and received permission from the General

Executive Board to participate in the Wallace campaign. In announcing that Wallace would address the convention, Fitzgerald stressed that this in no way constituted an endorsement or an indication of agreement with his program. The first voice of UEMDA opposition was raised at that point. Harry Block told the convention that he did not object to Henry Wallace addressing the convention, but he felt the CIO should have equal time. He inquired as to why Philip Murray had not been invited to address the convention. Fitzgerald answered that Murray had not been invited because it would have been unfair to put him in a position where he would be forced either to take sides with one of the UE factions, or to be used by one or the other factions to further their own aims. He claimed that Murray had agreed to this. Carey, said Fitzgerald, gave the CIO adequate representation.[77]

Despite the solid pro-Wallace sentiment among the UE officers, the convention did not endorse the Progressive Party candidate. The chief advocate of this neutral position was Fitzgerald who, though sure he had enough votes for an endorsement at the convention, realized that the rank and file probably favored Truman.[78] In the face of this situation an endorsement would have had the effect of being a bonus to UEMDA. Matles agreed. The UE's leadership knew the limits of their influence, no matter what the Communist Party might have wanted.[79]

The thirteenth convention proved to be the bitterest on record. Minority reports were issued by the insurgents on a variety of key issues. Although the convention stayed firmly in the hands of the left wing, the UEMDA forces were buoyed by successes in various locals and by the obvious alignment of Murray with the right wing within the CIO. They probably rejoiced privately at the support of Wallace by the general officers, realizing that this would drive them still farther from Murray.

In all cases the UEMDA minority resolutions clearly supported the CIO line. On political action they called for adherence to CIO policy and rejection of Wallace. When the majority resolution condemning raiding and calling on the CIO to withhold financial support from raiding unions came to the floor, a UEMDA minority resolution also condemned raiding but placed the blame for it squarely on the actions of the officers because of their refusal to support CIO policy on the Marshall Plan and Henry Wallace. In calling on the CIO unions to stop raiding, the right wing asked the seceding unions to come back to help the forces in UE whose efforts were directed toward restoring "real trade unionism" instead of "foreign and alien loyalties."[80]

Following bitter floor fights on political action, raiding, and foreign policy, the convention passed a resolution condemning James Carey for testifying before the Kersten Committee.[81] Immediately following the convention, the executive board of Local 101, Carey's home local, set itself up as a trial board and exonerated the right-wing leader of the charges directed against him by the convention. Fitzgerald called it a publicity stunt. He noted that UE had not expelled Carey or tried to take his membership away.[82] In the balloting for officers, the UEMDA showed some increase in strength, but the incumbents still won handily, Fitzgerald by a five to one margin.[83]

Although the convention had taken place during a recess of the Kersten Committee hearings, the specter of government harassment was constantly present during the meetings. Even as the UE delegates debated political policy, Clarence Jackson, Canadian vice-president and nine fellow Canadian delegates were taken into custody by United States immigration authorities as they attempted to enter the United States to attend the convention. Washington claimed that those apprehended were members of "excludable classes," under which category Communists were included. Eight Canadian delegates from right-wing locals crossed without incident.[84] From that point on Jackson continued to be *persona non grata* in this country.

Government pressure also came from another side. In mid-1948 the UE began to organize atomic energy workers in General Electric Laboratories. Apprehensive over the presence of UE members in such sensitive areas, Atomic Energy Commission Chairman David Lilienthal tentatively barred the union from some laboratories, but called a conference in Washington to discuss the issue. The UE refused to attend and on September 28, 1948, Lilienthal directed the General Electric Company not to recognize the UE as the bargaining representative of any persons to be employed by it at the new Knolls Atomic Power Laboratories in Schenectady, New York.[85] The union filed a million dollar suit against the AEC and GE, which was later dismissed.[86]

Between the UE convention in September and the Portland, Oregon, gathering of the CIO in November, Harry Truman won the 1948 election. Wallace's unexpectedly small vote dealt a serious blow to the left-wing unions. Conversely, the influence of organized labor in the Truman victory, though inflated, was indicated by Truman's own words upon learning of his triumph, "labor did it."[87]

The Portland meeting had the air of a victory rally about it. Flush with Truman's triumph, the convention, under the adroit leadership of Murray, turned into a tongue-lashing session with the left-wing unions on the receiving end. Murray raged against them for their support of Wallace and their attacks on the Marshall Plan. He called them "ideological dive bombers" and "afflictions on mankind." Murray ran the convention with an iron hand, refusing to allow minority reports to be discussed on the floor, and bitterly attacking the smaller left-wing unions such as the Farm Equipment Workers (FE), UOPWA, and the Food, Tobacco and Agricultural Workers, but he did not openly mention the UE.[88] The convention granted Murray unprecedented centralized powers when they authorized him to take over CIO affiliates.[89] The UE opposed this resolution as well as the ones concerning foreign policy, political action, and an increase in per capita.[90]

Yet for all the stridency at the convention, there were signs that Murray still had hopes that a showdown could be avoided. Patience had paid off in the cases of Mike Quill and Joe Curran, and Murray apparently hoped that Fitzgerald and the UE could similarly be salvaged. Fitzgerald himself took a stance at the convention which gave this theory some plausibility. In a strangely incongruent statement, he charged the Soviet leaders with being "war mongers" and suggested that he might, under certain conditions, "tell the Progressive Party to go to hell." The conditions were an effort by Truman to carry out the promises that he made in his platform, particularly about repeal of Taft-Hartley.[91]

Fitzgerald's actions may have been sincere or they may have been motivated by a desire to retain his CIO vice-presidency, the only one still held by the head of a left-wing union. In any event, Murray's actions concerning Fitzgerald's re-election as a CIO vice-president pointed out the ambiguity of the CIO leader's stand at the time. Murray could easily have had the UE president replaced as Walter Reuther and George Baldanzi urged. But instead, he offered to have his steelworkers' secretary-treasurer, David McDonald, nominate Fitzgerald for his vice-president's seat. Fitzgerald refused because Emspak had always done the nominating before.

The significance of this kind of personal approach, however, was a good indication that Murray had by no means completely written off UE as of November 1948.[92] With no opposition from Murray, Fitzgerald won unopposed.

Somehow, while the ideological fight raged, the everyday functions of the union continued. Average membership in UE for the year from August 1946 to July 1947 was at an all time high. During that 12-month period, 179,247 workers joined the union for the first time. Of these some 60,247 were veterans whose initiation fees were waived by the local unions and the international. It amounted to the largest number of workers ever to join UE in a peacetime year. Only in 1943 and 1944 were there greater gains.[93] As a result of this activity UE had collective bargaining rights in 1,536 plants employing 600,000 workers. UE won 245 plant elections and card checks and recognition agreements covering 32,034 workers.[94]

By 1948, a business recession had somewhat slowed organizational growth. The Bureau of Labor Statistics reported that employment in the electrical machinery industry fell by 42,000 workers in 1948.[95] While no figures are available, the refusal of the UE's officers to sign the Taft-Hartley affidavit no doubt provided an obstacle to growth. Add to this the problems of internal disruption and raids by CIO and AFL unions. In the face of these difficulties the union's performance was credible. One hundred twenty thousand two hundred and thirteen new members, off some 50,000 from the previous year, joined UE in 1948. Some 38,000 were veterans.[96] But the union lost approximately 30,000 more members than it gained. Considering the adverse business conditions, the drop in overall strength was acceptable. The loss from raids is difficult to assess. During the year some 35 shops with which UE previously had contracts were lost, some as the result of raids but most because of company failure during the economic downturn.[97]

In wage negotiations, UE generally kept pace with settlements gained in steel and auto. Up against an industry whose profits were at an all time high in 1947, UE negotiated agreements with General Electric and Westinghouse that amounted to 11.5 cents for wage increases and 3.5 cents for improvements in holidays and vacations. Three weeks vacation with pay for workers with 20 years service were included as well as pay for six holidays not worked. In steel and auto the wage settlements were 12.5 and 11.5 cents respectively, with comparable fringe benefits.[98]

On January 6, 1948, representatives of the workers in General Electric, Westinghouse, Sylvania, and the electrical division of General Motors met to plan the wage drive for the year. In addition to wage increases, the delegates voted for adequate pensions, health and welfare plans, severance pay for laid-off workers, improved vacations, paid holidays, and equal pay for equal work.[99]

The union settled with General Motors, RCA, General Electric, Westinghouse and Sylvania without a strike. At GE the offer included an 8 percent increase in total earnings with a minimum raise of nine cents per hour. At RCA the union gained a three week vacation period after ten years of service—a first for any major company in the United States.[100] Once again the settlements compared favorably to auto where at General Motors six cents were added to base rates and eight cents in cost-of-living float, which could move up or down, and steel where United States Steel agreed to a package that gave the United Steel Workers nine and one half cents an hour in general wage increases.[101]

By the beginning of 1949, it appeared that an ultimate break between the CIO and the left-wing affiliates had become unavoidable. The left had hoped in vain for some relief at the 1948 Portland CIO Convention, but none came. Murray obviously had refused to do anything about UAW's raiding of UE. In fact, by this time, Murray's steelworkers were themselves engaged in raiding another left-wing CIO union, the Mine, Mill and Smelter Workers.[102]

If any other indications were necessary, one came on January 18, 1949, when Murray pulled the CIO out of the World Federation of Trade Unions. The final split came over the WFTU's stand against the Marshall Plan, but the CIO's growing cooperation with the AFL and the Central Intelligence Agency to weaken Communist influence in the European labor movement made the decision inevitable anyway. Faced with the unquestioned Communist domination of the world organization, the 1948 CIO convention authorized Murray and the executive board to take any action, in consultation with the British Trade Union Congress, which it felt necessary with regard to WFTU. Soon after, the CIO, AFL, and the TUC joined with other anticommunist labor movements from around the world to create the International Confederation of Free Trade Unions.[103] It was a considerable victory for Carey who had long been lobbying for withdrawal from the WFTU. In the face of the CIO move, the UE continued to support and pay dues to the WFTU.

Beset by enemies on all sides, the UE's leaders struck back at their tormentors when they could. A flurry of action against UEMDA members resulted, most of it in vain. In Sylvania Local 608, Huntington, West Virginia, Mildred Turner, an ACTU member was charged with 20 violations of the union's constitution including collaboration with the company.[104] District Council 6 expelled John Duffy, an old thorn in their side and a close ally of Father Rice. Although Duffy's Local 613 at Allis-Chalmers, a UEMDA stronghold, disregarded the council's action, from then on his salary was largely paid by Father Rice with money supplied by the Steelworkers.[105] In District 9 where the administration-controlled District Council expelled right-wingers Viola and James Pascoe, their local also disregarded the order.[106]

As if their inability to discipline the dissidents was not frustrating enough to the UE's officers, by 1949 the insurgent candidate for secretary-treasurer served as chairman of the important Westinghouse Conference Board.[107] Not to be outdone, the right wing went after even bigger game. Local 1102, under the leadership of James Click, charged District 8 president William Sentner with having used the union to further the aims of the Communist Party and expelled him from the local.[108] When the District Council and the General Executive Board ordered his reinstatement, they were ignored.[109] Thus Sentner, the only avowed Communist Party member on the General Executive Board, had the dubious distinction of being president of a district without having his union membership acknowledged by his local. Other left-wingers in Local 1102 suffered as well. Opal Cline, a shop steward, was denied access to classified material and suspended in 1948 for "associating" with Communists and for voicing too many complaints against piecework rates and stirring up the other women. Unfortunately for Mrs. Cline, the right-wing executive board of 1102 took the position that workers removed for security reasons had no grievance. When the Industrial Employment Review Board upheld her appeal and ordered her reinstated, Emerson Electric refused with the local union's support. A similar fate befell two other radicals at Emerson Electric: Helen Sage, an outspoken Communist, and Matt Randle, a militant black worker.[110]

The ideological battle also raged across the border in Canada. There nearly all of UE's approximately 25,000 members were located in Ontario, with a few scattered locals in Quebec. By the beginning of 1949, there were four Canadian locals under right-wing control, with membership of some 4,000.[111] Of even more significance, in Canada where they had never been hampered by Murray's refusal to sign the Taft-Hartley affidavit, the main raiding union was the United Steelworkers of America. The USWA had captured the UE locals at Coulter Copper and Brass in Ontario, and English Electric in St. Catherines. Another plant had been lost to IBEW.[112] Added to this was the policy of the United States Immigration Service which refused to allow the Canadian district director and open Communist Clarence Jackson into the United States to attend UE General Executive Board meetings and convention.

With their fortunes steadily improving, the actions of the right wing became bolder. In District 1, Harry Block's Local 101 contributed $1,000 to UEMDA for work to capture Local 103 from the administration. When charged, the local arrogantly admitted the allocation but denied that it had been specifically earmarked for

Local 103; rather it was to be used by the Carey group "as it sees fit."[113] So confident was UEMDA becoming that Rice wrote a chiding "Dear Al" letter to Fitzgerald informing him that his aides were painting an unduly rosy picture for him.[114] Rice's optimism had undoubtedly been buoyed by the ACTU estimate at the beginning of the year that UEMDA controlled some 140,000 members or about one-third of the union's strength.[115]

Not all the news was good for the right wing, however, On April 13, W. V. Merrihue, General Electric's manager of employee and community relations told a meeting of the Pittsburgh Personnel Association that he expected the company to be free of "left-wing" elements in the UE soon. He further claimed that James Carey had come to GE management before the 1948 UE convention to ask their help in breaking the Communist hold on the union, but had been turned down.[116] Carey immediately denied any such action. He claimed that statements like Merrihue's helped the interests of the Communists.[117] On April 16th, Merrihue mysteriously denied having made the statement about Carey's visit. Delighting in Carey's embarrassment at the exposure of his collaboration with the company, *UE News* gave the story wide publicity.[118]

Apparently convinced that a conflict with Murray could not be avoided short of a complete surrender, the UE began openly to attack the CIO. *UE News* blasted the CIO for its lack of zeal in pushing for repeal of Taft-Hartley and blamed its ineffectiveness on the fact that it had tied itself to the tail of the Democratic Party.[119] The UE General Executive Board officially set itself against Murray on April 24 by blasting "labor leaders" who had subordinated the interests of the membership to the dictates of the federal administration on domestic and foreign policy.[120]

The UE had judged the situation correctly. The CIO Executive Board met in May and set the final course for driving out the left-wing unions. The board in a hostile mood demanded the resignation of those who did not actively support CIO policy on the Marshall Plan and political action, and called on unions to replace officers who refused to do this.

At the same meeting the left-wing Farm Equipment Workers were ordered to merge with the UAW or face possible revocation of their charter. The CIO Executive Board also ruled that individual union affiliation with the World Federation of Trade Unions, as in the case of the UE, would be considered a violation of CIO policy. On all these issues Fitzgerald was in opposition along with the other left-wing unions.[121]

The UE moved quickly to counter the CIO policy. On the question of the Farm Equipment Workers, it condemned the CIO Executive Board's stand that recommended the revocation of FE's charter because of its refusal to merge with the UAW. The UE had already become the champion of that small, left-wing union against the Murray-Reuther alliance. Earlier, delegates to the FE convention had expressed their appreciation to the UE for having given all the assistance at its command in helping FE to fight off the UAW raids.[122]

To make matters worse, on July 27, Murray eliminated the last common bond which he had with UE when the executive board of the United Steelworkers of America voted to comply with Taft-Hartley and file the noncommunist affidavits.[123] Almost immediately the steel union engaged in two raids against the UE. They moved against Local 155 where a secessionist right-wing group had been trying to break away from the local.[124] The other raid took place at a runaway Sylvania plant being set up to manufacture television tubes at Seneca Falls, New York. The plant had been moved from Emporium, Pennsylvania, where UE Local 639 had jurisdiction.[125]

The federal government stepped into the fray again at this point. HUAC announced that it would conduct hearings concerning Communist influence in Westinghouse Local 601 in Pittsburgh. The hearings were scheduled for August 9-11, which happened to be only a few days before elections for convention delegates were to be held in the deeply divided local. The UE immediately charged that Father Rice, in an attempt to help the UEMDA hold onto power on Local 601, had enlisted the aid of HUAC. UE charged Rice and John Duffy with having convinced the committee that the "good" that was done when the right wing took over the union was about to be "undone by Communist infiltration."[126] A member of the committee, Congressman McSweeney, denied the UE charges. Disingenuously, he claimed that he had "been in constant contact with men, including Father Rice and others, trying to ascertain whether a delay in the hearings would be beneficial. . . . After getting all the information I could from every source, it was decided it was best for the hearings to proceed."[127] All four UE left-wing members subpoenaed to testify were candidates in the Local 601 elections. Once again the hearings provided the press with the opportunity to publicize the charges against the UE left wing. The Pittsburgh newspapers seized the opportunity, and the right-wing slate won handily on August 14. In addition to the barrage from the press, ACTU orchestrated a sophisticated campaign in the churches in the Pittsburgh diocese. Priests read the following communication from their pulpits as "a matter of moral counsel to our people":

We consider that you have a moral duty to vote in this election and to vote not to uphold Communism. The leaders of the International UE support the attackers and persecutors of Archbishop Stepinac, Cardinal Mindzenty and the heroic priests and nuns and Catholic people behind the Iron Curtain. The people over there cannot vote against Communism. You still can.[128]

In addition to sermons, the various parish priests ran an efficient get-out-the-vote campaign replete with letters, leaflets, phone banks, and house calls. The task was made easier by the organization of ACTU chapters in the individual parishes, a task that had been accomplished by 1947.[129]

A worried group of General Executive Board members gathered in New York's Abbey Hotel on August 10, 1949. Continuous harassment by the rebels, the CIO, and the government had begun to crack their composure. Everywhere they looked they saw enemies, and try as they might to hide the fact, nonadherence to Taft-Hartley combined with raids by other unions had resulted in losses of some 88 shops with approximately 34,000 workers.[130] In 1949 alone there had been raids of one degree or another on 456 UE shops.[131] Nor had actions by the Board to stem the tide had much effect. In case after case right-wing locals were continuing to disregard the board's orders concerning expelled members. To meet these challenges, the General Executive Board feebly recommended that a pamphlet be issued that would expose the "efforts of the companies to destroy our union and those forces within the CIO that are helping the companies to do this."[132] Even more important, the board voted unanimously to recommend to the convention an amendment to the constitution dealing with charges relating to secession, raiding, and dual unionism. The proposed amendment would have given the General Executive Board absolute jurisdiction to conduct a trial of any UE member charged by any member of the General Executive Board with participating or encouraging secession from UE, raiding against UE, or dual unionism. The accused could appeal the verdict only to the convention.[133] The pressures had finally forced the administration to go against the principle of local autonomy that it had so long championed.

An even deeper indication of the seriousness with which the UE officers viewed the coming right-wing offensive at the UE and CIO conventions was their decision to recommend to the convention that it direct the general officers to file Taft-Hartley affidavits in order to place itself in a position to use the election machinery of the NLRB.[134] Vice President James Price of District 1 claimed the action constituted a defensive action against raiding.[135] It is also probable that the action was taken because the officers realized that should they retain control of the union at the coming UE convention, expulsion from the CIO would likely follow. The *New Republic* predicted such expulsions at the UE's Cleveland convention.[136] The raiding CIO unions would decimate the UE if the union could not participate in NLRB representation elections.

There was little doubt that the upcoming UE convention would be the most bitterly contested in the union's history. Some overly optimistic UEMDA leaders counted 1,650 votes in the right-wing column, enough for victory. While Carey was more cautious and told Murray not to accept the UEMDA count as gospel, for the first time it did appear that the insurgents had a chance to win.[137] As far back as May, UEMDA had met in Dayton to plan their strategy for Cleveland. At that time a slate of officers was chosen and instructions were given as to how to elect right-wing delegates.[138] Directing the effort was Father Rice who wrote to ACTU-UE members in August and asked for names of delegates to the UE convention and also their left-wing, right-wing status. He instructed them to resist a move to instruct the delegates to vote left wing. If such an attempt should succeed, he advised them to disregard the instructions and vote right wing anyway. In closing he told them to:[139]

1. Vote and fight against attempts to push WFTU

2. Resist all attacks on Philip Murray

3. Expect a new barrage of vilification against Rice over the HUAC investigation of Local 601.

The fourteenth UE convention in Cleveland did not disappoint the huge press corps present. From the beginning the floor fights proved to be long and bitter. The rules of the convention and the credentials committee report were challenged the first day. It became apparent from the response of the delegates that this convention was more evenly divided than any previous one. The efforts of the administration to turn back the challenge showed clearly in the majority statement on collective bargaining. After a long preamble describing the union's progress since its inception, the statement called upon the membership of UE to close ranks and fight to achieve the UE demands of $500 per year, per employee, to be applied toward an increase in wages and salaries, reduction of hours, and improved pensions and health insurance plans.[140] Carey blasted the statement as the feeblest report on the subject that he had ever heard.[141] The debate on this issue, which was the first test of the strength of the two factions, took the better part of the first two days of the convention. The administration finally won by a vote of 2,404 to 1,479.[142] The tally showed that while it would be closely contested throughout, the administration had the votes to turn back the UEMDA challenge.

Perhaps the most significant test of the convention came on the resolution condemning raiding and dictatorship in the CIO. The title left no room for misunderstanding the intentions of the officers. It accused both the UAW and the USWA of raids against UE. It reiterated the fact that between March 12, 1948, and January 7, 1949, the UE officers conferred with Murray on this subject with no satisfaction. In consideration of these facts UE listed six demands to be presented to the CIO. They included:

1. The CIO must stop all raiding and return all raided shops to UE.

2. If CIO unions failed to stop, Murray was immediately to file charges against them with the CIO Executive Board.

3. Anyone on the CIO payroll who had taken part in the raids was to be fired.

4. Carey must be stopped immediately from using his CIO position to lead the insurgents in UE.

5. A monthly financial report from CIO to member unions must be furnished.

6. No interference with the UE's internal affairs was to take place.

In the event that Murray and the CIO Executive Board did not comply with the six demands, the convention authorized the General Executive Board to withhold per capita tax from the CIO.[143] The hotly debated resolution carried by 2,393 to 1,477 over a minority report in support of CIO policy.[144] The stern tone of the resolution again indicated the resolve on the part of the UE's leaders to force the issue with Murray. No one had any illusions that Murray would comply with the demands.

The convention delegates demonstrated their unease with tampering with the UE constitution and their deep adherence to the principle of local autonomy when the question of the amendment to the constitution giving power to the general officers to punish insurgents came to the floor. Even though the leadership clearly had the support of a significant majority of the convention, the delegates could only be persuaded to agree to a toned-down amendment which stipulated that in case of raiding or secession by a UE member, a trial must be conducted at the local level within ten days and the district must act in seven days. If they did not, the General Executive Board could take jurisdiction. On the vote the left-right pattern held as the administration carried the issue by 2,360 to 1,486.[145]

The climax of the convention came on Wednesday afternoon, September 21, when the delegates convened to elect officers for the international union. By this time the right wing must have realized that the administration would carry the day. Nevertheless, there was feverish activity to line up votes on both sides. When the vote came the pattern did hold and the incumbents won re-election.[146]

The right wing claimed the election had been stolen because delegates who were instructed by their locals to vote right wing disregarded their instructions and cast their ballots for the administration. According to the right wing, the key local was Fitzgerald's home local, 201 in Lynn, Massachusetts. Fitzgerald's opponent, Fred Kelly, also came from Lynn. He had been carefully chosen because of his home local and because of his Catholicism. According to Harry Block, the entire slate of 201 delegates had been instructed to vote for Kelly, including Fitzgerald who was himself a delegate.[147] Fitzgerald disagreed with Block's analysis. He claimed that the Lynn UEMDA group started a campaign to instruct delegates to the convention. They set up an election and had two slates, one consisting of the incumbents and one of the UEMDA slate, although no one had as yet been officially nominated. Fitzgerald claimed that the election had been rigged by UEMDA although he admitted that the right-wing sympathy in the local was considerable. He attributed this strength to "red-baiting" and to the fear that if the incumbents were re-elected the shops would lose their defense contracts.[148] Fitzgerald also claimed that only the four at-large delegates were elected at the special meeting and they were the only ones actually instructed. The other delegates, including Fitzgerald, the head of the union's GE department, the business agent, and the local president, all of whom were automatic delegates, were for Fitzgerald. When time for the vote came, Fitzgerald was polled first and cast a ballot for himself.[149]

It is almost impossible to ascertain the accuracy of the two claims. By that time the split in Local 201, as in the rest of the union, was so severe that the two contending factions were acting almost as separate locals. The dispute had clearly gone beyond the point where instruction from one or the other would have had any effect.[150]

Block pointed to the importance of Local 201's vote. Since District 1 had been polled first and had gone for Kelly, if 201, which came next, had gone for Kelly too, it might have started a bandwagon effect.[151] In retrospect, however, this seems unlikely since on the two previous roll call votes on raiding and collective bargaining the voting pattern remained remarkably stable. By the time the delegates arrived in Cleveland the lines had hardened to the point that a stampede of the convention was a remote possibility at best. In a report on the convention authored by Harry Block, he listed 17 locals in which he claimed that delegates instructed to vote for Kelly voted for Fitzgerald.[152] Granting all of these contested locals to the right wing, which is open to question, the vote would have been 2,022 for Kelly and 1,877 for Fitzgerald.[153] There is one glaring omission in the Block totals. Some 81 delegates from 26 Canadian locals were barred from entering the country to attend the convention.[154] These delegates represented some 190 votes that would have been cast for Fitzgerald.[155] Only one Canadian local, right-wing Local 524, attended the convention and it cast 30 votes for Kelly. Had Fitzgerald received the 190 Canadian votes, even with the disputed votes for Kelly, he would have won by 2,067, to 2,022. It is likely that there were irregularities on both sides in the selection of delegates to the 1949 UE convention. But there was apparently little question where the blame lay in the minds of the members of Local 201. Following the convention, Albert Fitzgerald and his three fellow left-wing delegates were tried by the local for disregarding instructions and expelled.[156] What the 1949 convention showed conclusively was that UE had become hopelessly split, but that after nearly ten years of struggle, the right wing had failed to win control of the union. The possibility of holding the organization together after the convention was nonexistent.

One day after their defeat at Cleveland, UEMDA leaders issued a call for wholesale secession from UE. They established a committee of ten and announced that they intended to confer with the leadership of the CIO's Auto Workers and that they would seek a CIO charter in order to set up a dual union with the same jurisdiction as UE. They labeled UE's six demands to the CIO an "impossible ultimatum."[157] In response the General Executive Board bitterly condemned the UEMDA group and called upon the membership to "repudiate them, to unite against them and the employers, and to drive the traitors out of their locals and the union."[158] The action of UEMDA coming so soon after the convention indicated that the strategy had been to make one last attempt to defeat the administration from within. If that failed, machinery had already been established to create a dual union in the electrical manufacturing industry. Central to any such strategy would have to be the expulsion of UE from the CIO. Preparations for this were under way several weeks before the CIO convention. CIO official Les Finnegan wrote to right-wing district and local officers across the country reminding them that the CIO was "extremely anxious to obtain" copies of their contracts, constitutions, and the names of company officials with which they dealt. He also asked for information on all right-wing and left-wing locals, including their membership. Fund raising was also under way. Local 801 in Dayton wired the CIO $2,500 as its contribution for the formation of "a U.E.- C.I.O. International Union free from Communistic domination.[159]

The UE general officers carried out the instructions of the convention and met several times with Murray to discuss the six demands before the CIO convention in November.[160] Murray urged the UE officers not to press the demands, launching into a tirade, according to the UE account. Nevertheless, both Fitzgerald and Matles believed that had the UE not pressed the demands, Murray would have been satisfied to let the convention verbally castigate UE and the other left-wing unions.[161] This is highly unlikely. Murray knew that, in light of the Cold War pressures building in the country, there could be no compromise. He also knew that Reuther and the other right-wing forces in the CIO would accept no more temporizing on the question.

On the eve of the CIO convention, the general officers met with Murray for the last time. They proposed that the CIO, UAW and USWA enter into no-raiding agreements with the UE. They showed Murray examples of such agreements which some CIO unions had signed with AFL unions. Murray still refused to accept what was a softening of UE's position. With this final rebuff, UE's General Executive Board voted unanimously to put into effect the UE convention mandate to withhold per capita from the CIO "until such time as the CIO returns to the principles of free, democratic, industrial unionism."[162] After 12 years, UE had severed ties with the CIO. At the same time the general officers were negotiating with Grant Oakes, president of the Farm Equipment Workers, to merge the two organizations. By the time the CIO expelled the FE at the 1949 convention, the FE's members had already voted to become a part of the UE.[163]

There remains the question of whether UE's action resulted from orders from the Communist Party. Some observers believed that the Communists wanted the left-wing unions out of the CIO in order to form a new federation with the UE and Harry Bridge's longshoremen as the nucleus.[164] The weight of opinion, however, was on the other side. According to one source a "conference on autonomy and democracy in the CIO" consisting of all the left-wing unions was held prior to the CIO convention and resolved unanimously to "fight to remain in the CIO."[165] Even Victor Riesel, a persistent critic of the left wing, endorsed the interpretation that the Communist Party opposed withdrawal from the CIO.[166] UE's actions did not fit either analysis. If the Communist Party wanted an independent left-wing federation why not, assuming it had the power, have all the left-wing unions withdraw, not just UE. Also, why merge UE and FE if an independent federation was the goal? If the opposite was true, that the Communists wanted the left-wing unions to stay in the CIO, why allow its supposed single most powerful unit, the UE, to take such a hard line that ultimate withdrawal from the CIO became inevitable?

Walter Reuther sounded the keynote of the eleventh constitutional convention of the CIO when he told the delegates that, "we have come here to cut out the cancer and save the body of the CIO."[167] When he spoke he realized that UE was not in attendance. He castigated them because instead of coming to the convention to defend themselves, "They chose to walk out and issue a statement to the press saying that because the CIO is unwilling . . . to accept the points laid down in their ultimatum they are withholding per capita tax."[168]

One by one the CIO leaders went to the rostrum and poured years of frustration and hostility on the left-wing unions. The first to be expelled was the UE. The resolution on expulsion started off by stating that the family of the CIO could no longer tolerate the Communist Party masquerading as a labor union. It claimed that what the UE called raiding was merely a movement of workers throwing off their "yoke of domination" from a "gang of men who are without principle other than a debased loyalty to a foreign power." The bill of particulars against the UE emphasized its dissent on the Marshall Plan and the 1948 election. The only part of the indictment that approximated a trade union reason was criticism of the UE-FE merger. There were no charges that in any way reflected on the performance of the UE in terms of benefits for its members, no charges that the UE had not organized, had not improved wages and obtained seniority, union security, and welfare plans.[169] After expelling the UE, the convention took similar action against the Farm Equipment Workers. In a formal ceremony at the convention, Murray then presented James Carey with a charter for a new union, the International Union of Electrical, Radio and Machine Workers (IUE).[170] Carey was named the first president. The fact that the elaborate charter was ready indicated that no one was surprised when UE did not appear at the convention.[171]

Finally, after nine bitter years of internal strife and stubborn obstinacy on both sides, the end result, abhorrent to all unionists, was dual unionism in the electrical manufacturing industry. Emotions on both sides ran high at the convention. Finally internal and external pressures had brought the issue to a head. As in all disputes where the possibility of compromise had been exhausted, the end became predictable. The delegates on both sides acted out their roles as if following some predetermined script. An amendment to ban Communists from CIO office passed overwhelming, followed by one which empowered the CIO Executive Board "to refuse to seat or to remove" any board member whom it deemed ineligible by virtue of the anticommunist amendment. Another gave the executive board further power, upon a two-thirds vote, to revoke the charter or expel any affiliated national or international union whose "policies and activities . . . are consistently directed toward the achievement of the program or the purposes" of the Communist Party.[172]

Yet for all this rabid emotionalism, the delegates also had good reason for somber reflection as they were being applauded in print by a huge press corps that had never before been noted for a prolabor bias. The immediate prospect was for civil war in the labor movement. The ultimate benefactors of such warfare would not be UE or IUE, but GE, Westinghouse, and the other corporations in the electrical manufacturing industry. Even more significant, however, was the fact that by basing so much on the question of orthodoxy on the Marshall Plan and the Wallace candidacy, the CIO leadership established a precedent for using political tests to suppress dissidents in what was basically not a political movement. Somewhat apprehensively the *New Leader*, a journal hostile to the left-wing unions, noted that, "In expelling the Communist led unions the CIO granted to its executive board the right to determine CIO policies on non-trade union matters and to expel its affiliates for nonconformity. In curbing the rights of Communists the CIO is in danger of moving down the road to oligarchy."[173]

6

A HOST OF ENEMIES

The dismemberment of the UE became the centerpiece of the CIO strategy after the expulsion of the left-wing unions. The decision had been made in 1948 that the labor movement would give full support to the Democratic Party and the emerging anti-Soviet foreign policy underpinned by the Marshall Plan and the rearmament of Western Europe. Not only did the UE, as the biggest of the left-wing unions, stand in the way of this policy, but it was centered in a critical war industry, especially in the new electronic branches making equipment for the Korean War and advanced weapons systems for the defense department.

The newly created IUE was to be the chosen instrument of this policy. The new dual union held its first convention at Philadelphia in November 1949. The symbolism of the location was obvious. More than any other place, it could lay claim to being the founding city of the UE. Carey began his career there as an organizer of the Philco local. All throughout the bitter civil war, District 1 had remained the stronghold of the right-wing forces. In fact, the night before the opening of the IUE's founding convention, some 1,800 members of GE Local 119 in Philadelphia met with Carey and voted to withdraw from the UE and join the IUE. Carey spoke to the group and urged them to affiliate with "clean American unions."[1] District 7, under the control of the right wing, was another Carey stronghold, and had already voted to leave the UE as soon as the break with the CIO became official.[2]

Addresses by Philip Murray and Secretary of Labor Daniel Tobin gave the first IUE convention the imprimatur of the CIO and the government. In case the point was missed, Secretary of the Air

Force Stuart Symington also spoke and President Truman sent a letter hailing the new union for its anticommunism. An administrative committee, headed by James Carey, was appointed by the CIO to run the IUE for its first year. Amidst the rhetorical shelling of the UE, a war council chaired by Carey drew up a plan for the final campaign against the UE. Crucial to the IUE's hopes was aid from the CIO. In all, the industrial federation would donate over $800,000 in cash to the IUE by mid-1950, in addition to paying for the publication of its newspaper and providing it with hundreds of thousands of dollars worth of staff time and legal aid.[3]

Tactical sparring began at once. The IUE promptly asked the NLRB for representation elections at the plants of the three most important UE-represented chains, General Motors, Westinghouse and General Electric. The strategy was to schedule the GM election first because the right wing was strongest there and the IUE hoped a victory would give momentum to the campaigns in GE and Westinghouse plants.[4] The UE urged a common date for all three chains, but the right wing had taken care to cover all the bases, including the NLRB. No one was surprised when the Board set the order of elections precisely as the IUE had requested.[5]

The UE did its best to prepare for the onslaught. Twenty-one new staff members were added and provided with a special series of eight pamphlets aimed at countering the charges they were likely to face. But the truly significant change was the decision to ask local union officers at GE and Westinghouse to sign the noncommunist affidavits. This retreat was the clearest sign that the UE understood that it had no hope without at least having access to the electoral machinery of the NLRB.[6]

The NLRB ordered an election at the UE's GM plants for February 28. About 28,000 workers were at stake at five locations, the biggest of which was the right-wing stronghold at Frigidaire in Dayton. The campaign stressed red-baiting and the IUE's ties to the rest of the CIO, particularly to Walter Reuther's UAW. The result was predictable. All five plants went IUE and the overall margin was 8 to 1.[7]

With the General Motors elections out of the way, the focus shifted to Westinghouse. The NLRB had begun hearings on the hastily thrown together IUE representation election petition. Many plants were not listed and no authorization cards were filed.[8] Seizing the opportunity, the company filed its own representation election petition, something it was permitted to do under the new Taft-Hartley Act. On the pretext of clarifying the disputed situation, Westinghouse proposed splitting the current 59 bargaining units into 76. Westinghouse's action saved the day for the IUE. Without the company petition, the right-wing forces would not have been on the ballot in a number of key plants. The IUE did not even have locals at crucial locations such as Lester in Pennsylvania, Baltimore, Bridgeport, Newark, and Trenton. Through its petition guaranteeing the IUE a place on the ballot at each bargaining unit, the company undercut an important UE argument that only by voting to preserve the UE could workers maintain companywide bargaining unity.[9]

After 32 days of hearings, the NLRB scheduled the Westinghouse elections for April 27, 1950.[10] The huge East Pittsburgh plant would be the focus of the conflict. The plant had long been a battleground between left and right. The workers were very evenly divided. A majority of the stewards backed the UE, but a majority of the local officers, elected six months earlier, were behind the IUE.[11]

The IUE pulled out all the stops for this campaign. In a well choreographed effort, Philip Murray and Transit Worker union head Michael Quill were brought to East Pittsburgh for anti-UE rallies. The IUE Local 601 newspaper launched weekly red-baiting tirades and was joined by the Pittsburgh dailies, which featured cartoons of Philip Murray squashing a bug-like UE and editorials endorsing the IUE and stating that Communism was the issue.[12]

Local politicians and FBI agents spoke at IUE rallies. The HUAC held well-publicized hearings during the campaign, using the testimony of Matt Cvetic, who had gained a great deal of notoriety as a paid FBI informer inside the Communist Party, to vaguely hint at sabotage at East Pittsburgh.[13] Finally, the Catholic church intervened massively, spurred on and organized by the local ACTU head, Father Rice. Anti-UE sermons were preached and anti-UE leaflets passed out at almost all the Catholic churches in the area on the Sunday before the election. Typical was that at St. William's, where parishioners were warned that "Russia was pouring fabulous sums of money into the fight" and that Christian duty required a vote for the IUE.[14]

The election was razor-close. The IUE garnered 5,763 votes to the UE's 5,663. Since there were 170 votes for no union, a runoff between the two unions was ordered for June 1. The intensity of the anti-UE campaign did not slacken. CIO billboards appeared in a 40-mile radius of the plant at a cost of some $150,000. The state commander of the Veterans of Foreign Wars wrote to every East Pittsburgh veteran denouncing the UE.[15] The *Pittsburgh Post Gazette* warned that the UE had "imported 20 Communists from the Chicago area to cause racial tension."[16] Finally, on Memorial Day, the UE was denied a rally permit by the East Pittsburgh authorities on the grounds of public safety, but the IUE rally went on without interruption. Judge Michael Musmanno, the Democratic Party Candidate for lieutenant governor and a reserve naval officer, arrived in uniform escorted by an armed National Guard unit and denounced the UE as "traitors, who would dance on the graves of the sainted martyrs whom we honor on Memorial Day."[17] Not surprisingly, the IUE picked up most of the nonunion votes and won the runoff, but the 5,964 to 5,706 totals were impressive testimony to the ability of the UE loyalists to stand firm in the face of overwhelming pressure.[18]

A similar attack was pressed on the UE at other Westinghouse plants. At Lima, Ohio, after IUE supporters submitted a petition against working with him, Westinghouse told Jake Staas, a key UE third shift leader, that "recent developments have introduced unexpected complications that prevent returning you to work."[19] Fistfights punctuated attempts by UE loyalists at Sharon, Pennsylvania to conduct a meeting, while 34 Sharon police guarded the IUE meeting from similar disruption.[20] At the huge Mansfield, Ohio, complex, Westinghouse withdrew recognition from the UE stewards in January, 1950, and granted it to those of the IUE.[21]

The election results were mixed. The IUE won most of the larger plants, including Sharon, Mansfield, Lima, Cleveland, and Springfield. The new union won a lopsided victory, 2,372 to 385, at the huge Bloomfield, New Jersey, lamp plant, and narrowly squeaked out a win at the big Buffalo, New York, motor factory.[22]

The UE, however, held onto some important plants. The largest of these was its stronghold at Lester, PA. There, almost every steward had remained loyal to the union and the UE won easily. Other big UE victories included Newark, New Jersey, Bridgeport, Connecticut, and Sunbury, Pennsylvania; all plants with at least 1,000 workers. In all, the UE retained representation rights for about 15,000 Westinghouse workers, a credible showing considering the forces arrayed against it.[23]

As planned, the campaign to wrest General Electric from the UE came last. The hope had been that the IUE would be riding the crest of the momentum gained at General Motors and Westinghouse. The stubborn resistance of the UE in Westinghouse had, however, slowed the momentum. Here once again, the company provided the IUE with a major boost by filing NLRB representation election petitions for all its plants on December 16, 1949. The NLRB postponed the election beyond the April 1, 1950, contract expiration date, so that the UE was deprived of the argument that workers should stay with the union to protect their contract. The Board scheduled the companywide elections for May 25 at 57 locations.[24]

The IUE and the CIO launched a vast campaign, spending over $5.5 million on organizers, advertising, literature and outside speakers. General Electric's flagship plant at Schenectady was the key battleground, with a great deal of symbolism, (it was Emspak's home local and had always been a hub of the the union), and about 14,000 workers at stake. General Electric and the Atomic Energy Commission had already ruled that the UE was ineligible, on security grounds, to represent the workers at the Knolls Atomic Lab at the vast complex. Local landlords refused to rent meeting halls to the UE and GE denied the union dues checkoff payments unless it could get new cards signed by all its members. The union responded to the latter challenge by producing 10,500 signed cards in two days, and brought in 3,500 more within a week.[25] When the results were in, the UE had retained Schenectady, with a comfortable 7,761 to 5,847 spread.[26]

The Lynn, Massachusetts, plant was the opposite case. Important in the founding of the UE, it was a major jewel in the General Electric necklace of plants, but it had always been more conservative. Although it was the home local of Albert Fitzgerald, it had ultimately expelled him, throwing its support instead to the Carey forces. Lynn, it should be remembered, was also the home local of Fred Kelley, the right-wing standard bearer who challenged Fitzgerald for the UE presidency at the 1949 convention.

In a complete departure from normal Board practices, the NLRB included the more conservative salaried workers in the bargaining unit, which boosted the IUE's chances.[27] Secretary of Labor Tobin, in "what was believed to be an unprecedented appearance by a Secretary of Labor on one side in a fight between unions," spoke at an IUE rally in Lynn. He charged there that the UE had "one master—Stalin in Russia."[28] On election day, the IUE took the plants, winning by 7,935 to 6,358.[29]

At many of the other major GE locations, the results were not so close. At Bridgeport, for example, where right-wing forces had taken control of the official UE union apparatus and name, in the late 1940s, by a combination of force, expulsions and a court injunction, they prevented the loyalists from using the UE name. Not until February 1950 were the right-wingers forced to come out in the open as the IUE. There remained a reservoir of some support for the UE, but still, the union lost by a 2,553 to 1,130 margin.[30] The dispute at the GE switchgear plant in Philadelphia, where the ACTU played a major role, showed the bitterness and confusion resulting from the split. When a majority of the membership voted to go over to the IUE, the local president went with them, sending the local treasury to IUE headquarters in Washington for safekeeping. The UE continued to claim sole representation rights and held a new election to replace the defectors. Both unions claimed rights to the local's office across the street from the plant. Possession on any given day depended on who arrived first. The company, in the meantime, had recognized the IUE local. In the confusion, the company effectively stopped dealing with both groups, thus penalizing the workers. This state of affairs lasted for six months until the IUE won the representation election by a wide margin, 1,735 to 1,017.[31] Joseph Hughes, a UE steward who stayed with the union, later told of formerly close friends who never spoke to him again, so intense were the hatreds that resulted from the split.[32]

Most other large GE plants also went IUE. Among the more crushing defeats were Syracuse, where the right wing won by 4,390 to 255 and Pittsfield, where the vote was 4,392–1,803. In Fort Wayne, Indiana, the margin was a 3,988–1092 spread. Company-wide, the GE vote was 47,486 to 35,763 in favor of the IUE, and most GE shops left the UE.[33]

Still, the UE won some important victories in addition to Schenectady. The third biggest local, at the refrigeration plant at Erie, PA, went solidly UE, 6,608 to 4,373. There, the UE relied on a leadership team that skillfully incorporated workers of various ages, skill levels and ethnic backgrounds, and was led by liberal Catholics, less vulnerable to red-baiting.[34] The UE also triumphed at Newark, New Jersey; Ontario, California; and Tiffin, Ohio. When the smoke of battle cleared, the UE still represented 36,000 GE workers in the U.S., plus 8,000 in Canada, compared to 54,000 for the IUE.[35]

Events at RCA more or less followed the same script. By the time of the split, the UE had organized the three major RCA locations in the United States: Camden, New Jersey; Lancaster, Pennsylvania, and Pulaski, Virginia. Both unions had considerable support at Camden and Pulaski, but the IUE lacked strength in Lancaster. As a result, the IUE pushed to schedule the Lancaster election last. As usual, the NLRB chose the IUE's plan and scheduled the election for May 1950 at Camden and Pulaski. The IUE would later withdraw from the ballot at Lancaster.[36]

In the meantime, a ferocious barrage had been unleashed against UE backers at Camden and Pulaski. On November 7, 1949, led by IUE supporters in the plant, a Pulaski mob, angry at the UE's push for equal promotions for African-Americans, beat several UE organizers and activists, singling out Henry Rhine, because he was Jewish. The local police stood by and watched this attack and the UE men were forcibly placed on a train out of town. Both the UE local president, George Rhodes, and steward Archie Nestor had to go into hiding and be smuggled out of town. Rhodes's home was attacked and damaged by the mob. Rhine and Rhodes returned to town in January, 1950 and reorganized the local. They met in the local NAACP headquarters, the only organization in town that would rent them a hall. Nestor, more closely identified with the left and with the fight against discrimination, was unable to return to the plant.[37]

The Catholic Church was at the center of the anti-UE blitz in Camden. A UE organizer illustrated the impact of church pressure on a key Local 103 activist, in November 1949: "As a result of terrific pressure from his priest, John Crowson folded up."[38] The UE hit back by sending advance delegations of Catholic members to visit their parish priests, urging them to remain neutral. The union also heavily criticized the IUE's new contract at the nearby Philco plant and stressed the negative aspects of the CIO's record in the Camden shipyards. The vote totals at both plants were very close, but the IUE won both elections.[39] The UE did better at Sylvania, retaining a majority of the 9 plants, almost all of which had heavily female work forces.[40] In other companies the results were mixed. Battles with the IUE and other unions, most notably the United Auto Workers and the International Brotherhood of Electrical Workers at companies such as International Harvester, Sunbeam, Remington Rand, and Monroe Calculator were as bitter as the big wars at General Electric and Westinghouse, though they received a good deal less attention. In late 1949, the UE's membership rolls were boosted by the affiliation of the 50,000-member Farm Equipment Workers. The left-wing FE, under mounting pressure from the UAW for years, had first rejected a takeover bid by the Auto Workers in a referendum vote. In a second referendum, the members overwhelmingly voted to join the UE. UAW supporters challenged the legality of this vote, but in November 1949, the Supreme Court upheld the tally.[41]

At the 1949 convention, the CIO assigned the UAW complete jurisdiction over the farm equipment industry. The Auto Workers began an intense series of raids on the FE-UE. One of the key early tests was at the International Harvester complex in Louisville, where 3,200 workers were represented by UE Local 236F. The UAW campaign there had two main themes, unity with the auto industry and red-baiting. Both unions sought to appeal to the substantial African-American minorities in these plants, but the strong record of the FE pushed most blacks in its direction. When the ballots were cast in December 1949, the UE-FE won a nearly 2–1 victory over the UAW.[42] Later that month, the UAW was turned back in two other raids at Harvester, at the huge West Pullman works and at Canton, IL. International Harvester was still the UE-FE's.[43]

Several of these elections pointed out the uncertainty of intervention on the part of the Catholic Church. When the IUE raided Remington Rand in upstate New York, the Catholic bishop of Albany played a major role in the anti-UE campaign. Nevertheless, the heavily Catholic local rejected his advice and voted for the UE. In an election involving about 1,200 workers at the plants of Monroe Calculator in Orange and Morristown, New Jersey, Newark's Monsignor John Mechlen intervened, proclaimed a vote for the UE a mortal sin, and mobilized the local parish priests to support his stance. The workers rejected his advice, however, by a large margin.[44]

Nor was ACTU or other right-wing influence necessarily geographic. Pittsburgh was a case in point. Probably in no other city were the forces arrayed against the UE more formidable. After the loss of Westinghouse Local 601, the UE's biggest remaining Pittsburgh stronghold was Local 610. It covered the Westinghouse Airbrake plant in Wilmerding and the Union Switch and Signal plant six miles away in Swissvale. The latter plant had always been the soft spot in the local, organized four years later than the Airbrake. The IUE believed that it could win among the more conservative workers at the Switch and asked the Labor Board to schedule that election well before the one at the Airbrake. The NLRB complied.[45]

The election was held on June 15, 1950. The UE won by 735 to 602, using as its main issues unity with the Airbrake plant and comparisons of the Local 610 pension plan with those won by the CIO in the region. The two plants would remain firmly UE for the next 40 years, as the union crushed the IUE at the Airbrake later that year.[46]

Nevertheless, by late 1950, the UE had suffered serious damage. About 152,000 members had been taken away by the IUE and other rival unions. The old union had been wiped out in GM and was now the minority group in GE, Westinghouse and RCA. On the other hand, the UE had held onto over 100,000 workers in representation elections, had 300,000 members who had not yet even faced a raid, had been boosted by the affiliation of 50,000 members from the Farm Equipment Workers and had organized over 15,000 workers since the split. Against all odds, the UE remained a large, significant union.[47]

Was there any clear social basis to the division that had occurred? Why did some workers stay loyal to the UE, while others were more vulnerable to the appeal of its rivals? In a pioneering study of this question at two important plants, one historian has argued that, while skill, age and ethnicity were very important factors in determining which way workers would go in the split, the impact of these factors varied greatly from shop to shop.[48] Further investigation shows that skilled workers were a key group in most plants, and seemed to usually vote as a bloc. Their group loyalties, however, could push them in either direction in 1950. At the Pittsfield GE plant, according to one UE organizer, "the maintenance guys . . . with the exception of a few are with (the IUE leader). They honestly believe he is doing a great job for them."[49] At the nearby Springfield Westinghouse plant, however, the toolroom was one of the few UE strongholds in the shop. At Camden RCA, the predilections of the skilled workers were split by shift and by floor.[50]

There is considerable evidence that workers with higher seniority may have been more prone to stick with the union into which they had organized. At Springfield, each side claimed strong support from the senior workers, but comparisons of activists at the plant show that those of the UE were considerably older. At the Mansfield Westinghouse plant, the high service group was solidly loyal to the UE, but, unfortunately for them, the majority of the plant's workers had less than five years service.[51]

Both sides contended for the loyalty of women, who made up over one-quarter of the industry's workers. A clear pattern does not exist for women's preferences in the split. Women, especially those who were married, may have been drawn to the UE by its strong support for the principle of unified seniority lists. Some single women, however, may have supported the IUE, because many of its local leaders had favored placing married women below single females on seniority lists. Finally, because of their higher level of church attendance, women may have been more vulnerable to the anti-UE campaigns of the Church.[52]

Race and ethnicity were final factors. In the small number of electrical plants with a substantial African-American membership, both sides sought their loyalty. At the East Pittsburgh plant, for example, Blacks organized as a separate voting block and interviewed representatives of the UE and IUE. In this particular example, the key African-American leader, William Peeler, endorsed the

IUE. Elsewhere, particularly at International Harvester and in the St. Louis electrical plants, the UE retained considerable loyalty among blacks by effectively contrasting its record on race with that of other CIO unions.[53]

Ethnicity cut many ways in the 1950 crisis. Some old-stock Protestant workers, particularly Masons, tilted to the UE as a reaction to Catholic Church intervention in the situation. Poles, perhaps because of the strong Catholicism among the men, seem to have leaned to the IUE. Italians were a swing group and South Slavs were disproportionately pro-UE.[54]

In almost all cases, the success of the IUE hinged on its ability to win over all or a big part of the local union leadership. Neither red-baiting nor threats of job loss were generally enough to swing the vote to IUE, so long as the officers stayed loyal. The turning point usually came when the local leadership decided, for whatever reason, to defect. On the other hand, the IUE's success in winning in machine shop locals was less than in the electrical manufacturing chains. This may be due to the fact that James Matles, who had originally brought the machine shops into the UE, maintained, as Director of Organization, close relationships with local leaders and was able to persuade them to hold the line.[55]

After the initial round of elections, the UE was able, for the most part, to hold its membership steady for the next two years. In fact, in two very important cases in GE and Westinghouse, the UE almost regained its dominant position in those chains.

The most important battleground in GE in these two years was Lynn. Dissatisfied with the performance of the IUE after its victory in 1950, the sentiment of the workers in this huge plant had swung back to the UE and a majority of the blue collar workers petitioned for an election. Once again, despite the UE's objections and its consistent practice to the contrary, the NLRB included white collar workers in the bargaining unit. The election was set for August 16, 1951.[56]

A massive wave of red-baiting narrowly saved the day for the IUE. FBI spy Herbert Philbrick, the subject of the popular book and television series, "I Led Three Lives," charged that key UE Lynn leaders had "associated" with Communists who were somehow linked to espionage. Two days before the election, the IUE announced that UE leader Don Tormey would be subpoenaed by the HUAC. Later that day, federal marshals burst into the Lynn UE headquarters with reporters and photographers in tow to serve the subpoena on Tormey. That night, local headlines announced, "Red Probers Summon UE Agent on Eve of GE Election Here." The night before the election, HUAC subpoenaed the NLRB for the UE's authorization cards, allegedly to check for forgeries. The next day the IUE polled 6,927 votes to 5,887 for the UE.[57]

During the Lynn campaign the IUE had filed a petition at Schenectady. One week before the election, a grand jury, with advance warning to the IUE, cited UE officers for contempt for not revealing information about alleged "Communists and spies" in the plant. Two weeks after the election, a judge quietly dropped all charges. The tactics failed and the UE held on to the plant with a greater margin than in 1950.[58]

The UE mounted a major comeback effort of its own at the East Pittsburgh Westinghouse plant in 1951 and 1952. The IUE local leadership was badly split and shop floor conditions had deteriorated under the IUE.[59] In May 1951, the UE filed for the election and optimistically began a campaign. In July, however, the NLRB dismissed the UE petition. The Board argued that the IUE's contract was a bar to an election, a policy it had overturned when the IUE had sought elections in 1950.[60]

The UE re-petitioned in 1952, once the contract bar expired. The IUE counterattacked by once again enlisting its anticommunist allies. The burgess of East Pittsburgh, a United Steelworkers officer, barred the UE from using loudspeakers in the borough, while permitting an IUE sound car.[61] There was the familiar redbaiting. The issue is "pure and simple Communism," editorialized the *Pittsburgh Press*. Matt Cvetic once again entered the fray. The FBI informer issued lurid statements about alleged Communist cells in the plant.[62] All these factors took their toll, and the UE lost the election by 6,781 to 4,825, a significantly bigger defeat than two years before. The longstanding bitterness of the battles at East Pittsburgh spilled over the night of the election when IUE members invaded the UE headquarters, severely beat UE activists, and wrecked the office.[63]

Away from the major chains, there was a limited erosion of the UE's position. A protracted battle with the IBEW at Chicago's Stewart-Warner, reaching back to the late 1940s, resulted in a victory for the AFL union and the UE rescinded its charter in early 1951. At the Reliance Electric plants in Cleveland and Ashtabula, OH, the UE local officers suddenly resigned. The former president, John Janowitz, announced that he had been an FBI undercover agent for eight years. The local officers declared that they were asserting their "loyalty as American citizens by severing all connections with the UE International." The UE did not appear on the ballot and the 1,350 workers there were lost.[64] At the 3,000-member

Seeger plant in Evansville, the UE finished third, behind the IUE and no agent, in a bitter campaign in which UE activists were frequently arrested and beaten.[65] In spite of these losses, the UE successfully defended itself in most of the plants. The worst was yet to come, however, as the nation slipped inexorably into the darkest years of anticommunist fear.

A massive, sustained campaign of red-baiting was directed against the UE by the government and corporations. While anticommunist charges had been a part of the union's history since its inception, they appear sporadic and restrained by comparison with the attacks of the decade of McCarthy. These red-baiting efforts were continually utilized to smear the union and, as we have already seen, tip the balance in close NLRB representation elections. The attacks also necessarily tied up substantial amounts of union time and energy, and threatened, at points, to put top union officers in prison. Finally, there were several attempts, one very serious, to outlaw the UE entirely.

In addition to the 1950 HUAC hearings timed to coincide with the East Pittsburgh Westinghouse election, the Committee attacked the UE in other locations. HUAC convened that spring in Cincinnati, partially in response to a petition campaign by the *Cincinnati Inquirer*, and called a number of Queen City UE activists. HUAC also subpoenaed key UE Sylvania militants during the 1950 campaign there. At all of these hearings, some UE leaders invoked the Fifth Amendment.[66]

On July 18, 1950, HUAC lodged contempt citations against Emspak, Matles, UE East Pittsburgh leaders Tom Fitzpatrick, Tom Quinn and Frank Panzino and Cincinnati UE activists Esther Tice and Talmage Raley, based on their refusals to testify at hearings earlier in the year. All seven pled not guilty and were released on bail.[67]

The union established a National Defense Committee to raise funds and to coordinate the search for public support against the charges. Several districts of the union, led by Four and Six, set up their own defense committees, as did some of the larger locals.[68] The cases were heard before various Federal District Court judges in Washington, during February 1951. Matles, Tice and Panzino were the first to be acquitted, on the grounds that they had properly utilized the Fifth Amendment, and Raley and Fitzpatrick were found not guilty a month later. Judge F. Dickinson Letts, however, found Emspak guilty and sentenced him to 4–12 months in prison and a fine of $500. The conviction rested on the technicality that Emspak had not directly cited the First and Fifth Amendments, choosing instead to argue, "I do not think this Committee has the right to pry into my associations."[69] In a separate case, the court sentenced Quinn to 4–12 months in jail, with a fine of $1000.[70] In sentencing Quinn, the judge read a statement that blamed Quinn for the deaths of American soldiers in Korea.[71]

Fund-raising for an appeal was difficult for the hard-pressed union in the hysterical atmosphere of 1951. At one point, Matles intervened to tell union officers that the "drive for the fund to date has been a failure."[72]

The UE appealed Quinn's conviction all the way to the Supreme Court. In a landmark decision the court overturned the conviction on the grounds that a valid legislative purpose was required before a congressional committee could question an individual. Quinn's ultimate victory in the courts did him little good at Westinghouse. The company fired him in 1953 from his job as a welder. Quinn took the fifth amendment again in 1954 before Joseph McCarthy's Senate investigating committee, but when the HUAC tried one last time in 1959, Quinn disregarded the advice of his lawyer and swore under oath that he had never been a member of the Communist Party, directly refuting the testimony of an FBI undercover agent whom Quinn swore he had never met. Quinn's principled stand brought an end to ten years of harassment by the Congress of the United States.[73]

In 1951, new charges were filed against the top UE officers and the union itself. Matles and Emspak were called before a Federal Grand Jury meeting in New York and were charged with "obstructing its work," when they refused to answer questions about their political affiliations. This flimsy set of accusations, timed to coincide with a raid on the GE Schenectady plant, was dropped by a judge in August, after the UE had retained the plant.[74]

In November 1952, another New York Grand Jury issued a "presentment," asking the NLRB to withdraw the UE's certification rights. The three top UE officers had been called in and questioned about the truthfulness of their Taft-Hartley affidavits.[75] The NLRB then sent the UE officers a list of six additional questions about their political affiliations. If they did not respond to these, the Board warned, the UE certifications might be withdrawn. The UE was able to obtain an injunction in January 1953, blocking this extra-legal move.[76]

The most serious attack on a top officer was launched in 1952. In October, the Immigration and Naturalization Service told Matles that he would be ordered into court in an effort to revoke his citizenship. Matles, who had come to the United States in 1923, as a

19-year-old, had immediately applied for citizenship and been naturalized five years later. The government charge was that he had concealed membership in the Communist Party on this 25-year-old application. If citizenship were revoked, he would be deported to his native Romania.[77] Matles denied having lied on the application and dozens of locals sent protest letters to the Attorney General, asking that the case be dropped. Matles's older brother, an invalid, resisted threats by the government to deport him unless he agreed to testify against his sibling.[78] Curiously, after a flurry of initial publicity about this case, all of it damaging to the UE, the government took almost no action for five years, but refused to drop the charges.

In 1952, Senator Hubert Humphrey conducted Senate hearings on the need for additional legislation to be used against Communists in unions. Although the UE testified against such legislation and used the occasion to attack the government's anticommunist campaign, its opponents used the hearings as a forum to push for more Draconian measures. Gwilym Price, CEO of Westinghouse, testified and called for a bill to outlaw "Communist dominated unions" and for a free hand in firing individuals deemed to be leftists. James Carey joined in the clamor, telling the committee that he supported the appointment of a special, tripartite government, business, and labor board, which would have the power to cancel government contracts to companies with left-wing unions. Carey also resigned from the government's Mutual Security Agency, to protest the government's failure to drop all contracts with GE unless they stopped bargaining with the UE.[79]

The hearings were suspended until after the 1952 presidential elections, but a new round of major media attacks began. In October 1952, the *Saturday Evening Post* featured an article on the UE filled with lurid charges which vaguely linked the union to Communist espionage. The article focused on Schenectady, Sylvania's Mill Hall, Pennsylvania, plant and on the Rome, New York, General Cable plant, where a lengthy strike was underway. *Reader's Digest* followed with an article entitled, "We Are Protecting Spies in Our Defense Plants." This article, devoid of hard evidence, charged the UE with espionage at the Salem, Massachusetts, factory of Sylvania where an election campaign was under way.[80]

These articles set the stage for the intensification of governmental and corporate attacks, which reached a crescendo in the 1953–57 period. Matles was called before Senator Joseph McCarthy's Senate subcommittee, which held election-coordinated sessions in Schenectady and Lynn.[81] The same committee staged hearings in Pittsburgh in spring 1953 and subpoenaed a number of

UE activists. The hearings featured the bizarre claim that an unnamed East Pittsburgh worker had been blown up by a bomb, allegedly detonated by Communists using magnetic waves.[82]

The leadership's only admitted Communist Party member, William Sentner, was indicted for "conspiracy to overthrow the government" in September 1952 and went on trial in 1953. Separate grand juries began investigations of District 2 President Paul Seymour and District 6 President Stanley Loney. Loney's threatened arrest led to a successful move by Locals 506 and 610 to replace him as president with 610s Dan Marguriet, a man less identified with the organized left.[83]

In the midst of these attacks, in December 1953, GE issued the "Cordiner Memo," stating that any GE employee who pled the Fifth Amendment before a governmental investigative body would be fired. Other companies, including Westinghouse, promptly followed suit and over 50 current or former UE members were fired.[84]

The cases of Tom Fitzpatrick and Evelyn Darin, both from the East Pittsburgh plant, are representative. Fitzpatrick, while still paying dues to the UE, had joined the IUE local that now represented the workers at the plant. Popular and able, he had promptly been elected as a delegate from the IUE local to the state CIO convention. James Carey intervened, however, to have the Pennsylvania CIO Council refuse to seat him, on the grounds that he had taken the Fifth Amendment. Emboldened by this example, Westinghouse announced the next day that Fitzpatrick and Frank Panzino had been fired, calling them "a disturbing influence among our employees for many years."[85] IUE Local 601 filed a grievance against the firm for the dismissal and pursued it to the national level. There, however, Carey allowed it to drop, telling the IUE's Westinghouse Conference Board that Fitzpatrick and Panzino should "go jump in a river and drown themselves."[86] Soon the FBI was visiting most strong UE supporters at East Pittsburgh, threatening them with being called before similar committees. "It is quite evident," noted the main UE organizer in the area, "that this sort of harassment is having the desired effect on many of the questioned. They want to run and hide."[87]

Nor were their fears unfounded. Evelyn Darin, a coil winder for 27 years and the main UE woman leader in the plant, was among six East Pittsburgh workers subpoenaed to go before McCarthy's Committee in January 1955. Darin did not appear, asking to be excused on grounds of illness. The next day, she and the four others received word from Westinghouse that they had been fired. Once again, the local filed grievances, but to no avail. When Darin applied for unemployment compensation, Pennsylvania denied it to her because she refused to answer the questions of the hearing examiner about Communist Party membership on Fifth Amendment grounds.[88]

Bad as the government harassment had been, for the most part it had been directed against individuals, not the legal status of the union. The most serious legal challenge to the survival of the UE came with the passage of the Communist Control Act in 1954. This legislation established the Subversive Activities Control Board (SACB). If the SACB found a union to be "Communist-dominated" or "subversive," decertification by the NLRB would follow.[89] In December 1955, in the midst of the Westinghouse strike, Attorney General Herbert Brownell filed charges against the UE. Brownell claimed that the Communist Party, working through front groups, controlled the union. Through such control, the indictment went on, the Communist Party had used the UE's halls, mimeo machines and paper to solicit aid for those on trial under the Smith Act. As further evidence of this alleged control, they noted that the UE had opposed the Korean War, the Smith Act, Taft-Hartley and the Communist Control Act itself.[90]

The Attorney General sought extensive pre-trial depositions from the UE leaders, who refused to complete the depositions on Fifth Amendment grounds. In November 1956, Matles was found in contempt of court for refusing to submit them. The Judge in the case, James Abruzzo, sentenced Matles to three months in jail. In June 1957, a divided Circuit Court of Appeals upheld the conviction 2–1. Matles appealed to the Supreme Court.[91]

The UE mounted a strong campaign to have the SACB suit dismissed, and lined up more support than in any previous efforts since 1950. The government's case was damaged by contradictory statements by its informer witnesses, and by revelations about their past criminal convictions. In 1958, the Supreme Court further weakened the government's case by ruling that the defense was entitled to see government notes about their conversations with the informers and any background information on them that the prosecution possessed.[92]

The prosecution made one last effort. New hearings were slated to begin on February 24, 1959. The UE renewed its pressure to drop the case. Faced with mounting public opposition to red-baiting and with the collapse of its case, the new Attorney General, William Rogers, ordered the Justice Department to ask that the case be dropped. On March 31, 1959, the SACB did so. The most dangerous legal attempt to put the UE out of business had been turned back.[93]

This was the signal for the end to most of the intense, systematic legal harassment of the union. Matles's citizenship revocation trial had been resumed, after a five year hiatus, in 1957, but this case had also been dropped.[94] John Killian, a former leader of UE's Local 1111 in Milwaukee, had been convicted in 1955 of falsely swearing Taft-Hartley affidavits. In late 1957, the Circuit Court of Appeals overturned his conviction.[95] The government's abandonment of prosecution came too late for some. Former UE District 8 leader William Sentner died suddenly on December 10, 1958, in the midst of legal appeals. When the Circuit Court of Appeals ruled in favor of John Nelson of GE Local 506 in Erie, Pennsylvania, in late 1958, the popular leader was already ill with the disease that would kill him within a year.[96]

The waning of these legal attacks was an important victory for the UE. It had survived, and would be able to mount a serious rebuilding attempt in the late 1950s. Charges of Communist control had been defeated and its top officers had turned back the attempts to jail them. In truth, however, the anticommunist campaign had achieved its purposes. Dozens of UE activists had lost their jobs and hundreds, perhaps thousands, of others had been silenced or intimidated. Most importantly, the union had suffered devastating membership losses, and by 1954 had lost about two-thirds of its half million members.[97]

Although the union had suffered grievously from the raids of the IUE and other unions, an equally great hemorrhage would take place in the mid-1950s, as a result of defections of whole locals and districts to various rivals. There were basically three reasons for this. First, was the ongoing, cumulative effect of the red-baiting, which reached a crescendo in this period. Second, from 1953 to 1955, serious, and ultimately successful merger talks took place between the AFL and the CIO. Third, desiring to move its labor cadres back into the mainstream of the labor movement, the Communist Party ordered its followers in the unions that had been expelled from the CIO to make peace with their rivals and take their unions into the new AFL-CIO.

Disaster at Schenectady was the harbinger of things to come. Longtime business agent Leo Jandreau, a union founder; his wife, Ruth Young, once the most powerful woman leader in the UE; and Chief Steward William Mastriani, defected to the IUE in 1953. A desire for unity, fatigue at fighting off constant IUE pressure and red-baiting, and the conversion of Ruth Young to Catholicism all played a part in the decision. GE quickly joined the fray, firing a number of UE loyalists under the Cordiner memo. The UE, realizing the meaning of the loss of Schenectady, threw everything into the campaign, but could not overcome the combination of the Jandreau organization and company pressure.[98]

The loss of Schenectady signaled the end of hope for regaining lost ground on the part of many who had supported the UE in the first round of battles. As the drama at Schenectady unfolded, so too did the unity talks between the AFL-CIO. These talks, and the subsequent merger of the two labor federations in 1955, were catalysts for a series of devastating developments for the UE.

The possibility of labor unity on the national level led many inside the UE to push for the UE to re-enter the house of labor either as a separate entity or through merger with one of its erstwhile rivals. Mergers with the IUE, the UAW, the IAM, and the IBEW were given serious consideration. In the spring of 1955, the UE's General Executive Board, while offering a critique of the formal policies proposed by the AFL-CIO, authorized the officers of the union to discuss possible terms for affiliation, laying down the following conditions: an end to all raids, the guarantee of local autonomy and union democracy, and cooperation in collective bargaining while merger talks progressed.[99]

Amalgamation talks went nowhere, however, owing to differences of opinion on the General Executive Board, and also to the decision by Carey and the IUE to reject the UE's conditions and to offer the UE only total absorption into their bitter rival. Carey made a point to stress that the ban on Communist Party membership would be maintained in the IUE.[100]

The momentum of the AFL-CIO merger also led to a change in the trade union policy of the Communist Party. It ordered its union cadres to try to lead their unions back into the mainstream of the labor movement. The Party believed that the independent left-wing unions could not survive outside of the huge, unitary labor federation. For most of the expelled unions, such as the Fur Workers and the Mine, Mill and Smelter Workers, grievously wounded by raids and the legal fees required to defend their leaders against government attempts to send them to prison, continued independence seemed a sure recipe for extinction. But the UE was different. After five difficult years its membership had stabilized at about 180,000 and it still retained control of important locals. In addition it was still an attractive potential partner and in a relatively strong position to exact reasonable conditions in any merger with an AFL-CIO union. Disaster was, however, about to strike, and the Communist Party's "enter-the-mainstream" line would be a contributor to it.[101]

In November 1955, District 8, based in Iowa and Missouri, was the first to go. The former Farm Equipment Workers locals, under heavy Communist influence, led the way into the UAW.[102] Worse disaster hit in the spring of 1956. District Four, in New York and New Jersey, had lost 60,000 members to the IUE, but still had 20,000 members. Of all the remaining districts, it was the most solidly under the control of Party loyalists. The entire district went over to the IUE, claiming that the merger offered the only hope for reuniting all the workers in the industry. With almost all of the district's officers and staff behind the secession, (all current UE staff members were to go on the IUE payroll), the UE lost nearly every local. The IUE promised that no UE staff members would be fired for using the Fifth Amendment, and that the five large amalgamated locals would retain their autonomy. Shortly thereafter, however, many were fired from their IUE jobs in the wake of HUAC hearings in Newark.[103]

A few weeks after the District 4 secession, the other shoe dropped. Almost all of the District 3 staff engineered a secession of that district to the IAM, using the familiar arguments about unity and effectiveness. Most of the Ohio District 7 staff and officers left the union in August 1956, with most going to the IAM. District 9 was the last to go—President John Gojack took most of the district to the IAM.[104] At the end of the carnage the UE had lost over half of its already depleted membership. Only about 75,000 members remained.[105]

Throughout this trying period, the UE continued to doggedly pursue its collective bargaining responsibilities. It did so in an atmosphere affected by contradictory forces. On the one hand, it was under attack at all times and the workers in the industry were badly divided in their dealings with management. On the other hand, the industry was expanding rapidly throughout most of the decade and workers brought with them the legacy of the militancy and gains of the 1930s and 1940s.

General Electric remained the pattern setter for the industry. The firm took advantage of the division of the UE to institute, in the 1950s, a collective bargaining program known as "Boulwarism," named after the company's new Industrial Relations Vice-president, Lemuel Boulware. At bottom, this was a take-it-or-leave-it approach to negotiations. GE itself described it as a program "to determine, and to put into place voluntarily all that is warranted in the way of wage and fringe benefits and adjustments for all employees." The strategy relied on the ideological divisions among its three major unions, the UE, IUE, and IBEW, its geographical decentralization program (GE opened several dozen new plants in the South and West), and a slick campaign of "communicating fully to employees, throughout the year, on all matters which affect their relationship with the company." GE would, with great publicity, announce a wage package, then put it into effect at its nonunion plants and at those represented by smaller unions. It would then refuse to move from the offer unless the UE or IUE could mount great pressure.[106]

In 1950, GE instituted Boulwarism in its fullest form. The UE, by threatening to strike and demonstrating its willingness to do so, was able to modify the firm's initial offer, but only modestly. In the September 1950 contract, wages were increased by 3 percent, with an additional 5 cents an hour for skilled workers and some pension improvements. Instead of the five year deal GE had sought, the UE maintained its opposition to multi-year contracts, achieving a one-year contract with a wage reopener in 6 months.[107] The wage reopener agreement, reached on May 17, 1951, brought a 9 cents an hour raise, contingent on its approval by the Korean War-instituted Wage Stabilization Board. The UE reluctantly accepted this offer, noting that "it falls far short of meeting the needs of GE employees, and does not even make up the ground they have lost since the last increase."[108] The UE attributed the inability to win more to Boulwarism, the split, the IUE's acceptance of GE's offer, the Truman administration's wage freeze and the participation by the AFL and the CIO in the functioning of the WSB.[109] When another reopener came due in September 1951, the UE pushed GE for a general wage increase and for increases to minimize geographic, day work, and gender differentials. The UE took a strike vote, which won a majority, but failed to carry Taunton, Elmira, Decatur, DeKalb and, most importantly, Schenectady. As a consequence of this and other factors, in December the union was forced to settle with GE for a 3 percent hike.[110]

The WSB moved very slowly on the approval of this and other major UE contracts, including those with Westinghouse and Sylvania. The union conducted petition campaigns among its members and ran advertisements aimed at the public in an attempt to speed approval, but the increases remained stalled, as they did for the other unions involved, past the expiration date of yet another GE contract. In September 1952, the UE signed a one-year pact, with a 5.8 percent hike. The UE then began a major campaign of publicity and delegations to Washington, with similar actions by the IUE and other unions, which finally brought approval by the WSB.[111]

The next contract, an 18-month one signed in 1953, saw GE double its original modest offer, following a larger than expected settlement in the automobile industry.[112] When that pact expired in 1955, the UE's position versus GE had been dramatically weakened, since by then it had lost the Schenectady plant. The IUE accepted a five-year pact from GE, which it hailed as a model. The UE regarded both the wage and benefit components and the productivity clauses as unacceptable and refused to sign, awaiting the outcome of the probable strike at Westinghouse.[113]

The Westinghouse negotiations roughly paralleled those at GE from 1950 to 1955. Once the representation elections were over in 1950, the UE called on Westinghouse to reinstate the old contract. Facing the now-divided workers, the firm sought contract language concessions.[114] The negotiations went on through the Summer while the IUE accepted a barebones agreement. The UE mounted a convincing strike threat. At this point, the IUE signed a full contract, which included many concessions on shop floor issues. For awhile it appeared that there would be a strike, but the UE reached an agreement on November 1, retroactive to September 8, protecting most of the old contract.[115]

Negotiations reopened in April 1951. Tentative agreement was reached on a contract, but a dispute remained over whether the raise was contingent on War Stabilization Board approval of a price hike for Westinghouse. The IUE signed such a deal, but the UE, ultimately, was able to resist it.[116]

The UE waged two long strikes at Westinghouse plants in 1952. At the Trenton plant a dispute, leading to a lockout, began on January 18, after the firing of a worker who failed to meet new production quotas unilaterally established by Westinghouse. The firm put heavy pressure on the primarily female work force and threatened to move the entire plant to Little Rock. After almost eight weeks off the job, a mixed settlement was reached in April.[117] That same month, the 675 workers at Pittsburgh's Nuttall plant struck over proposed cuts in incentive time values. The company made a serious effort to break the strike, using police attacks on picket lines, heavy red-baiting, and an expensive public relations effort. The workers, however, held firm, and won a favorable contract.[118]

In July 1953, the UE signed another contract with the firm, with wage increases that averaged 4.7 cents an hour.[119] This document was renewed in July 1954, after the UE turned back Westinghouse's efforts to add an explicit clause committing the union to productivity drives.[120]

The biggest picket line battle of the decade came with the 1955–56 Westinghouse strike. On October 25, 1955, the UE struck Westinghouse locations nationwide, joining the IUE, whose contracts had expired a week earlier. Relations between the two unions had temporarily warmed. The IAM and IBEW locals at Westinghouse also joined the strike. At stake in the national battle were contract length, wages, and a host of concessions that Westinghouse hoped to impose on its now badly divided workers. The strike was strong at almost all UE locations. The union embarked on a massive campaign to generate support and solidarity for the strikers. For the first time since the 1940s, the UE was fairly successful in breaking through the wall of isolation imposed upon it and reaching the public with its case. Many ties with local AFL-CIO unions were forged or renewed during the strike, although raids on the UE continued, as did court injunctions and other legal attacks.[121]

As the strike dragged on into 1956, the UE and IUE encouraged the formation of a National Citizens Committee, with Eleanor Roosevelt as its titular leader, which sought an arbitrated settlement to the strike. The UE also encouraged and attended a conference of the mayors of 16 cities with Westinghouse plants, and succeeded in convincing them to intervene in the strike in a positive way. In some areas, such as Pennsylvania, the strikers were awarded surplus food, but in others, Illinois, for example, it was denied.[122]

In late January, the IAM and the IBEW locals signed a five-year deal with Westinghouse on terms close to those sought by the firm, but the IUE and UE stayed out.[123] In March, after 154 days, a national agreement was reached. The UE achieved the withdrawal of Westinghouse's onerous speed-up and measured daywork proposals and both unions won substantial monetary gains.[124]

The strike was not over, however, for UE Local 107 in Lester, PA. For four more months they remained out over local issues, including a plan to scrap the plant's high incentive rates and replace them with measured daywork. Injunctions were obtained against the large and militant picket lines, but the strikers held firm. Twenty-six local leaders were jailed and fined. The UE redoubled its aid to one of its biggest remaining locals. Other unions in the Philadelphia area were contacted and made significant contributions. Local 107 was able to mobilize considerable community support against the lock-out. This included thousands of dollars worth of food raised in house-to-house canvassing, and a statement by five Philadelphia congressmen endorsing the UE's refusal "to accept Westinghouse's drastic proposal."[125] Finally, in August, the company was forced to give in and abandon most of its takeaway proposals, including the attempt to fire 14 of the union's activists.[126]

Collective bargaining at Westinghouse by the UE and the IUE demonstrated the differences between the two unions with regard to restrictions on management prerogatives. The issues of incentive pay and seniority provide an optic through which to view the different responses of the two unions to management's attempts to roll back earlier collective bargaining gains in these two critical areas of shop floor control.

Workers at Westinghouse worked under two different payment systems, daywork or incentive piecework. Daywork employees received a set rate for each hour; incentive workers received payment according to the amount they produced. Usually, this meant a low "base rate" received regardless of output, and a bonus or incentive payment for each additional piece produced above a certain target, or "100 percent." Westinghouse, using efficiency experts, conducted time studies of incentive jobs to set the "recorded value," 100 percent and the amount paid per additional piece. From the point of view of workers, a rate might be too "tight," that is, require too much speed and effort to achieve; or, from management's point of view, it might be too "loose," allowing workers to make a high wage without greatly increasing their work pace.[127]

Following the war, Westinghouse, like many other corporations, began to launch major attacks on incentive rates. Between 1946 and 1949, the UE fought off these attempts, arguing that "corporations have hogged all the benefits of such increased production . . . making all technical improvements a curse rather than a blessing to the vast majority."[128] By 1948, the UE had codified a formidable set of protections into its Westinghouse contract. Recorded values could only be changed when there was a clerical error or a change in method. Even then "only that portion of the value affected by the change" could be adjusted. If a worker thought that a value was too tight, it could be handled under the grievance procedure. This usually meant that workers could at least obtain a new time study. The company could not change the payment method of any group of workers, daywork or incentive, without negotiating first with the local union.[129]

The 1949 split and the resulting period of uncertainty over representation rights gave Westinghouse an excellent opportunity to attack these contractual protections and cut rates unilaterally. At the big turbine plant in Lester, Pennsylvania, the UE struck to maintain them.[130] On the other hand, rates were cut at the IUE stronghold in Mansfield, Ohio, where workers did not "want to stick their necks out" in the existing climate of red-baiting and interunion rivalry.[131] In October 1950, the IUE signed its first full contract with Westinghouse. The result was a step backward on incentive standards. The contract added a clause giving management the right to establish "time values for wage payment purposes by the following methods: by time study, from formula or data, by comparison or by estimate." Another provision allowed time study on an entire job when one element was changed. Most importantly, perhaps, the IUE contract gave up the right of the union to grieve changes in time values.[132] At the Cheektowaga, New York plant, the IUE supplement went even further, allowing the company to make time studies of all workers and pledging union cooperation in the effort.[133] In Sharon, Pennsylvania, values were cut on hundreds of jobs in 1951. When workers resisted, Westinghouse ordered disciplinary furloughs for 4,500 workers and threatened to close the plant.[134] The unorganized, newly opened plants and, in some cases, the 36,000 Westinghouse workers represented by the IBEW and other unions, further undermined conditions.

Attacks on incentive standards also took place in the UE's plants. But although there were some minor concessions, the attacks were largely turned back. Guaranteed rates at the UE's stronghold at Lester, Pennsylvania, ranged from 8 to 33 percent higher than those at the IUE's East Pittsburgh plant.[135]

During the 1955 strike, the biggest and longest in the history of the company, a central issue was Westinghouse's drive to weaken incentive protections and increase output. The company wanted three things: the right to time study dayworkers and impose production quotas on them, the right to restudy and reset incentive rates at any time, and the acceptance of a productivity clause.[136] Throughout the conflict the UE urged the IUE to stop negotiating over the ground rules for the study of dayworkers and to reject it totally. The two unions reached settlements in March 1956. Both had to agree that Westinghouse could conduct time studies of dayworkers under certain conditions, but the UE contract limited this to "measuring or improving production method analysis or for budget purposes." In other words, no measured daywork.[137] The IUE clause allowed Westinghouse to apply individual production standards to "direct dayworkers," those who did easily measured production tasks, and agreed to a very explicit productivity clause for them.[138]

There were clear differences between the approaches of the two unions on seniority as well. By 1949 the UE had succeeded in winning fairly broad seniority units. In most cases this meant departmental seniority, with units of a thousand workers or larger. In the case of smaller factories, UE contracts frequently called for plantwide seniority. Broad units were important because they were more equitable and tended to generate greater internal solidarity.[139] Finally, the UE had made considerable headway in achieving seniority lists undivided by race, ethnicity, and—more significantly—by gender. The latter was the most salient because of the firm's past practices. Westinghouse, supported by many of its workers, had maintained separate seniority practices for men and women, including pre-World War II provisions against hiring married women. Women were let go when they married. Following the War, when these provisions were relaxed owing to the labor shortage, Westinghouse attempted to return to the old policies. The UE successfully resisted and by 1949, most locals had unified seniority lists.[140]

As with incentive standards, Westinghouse took advantage of the 1949 union split to try to limit seniority protections. The company proposed that the upgrading procedure be "based on seniority if the employee can do the job. Management reserves the right to determine if the employee can do the job." Furthermore, Westinghouse called for the narrowing and fragmentation of seniority units.[141] The 1950 IUE contract codified a significant retreat. It explicitly favored layoffs over work sharing in times of economic downturn, and locals were authorized to negotiate over the configuration of seniority units.[142] Perhaps most ominously, the company won the right to grant from 1 to 2 percent of the workers in any unit exemption from seniority as it saw fit. None of these provisions were present in the 1950 UE contract.[143]

While the national IUE contract did not discriminate against women in seniority provisions, many of the supplements reached by its locals did. Local 202 in Springfield, Massachusetts, was representative of about a dozen such cases. Its contract specified that "married women will not be considered for employment if their husbands are able to work." If a female employee did marry, she might temporarily remain on the job but would be the first to go in case of a layoff.[144] On the other hand, there is no evidence that UE contracts narrowed seniority units or established separate seniority lists for women.

In sum, during the 1950s, most Westinghouse workers lost some ground on incentive and seniority issues, but there were clear differences between the unions. On both issues the UE had firm, well-thought-out positions, and was more firm in resisting concessions and protecting shop-floor conditions for its dwindling numbers of Westinghouse members.

The 1950–56 period was also a militant one at UE plants outside the GE and Westinghouse chains. International Harvester was a particularly stormy company. In 1950, the 35,000 new FE-UE members struck for three weeks, after International Harvester reneged on an earlier wage agreement. They won higher wages and an end to the lower wage scale for Southern plants.[145] By 1952, however, the situation had darkened. A long strike was provoked by Harvester's demands for concessions on incentive, classification, and grievance procedure, all of which had been agreed to by the UAW at IH plants where it had the representation rights. After 87 days, the strike was weakening and perhaps one-quarter of the workers had returned to their jobs. HUAC had scheduled hearings to investigate the union. Harold Ward, the treasurer of the local, had been charged with the murder of a strikebreaker and had been all but convicted in the pages of the *Chicago Tribune*.[146] The union was forced to, as it admitted, "give ground on a number of issues," in order to avoid total defeat.[147] The loss of this strike contributed to the UAW's capture of most of the old FE in 1955, when the next Harvester contract came due.

There were several major UE strikes in 1954. One was a 108 day clash at Detroit's Square D, where the company's hope to recruit strikebreakers among the unemployed autoworkers failed, in part, because of cooperation with the UAW. The *New York Times* called it "the first attempt to break a strike in Detroit since 1939."[148]

In July 1954, American Safety Razor, located in Brooklyn, announced that it was moving its plant to low-wage, Staunton, VA. The company locked out the workers in September, as they fought to delay the move and win pension and severance pay concessions. The workers eventually responded with a sit-in, but massive use of the police and red-baiting broke the strike, despite a national boycott of the firm's razors.[149]

In sum, throughout the 1950s, despite the savage attacks on it by the labor movement and the government, the UE was able to continue to bargain successfully for its remaining workers in the national chains. It resisted almost all the work rule changes proposed by the companies and won some improved monetary benefits. The divisions, however, did take their toll. General Electric and Westinghouse, once totally organized by the UE, now bargained with a number of unions and had important nonunion plants. As a consequence, wages in the industry began to lag farther behind those of steel and auto, a situation that would worsen in the late 1950s and early 1960s.[150]

7

SLOW CLIMB BACK

In early 1957, few would have predicted anything more than the continued decline and disappearance of the UE. Events during the next 15 years, however, were to give the UE a period of recovery and hope. These events included the improving economy during the military buildup associated with the Vietnam War, the waning of red-baiting, and the internal strife which nearly tore its main rival, the IUE, apart. Equally important was the fact that the fairly small group that remained in the UE was deeply committed to the organization. Hardened to the experience of red-baiting, they often had deep personal ties to veteran UE staff members, and a loyalty to its principles.

Over the early and mid-1960s, a profound crisis developed inside the UE's main rival, the IUE. Much of the coming apart revolved around the competence of James Carey, an old theme in the electrical union movement. During the early 1950s, Carey was protected by the fact that he was the instrument to drive the UE out of their principal trade union fortresses. In that effort he was supported by the resources of the CIO, the government, the Catholic Church, the electrical corporations, and the media. The death of his patron, Philip Murray, the elimination of the UE as the major union in the field, and the decision of the companies to exploit the division among their workers brought Carey's shortcomings as a leader into sharp relief. His downfall began with the GE negotiations in 1960.

After the unsatisfactory 1958 negotiations, Carey declared that General Electric would face a strike in 1960 unless IUE demands were met. Carey tightened his grip over the locals by having the 1958 IUE convention give him additional power to place locals in trusteeship, a threat for recalcitrant locals. Carey clearly needed a victory at GE. For one thing, the UE was showing signs of resurgence, having taken the GE foundry at Elmira, New York, back from the IUE in 1959. Carey blamed GE's refusal to grant the IUE supplemental unemployment benefits during the 1958 negotiations for the loss at Elmira, and warned that GE's continued hardline policies would lead to the loss of other plants to the UE.[1]

Carey's enthusiasm for a showdown with GE was not universally shared by his members. The IUE's negotiating committee initialy felt compelled to accept GE's offer. When, at Carey's insistence, strike votes were held in 1960, important locals at Schenectady, Bridgeport, Syracuse, and Pittsfield voted against.[2] Without the solid support of these locals, it was clear that any strike effort would be extremely risky. In addition, IAM and UAW locals had voted to accept terms very similar to those offered IUE.

The key Schenectady plant was the most important soft spot. Leo Jandreau, who had defected to the IUE and taken the Schenectady local with him in 1954, refused at first to support the strike. Under intense pressure, he relented, but then ordered his members back to work ten days later, blasting Carey for not having "the issues or the organizational strength or the other economic factors . . . necessary to lead a successful strike," and for not accepting a company truce proposal.[3] By the third week it was clear that the strike was lost. Strong back-to-work movements were developing at certain plants and decertification procedures were initiated at others. After having demonstrated its strength, GE then came to the rescue. The company had no interest in completely destroying the IUE—not with the UE waiting in the wings. GE made minor concessions and Carey called off the strike after three weeks. *New York Times* labor writer, A.H. Raskin, called it the "worst setback any union has received in a nationwide strike since World War II."[4]

Carey's troubles deepened after this debacle, as rivals began to surface within the IUE leadership. Carey succeeded in having Al Hartnett, the IUE secretary-treasurer, and an old UEMDA colleague, suspended and stripped of power after Hartnett challenged him. He also attempted to defeat another old right-wing comrade, James Click, in the race for IUE vice-president. Click won, but resigned in 1963, charging as Hartnett had earlier, that Carey was acting unconstitutionally, and that the IUE under Carey had become a "hopeless mess of dishonesties, confusion, and ineffectiveness in which all semblance of democracy . . . had disappeared." Following Click's defection, a movement began in St. Louis to swing several large locals to the Teamsters. Carey's personality had already alienated him from many other labor leaders, including AFL-CIO President George Meany.[5]

In the 1963 General Electric negotiations, Carey again ran into internal opposition to his negotiating style. Over his objections the IUE negotiating committee and the General Electric Conference Board voted to accept the GE offer. By 1964, a new opponent to Carey had surfaced, Paul Jennings, an IUE District Director. Jennings challenged Carey for the IUE presidency in an election in which the UE criticized both sides, but seemed to prefer a Carey defeat. The official tally showed that Carey had won a narrow victory, but it was to be short-lived.[6]

Early in 1965 the Labor Department released the results of an investigation into the election that showed massive vote-stealing by the Carey forces. A deal was arranged. In return for unanimous IUE Executive Board support for Jennings's installation as president, Carey was not prosecuted and was given a lavish financial settlement.[7]

The UE responded to Carey's fall aggressively. Walter Reuther of the UAW had already proposed a UAW takeover of the IUE in February 1965. Fitzgerald advised the IUE to reject this course and proposed an immediate merger of the two electrical unions.[8] Matles, in a hopeful mood, told the UE General Executive Board that IUE's problems had created the situation the UE officers had been working for since the split in 1949. Mobilization was necessary for "united action and one union in the industry." Unfortunately, leafleting of IUE plants and other actions had hardly started when the deal settling the IUE presidency was made. Jennings rejected the UE proposal, red-baited heavily, and successfully derailed the merger move.[9]

The UE's main efforts, however, were directed, not at merger, but at a come-back, and the older union was to come very close. The main battleground was a familiar one, the GE plant in Lynn, Massachussets. In mid-1959, the UE submitted a NLRB petition bearing the signed cards of more than 55 percent of the workers. For eight months the IUE stalled the election at the Labor Board, until a successful IUE walkout over grievances, (backed by the UE supporters), led them to hope that they could chance an election. Five days later, however, the IUE's hopes were shaken when its local business agent, a charter IUE member, declared for the UE and was followed, the next day, by the IUE local secretary.[10]

The IUE hit back with its two most important weapons: red-baiting and links to the Democratic Party. The Senate Eastland

Committee began a series of lurid investigations involving the UE. Stories of the Committee's findings appeared regularly in the Lynn newspapers. No stranger to these tactics, the UE had tried to prepare for them. District 2 President Paul Seymour had obtained a pledge of neutrality from Massachussets Senator John F. Kennedy, whom the UE had supported in the past. But when the IUE issued a re-dated presentation of a 1953 Kennedy endorsement of the IUE, the Senator, then campaigning for the Democratic presidential nomination, refused to repudiate the IUE's use of his remarks. The tactic hurt the UE badly, especially among Irish Catholics.[11]

It was, however, the UE bitterly charged, liberal Senator Hubert Humphrey who "stole the election. . . ." Humphrey, also a candidate for the Democratic presidential nomination, issued an election eve statement endorsing the IUE and raising the specter of lost defense contracts at Lynn if the UE were to capture the local.[12] With more than 4,000 of the plant's 7,000 workers directly employed on military projects, this threat had a chilling impact. When the election was held on March 25, 1960, the UE polled a tantalizing 48 percent of the vote.[13]

The other key setback for the UE's 1960 comeback try occurred at the Baltimore Westinghouse plant. An IBEW local had been installed, with company support, in the rapidly expanding Air Arm Division. The UE petitioned for the plant in October of 1959.[14] The federal government, the IUE, the IBEW, and the local media launched a furious red-baiting assault. The Eastland Committee, provided with an office in the plant by the company, subpoenaed UE supporters. Westinghouse issued a pamphlet raising the fear of lost defense contracts if the UE were to win.[15] Clarence Mitchell, the main IBEW staff representative on the campaign, later signed an affidavit stating that Westinghouse conspired with the IBEW to hire IBEW staff men and allow them free run of the plant. The strategy worked, and the UE was soundly beaten.[16]

The IUE disaster in bargaining with GE in 1960 also made it impossible for the UE to come away from its negotiations with the company with much more than its rival was forced to accept. Things improved somewhat in 1963 when the UE settled first with GE, gaining wage hikes and improved vacations, and fought off a company attack on its right to strike over unresolved grievances.[17]

Although the early years of the 1960s proved to be disappointing, during the latter two-thirds of the decade the UE experienced its biggest organizational surge since the 1940s. One key to this was a lessening of red-baiting. In the early 1960s, a lessened, but still substantial amount of anticommunist fire was directed against the union, including regular attacks by the old nemesis, Charles Owen Rice, in his weekly column in the *Pittsburgh Catholic*.[18] In the same period, the Supreme Court let stand the convictions, and allowed to go to jail, such former UE leaders as Marie Reed Haug of Cleveland and Jack Killian of Milwaukee. The IUE launched savage red-baiting attacks on UE Washington Office Director Russ Nixon in 1961 for having criticized the decision to drop atomic bombs on Japan, and on staff representative James Lustig for attending a rally for the *Daily Worker*.[19]

In the mid and late 1960s, however, low unemployment during the Vietnam buildup emboldened workers, and the shift of public opinion to the left as a result of the civil rights and anti-war movements removed much of the sting of anticommunism. There was also at least one change of heart. When the UE convention met in Pittsburgh in 1966, Monsignor Rice telephoned Albert Fitzgerald to wish the union well. When Fitzgerald answered that the wishes came too late, Rice replied that "twenty years is not too late for a man to change his mind."[20]

Some shops lost earlier in the decade were won back. Another major set of victories came in a complex of gear and cutting tool shops in Vermont and Massachusetts. Organizing victories in the midwest, most notably at GHR in Dayton, led the union to reconstitute its District 7, which now covered Ohio, Indiana, and Michigan. The West Coast Conference was again reconstituted as District 10. District 1 in Pennsylvania nearly doubled in size between 1962 and 1967. Similar good news flowed in from District 11's efforts in and around Chicago.[21]

A representative and significant example of these campaigns came after a victory at the GE specialty control plant in Waynesboro, Virginia. The UE's attempt to organize the plant's 1,000 workers in 1962 was bolstered by a victory at the nearby Staunton Westinghouse plant. GE followed the usual script, passing out leaflets attacking the union, holding captive meetings, and enlisting the support of the local newspapers. Two days before the election Waynesboro police barred UE organizers from leafleting at the factory gates. Nevertheless, the UE won the election held on May 7, 1965, by a margin of 531 to 443.[22] GE refused recognition and appealed the NLRB certification order. Finally, in October 1967, five years after the drive began, the US Circuit Court of Appeals rejected GE's protests and the company agreed to include the workers under their national contract with the UE.[23]

The renewed growth of the UE did not come as a result of any trimming of its independent stance. The *UE News* editorials continued to criticize rising military expenditures and the focus on the Cold War. With one exception, the union continued to remain independent of the Democrats at the national level. The exception occurred in 1964 when the conservative Republican candidacy of Barry Goldwater turned the presidential election into "no ordinary contest." The UE leaders equated a Goldwater victory with a "catastrophic setback" for working people,and gave a qualified endorsement to LBJ.[24]

Two issues dominated liberal politics during the 1960s—civil rights and the Vietnam War. The UE was heavily involved in both movements from the beginning. Actively involved in fund-raising for civil rights, the UE vigorously condemned the jailing of Dr. Martin Luther King and criticized the Kennedy administration for its "failure to assume moral and political leadership in the fight for full equality."[25] The UE sent an exceptionally large delegation to the 1963 March on Washington, and the union pushed hard for the passage of the 1964 Civil Rights Act.[26]

As US involvement in the Vietnamese War escalated over the decade, so did the UE's role in opposing the conflict. As early as 1964, the union criticized President Lyndon Johnson for putting "excessive trust in military solutions to political problems, a trust that if continued threatens us with at best another Korea." The UE joined and helped to organize labor activity against the war, including the National Labor Leadership Assembly for Peace. Both presidential candidates in 1968 failed the union's test on the war and the UE returned to its no-endorsement tradition. Throughout the war the UE called for immediate peace negotiations and the recognition of the National Liberation Front, as a key negotiating partner.[27]

The UE continued to give attention to the concerns of women workers. The union held a national woman's conference in 1962, and several of its districts did the same during the decade.[28] One of the topics at the 1962 conference was the development of female leadership within the union. An important step in this direction came in 1962, when Gertrude Southern, the new president of District 10, was added to the GEB. She was the first woman on the Board since the early 1950s.[29]

There were other changes in the UE's leadership during this period. In April 1962, Julius Emspak died of a heart attack at the age of 57.[30] When the UE convention met five months later, James Matles was unanimously named to the office. That left the third position in the UE's triumvirate, Director of Organization, vacant. Robert Kirkwood, the business agent of Local 610, edged Joseph Dermody, the Secretary of the GE and Westinghouse Boards, by one vote.[31]

Kirkwood was born in 1913 in Newton, Iowa. In 1937 he was chosen the first secretary-treasurer of the newly organized Maytag local in Newton. In the big strike at the plant the next year, Kirkwood was fired, and then joined the union staff, serving in a variety of roles in the Midwest and Pittsburgh over the next 25 years.[32]

By the mid-1960s, there was a growing recognition by the UE's rivals of the need for greater unity in collective bargaining at GE and Westinghouse. Only a minority of GE's work force was now unionized and they were divided into many different unions. In September 1965, the AFL-CIO organized a meeting of its major unions in GE to plan future negotiations strategy.[33] The biggest gap was the failure to invite the UE, with its more than 16,000 GE members. Accordingly, the UE denounced the AFL-CIO unity talk as hollow.[34]

Still, however, the UE did not abandon attempts to achieve real cooperation. In August 1966, Fitzgerald telegraphed Jennings of the IUE, urging an exchange of information and cooperation during the negotiations. The results were mixed. The AFL-CIO body was still unwilling to formally admit the UE, or even to issue a joint statement on cooperation, but there were a number of joint discussions of collective bargaining goals and strategy.[35] Even this, however, was mixed with public denunciations of the UE by the IUE, including intense red-baiting.[36]

Every GE and Westinghouse UE local voted for the strike authorization in 1966, and the 2,000 workers at Ashland did strike in a successful effort to force their inclusion in the national GE contract.[37] The militant UE members at the Lester Westinghouse also struck over local contract issues.[38] The results of this greater unity and militancy were substantial. There were important improvements in both the GE and Westinghouse contracts, including the reinstatement of a Cost of Living Allowance. The basis had been laid for a major showdown with GE in 1969.[39]

The 1969 answer to this fragmentation was one long sought by the UE—unity at the bargaining table. The Collective Bargaining Council brought ten unions representing GE workers together to coordinate bargaining. GE had not seen this kind of united front since the split in the CIO in 1950. With the talks at an impasse, a national walkout began on October 29. Some 140,000 of GE's 170,000 production workers joined the strike, including UE's 16,000 members. The most dramatic example of the UE's new-found respectability was a donation of $200,000 from the UAW for strike relief.[40]

Surprised by the unity of the forces arrayed against it, GE played its strongest card—a back-to-work movement. The utter failure of the tactic brought a settlement which included substantial movement from its original offer on the part of the corporation. The *New York Times* called it an "unmistakable departure from the take it or leave it spirit of past bargaining. In effect, "Boulwarism" was dead.[41] The UE, which had entered the 1960s badly weakened, but had experienced a decade of progress, seemed poised to reap large gains in the 1970s.

8

HOLDING ON

The promise born of the 1957-69 period was to go largely unfulfilled in the years after 1970. At precisely the moment when the impact of red-baiting seemed to be fading, new, perhaps more dangerous crises appeared. Increasingly severe recessions, soaring inflation, and a massive wave of plant closures threatened not only the UE's recent gains, but its survival as well. While these challenges were primarily economic, they took place in as hostile a political environment as the labor movement had seen since the 1920s. Like most American unions, the UE would be much smaller at the end of the period than at the beginning.

The era began on an optimistic note. The bill for the "guns and butter" policies of the Vietnam War years had not yet come due. Employment in the electrical industry, bolstered by defense contracts, remained high. For the UE, the victory in the 1969-70 strike at GE bore fruit in other firms, especially Westinghouse. Within three weeks of the victory at GE, the union could recommend a good contract to their members in Westinghouse.[1] "For the first time in a decade," the officers boasted, "this company has been prevented from undercutting an earlier settlement with the GE company."[2] The Westinghouse settlement did not come easily. Members of the militant Lester Local 107 spent 146 days on the picket line to win the local supplement they wanted.[3]

Perhaps most important, the GE strike had transformed the relationship between the UE and other unions in the industry. It signaled the virtual end to the bitter rivalry with the IUE. In an unheard of gesture, Albert Fitzgerald and Paul Jennings exchanged visits to their rival's GEB. In his speech to the IUE,

175

Fitzgerald urged "reunification of all the workers in our industry so that we're all again under the banner of one union."[4] Jennings replied by saying that "everything that has to be put together can be put together."[5] The *Wall Street Journal* predicted a merger.[6]

Relations warmed with other old rivals as well. Matles and Fitzgerald were invited guests at the 1970 convention of the United Auto Workers. In September of the same year, the UE and the United Steelworkers, Philip Murray's old union, ratified a formal no-raiding agreement, the first of its kind for the UE. In August 1971, an historic milestone was reached when the UE and the IUE signed a no-raiding agreement and developed a plan for cooperating on organizing campaigns.[7]

But although superficially it seemed close, no actual merger occurred. Given its reduced circumstances, the UE undoubtedly understood that a merger would mean the disappearance of the union into a larger partner, be it the IUE or some other union. Both unions were still led by men who bore the scars of the civil war— men for whom it was extremely difficult to forgive and forget. In addition, the reluctance to merge was still based on different views of unionism. Matles told the 1973 convention that merger speculation "reflected the lack of understanding that unity must be built from the rank-and-file, not the top down."[8] The differences with the AFL-CIO, though muted, remained. The UE leadership argued that the greatest danger from merger was that it might "blur our vision as to what rank-and-file unionism is."[9] For the UE, the important differences included the membership's right to ratify contracts and settle or start strikes, the UE's coolness to binding arbitration, and its dislike of secret negotiations and the use of negotiating specialists removed from the members. For the UE, mobilization of the membership remained the tactic of first and last recourse.

Although merger ultimately foundered, cooperation did blossom in negotiations in the major chains. At GE the UE and the IUE carried out what nearly amounted to joint negotiations in 1973, with the UE officially joining the coordinated bargaining council, winning a contract that the *Wall Street Journal* called an "end to an era of Boulwarism."[10] The unity carried over to the 1976 negotiations. This time cooperation included the UAW, the Teamsters, the IBEW, and the Machinists. The result was as good a contract as had ever been won at GE, including a substantial hourly wage and an uncapped cost of living clause.[11] When Westinghouse tried its time-honored tactic of rejecting the GE pattern, the UE, IUE, and IBEW struck for three days to achieve their goal.[12]

The waning of the intense inter-union rivalry allowed the UE the opportunity to concentrate its efforts on organizing, and the union organized or regained several dozen shops in 1970–71.[13] The recession which hit from 1970–71 did, however, slow down the organizing momentum of the late 1960s. The 1971 UE Officers Report noted that the union "cannot be satisfied with our last year's record."[14] In response, staff were reassigned to organizing and rank-and-file organizing committees were instituted, along with a targeting of the South, all steps that would quickly bear fruit.[15]

Early in the seventies significant victories at nonunion GE and Westinghouse plants in the hostile anti-union soil of the South buoyed the spirits of the organizers. Wins at the turbo generator plants of Westinghouse at Tampa and GE at Charleston were especially satisfying. Both plants had been part of the postwar wave of southern and western plant locations by American companies in search of lower wage rates and nonunion territory. Both GE and Westinghouse resurrected red-baiting during the campaigns, but even in the South the old charges had largely lost their bite. Westinghouse fired several union activists, and mailed anti-union literature stressing union violence to workers' homes. Worker Vernon DeWatt signed an affidavit stating that Westinghouse had tried to recruit him "to go to the UE meetings, report . . . how many people were there, the ratio of Black, white and Cuban. . . . "[16] Still, when the election was held in December 1972, the UE won by 207–180.[17] The UE overcame the same mix of company attacks at GE in Charleston, winning an election in 1975, after a narrow defeat in 1974.[18]

The UE fought important picket line battles from 1970 to 1975. These included a nine-week strike at Honeywell in Chicago, and a ten week battle at Litton in Athol, MA.[19] One of the most important tests was a nine week strike at the newly organized Tampa Westinghouse. There, the company and the FBI infiltrated a paid agent inside the local, who attempted, unsuccessfully, to disrupt the strike.[20]

The backdrops to negotiations in this period were the difficult economy and anti-labor Republican administrations. During the 1974–75 recession the plant closure and runaway problem became much more acute. At least a dozen UE shops closed in 1974. Layoffs hit other plants. At Bryant Electric the work force was cut by one-third, while at the Lester Westinghouse the company announced that an entire division of 1,000 would have its work shipped to Round Rock, TX.[21]

The situation worsened in 1975. The UE's secretary-treasurer reported that, despite the union's substantial organizing achievements of the past few years, membership had actually declined, due to unemployment, and stood at about 67,000. Some of the worst cases of job loss were at the GE Ashland plant, where employment fell from 2,200 in 1965 to 700 in 1975, mostly due to the exodus of operations to Singapore; Erie, where 1,600 were to be laid off by early 1976; and GE Allentown, which was almost closed.[22]

After the organizing breakthroughs in 1974 and 1975, there were high hopes for the UE, especially in the South. For the rest of the 1970s, however, there were no spectacular victories. Still, the union organized a score of small shops. Chicago, where a number of victories were won at low-wage, minority-staffed shops, was one such notable area of success.[23]

In 1980 alone, however, the UE won elections covering 5000 workers—no small feat in the midst of one of the worst periods in the annals of organized labor.[24] By far the largest of these victories was at Stewart-Warner in Chicago. This complex of factories had originally been organized by the UE in 1943, and been lost to the IBEW in the red-baiting of 1949. By 1979, frustrated by their failure to achieve reform within the IBEW, the workers, now overwhelmingly African-Americans, had voted them out and formed an independent group, the United Workers Association. The UWA, after a year on its own, voted by two to one to affiliate with the UE.

This was not, however, the end of the battle. The IBEW fought to regain the plant and the UAW intervened. In a first round election the UE narrowly edged the UAW, while crushing the IBEW. In the runoff the UE defeated the UAW by a 1372 to 936 margin, adding about 5 percent to its membership in one stroke.[25]

The other big victory of 1980 came at Litton's microwave plant in Sioux Falls, South Dakota. The UE already represented the workers at Litton's Minneapolis plant. In 1977 the firm had moved most of its operations to Sioux Falls, where wages averaged $2 less an hour. After a two-year organizing drive, the workers voted solidly for the UE.[26] But the election results did not ensure success. In a tactic that would become commonplace in industrial relations in the United States in the 1980s, the company refused to agree to a first contract with the newly certified union. In February, the UE hit back with innovative tactics of its own, calling for a boycott of Litton products, arranging appearances by Litton workers on popular television programs, and setting up informational picketing across the country.[27] Facing rising pressure from the boycott and a 1984 federal court ruling upholding the NLRB charges, Litton finally signed the contract in July 1984.[28] In all, the campaign had taken six years—four of them after the workers had clearly expressed their choice for union representation. For the UE, the victory meant 1,900 new members, but it had been costly in time, energy, and money.

One reason for the UE success was the relative absence of the Communist issue. Anticommunism no longer stirred the old passions at a time when American unions were experiencing shocking membership losses and fighting to survive in the midst of hostile political and economic circumstances. To be sure, some inter-union rivalry persisted on the organizing front, but it rarely centered on the ideological issue, and usually the opponents were corrupt or poorly functioning locals of unions like the Carpenters or Boilermakers.

Organizing successes, however, were not the central story for the UE and the rest of the American labor movement during the seventies and eighties. Rather, the period witnessed the virtual collapse of the great center of American unionism, the mass production industries. Electrical manufacturing was no exception.

The recession of 1980–83 led to a massive wave of plant closings. Most were small and medium sized shops, but the great blows came in what was left of the UE's strength in the electrical manufacturing chains.

The first of the Westinghouse plant closings came in 1980, when the company announced the closing of its Tampa plant with the loss of 700 jobs. This was an especially bitter pill for the union after the fierce battle to organize the plant in the early seventies.[29]

But the biggest blow was the shrinking and final closing of the old Lester plant, near Philadelphia, a UE fortress throughout the entire ideological war. The decline of Lester was typical of the era. Work was progressively moved to more modern, often nonunion plants, both in the United States and abroad. From 5,700 workers in 1972, employment fell to 1,100 by 1984. In December 1986, after 70 years of production, the plant gates closed for the last time.[30] With its shutdown came the end of the UE as a major factor in the company where so much of its history lay.

The script followed the same pattern in GE. The UE had retained a much greater presence in this company than it had in Westinghouse, so the losses there were even greater in numbers. Two hundred workers at the Niles, Ohio plant saw their jobs go to Brazil.[31] Half of the jobs at the Decatur, Indiana plant went to Mexico. GE opened new iron and toaster plants in Singapore and Malaysia, and a new motor plant in Mexico.[32] In July 1981, GE announced the closing of its Ontario, California plant. One thousand workers, mostly women, lost their jobs.

Once again, the closing of a southern plant was particularly telling. Organized with great difficulty and at great cost by the UE in the seventies, the Charleston, South Carolina plant shut down in 1985. Most of its work had already gone to Taiwan.[33] In October 1987, GE announced that it would shut the Decatur, IN plant and move the work to Jaurez, Mexico. The union mounted one of its strongest campaigns to keep this plant open, but GE would not relent.[34]

Other devastating blows fell outside the major chains. WABCO's Union Switch and Signal plant was closed and employment at the Airbrake was cut to just 500. Most of the jobs there were transferred to nonunion plants in GA and SC.[35] The Litton plant in Sioux Falls saw employment fall from 2,100 in 1982 to about 800 in 1987.[36] Stewart Warner was sold to BTR, a British conglomerate. Several of the unionized Chicago plants were closed and employment fell from 3,000 in 1980 to just 700 a decade later, with most of the jobs going to Mexico or to Johnson City, TN.[37] Of course, the IUE and other unions in the chain suffered just as severely.

The UE put up a staunch fight in almost all these cases. Occasionally, even in the conservative atmosphere of the 1980s, it achieved success. Probably the most dramatic such example was the case of Morse Cutting Tool, purchased by the Gulf and Western conglomerate. Between 1983 and 1986, by pressuring the New Bedford town officials to use their power of eminent domain, and by locating purchasers for the plant, the UE saved the 375 jobs at stake on two separate occasions.[38] As the *New York Times* put it, "the fact that Morse is open at all is widely acknowledged to be a result of the efforts of Local 277 of the UERMWA."[39]

The increasingly difficult economic climate had an impact on negotiations. The period began well. In 1973, at both GE and Westinghouse, the UE and IUE carried out what nearly amounted to joint negotiations, as the UE officially joined the coordinated bargaining council. Backed by strike votes and mass rallies, a good contract was won at GE.[40]

The unity carried over to the 1976 negotiations. This time, the UE and IUE negotiated separately, but closely coordinated their activities. The same held true for links with the UAW, IBT, IBEW and IAM. In June, a solid contract was reached with GE. An immediate raise of 60 cents an hour, the biggest in the history of bargaining at GE, was won, and the COLA was uncapped.[41] At Westinghouse, it took a three-day strike, in July, by the UE, IUE and IBEW, before a deal was reached that matched that at GE.[42]

In 1979, the unions in GE, especially the UE, IUE and IAM, met daily during the first five weeks of talks. In the final two weeks before contract expiration, two representatives of each union formed a special subcommittee to finish the bargaining. The contract reached in June averaged increases of $1.80 over three years.[43]

The Westinghouse talks were more difficult. All 14 unions at Westinghouse rejected the company's initial proposal to make the pension plan, which had been in effect since 1953, contributory. A strike began on July 15, 1979. Six weeks into the strike the firm dropped its take-away demand on the pension, but other issues remained. The IBEW now called for ending the strike, while the UE and IUE urged rejection of the contract. Westinghouse slightly sweetened its offer, and on August 30, the strike was settled.[44]

The 1982 round of negotiations at GE and Westinghouse were resolved without a strike. The GE contract brought a wage increase and modest improvements in other areas, at a time of contract give-backs in many manufacturing unions. A similar pact was reached with Westinghouse.[45]

The biggest UE strike of the 1970s and 1980s, came at WABCO in 1981–82, when the company proposed a takeaway contract, prompting a walkout on October 21, 1981, by 4,000 workers.[46] A month into the strike the company tried to re-start production, using managers, but mass picketing brought an injunction against both the re-start and the huge picket lines.[47] Finally, in June 1982, after a rally featuring folk singer Pete Seeger had lifted union spirits, a contract was reached that defeated most of the takeaways and brought a wage increase and a COLA.[48]

By the mid 1980s, the UE was no longer a significant factor in Westinghouse negotiations, but this was not the case at GE. The 1985 contract brought modest gains, stopping GE takeaway demands.[49] In 1988, the UE's bargaining position was weakened by an earlier decision by the IUE to accept wage cuts at the GE motor plants, a decision which caused considerable strife within that union. When the two old rivals bargained with GE in 1988 they accepted what they could get "reluctantly." The UE leadership admitted that they had no choice under the circumstances. A nationwide strike against GE was "impossible."[50]

In 1991, however, better co-operation with the IUE, and a successful international conference of unions at GE, resulted in an improved contract. It brought big gains on wages and pensions, and the union described it as a turnaround.[51]

Once the third largest affiliate of the CIO, the union entered the nineties with a membership of less than 40,000. In an effort to streamline and maintain its organizing efforts, the UE had sold its valuable Manhattan headquarters building, an old Vanderbilt mansion flanking St. Patrick's Cathedral, and moved to Pittsburgh in 1986.[52]

The UE experienced internal change in this period as well. The union had been led from its earliest days by a small group of effective and dedicated leaders, a factor of no small importance in explaining its resilience. In early 1971, Organization Director Robert Kirkwood fell ill and stepped down. He was replaced by Hugh Harley, a longtime UE staffer, who had mostly served in District 2.[53]

In 1975 at the UE's 40th convention, James Matles resigned as union secretary. Two days later, he died of a massive heart attack at the age of 66, after 38 years as a UE general officer. Boris Block, who himself had a quarter of a century on the UE staff, in New England and elsewhere, replaced him.[54]

Three years later, in 1978, Albert Fitzgerald followed his old companions into retirement after 37 years in office. Fitzgerald's successor, Dennis Glavin, a longtime skilled worker at the Lester Westinghouse, a leader of Local 107, and a veteran of 46 years with the UE, retired after only three years, and James Kane, a former business agent and president of District 2, replaced him as the UE's president.[55] Kane served for six years, overseeing the transition to Pittsburgh and to younger leadership. He was replaced in 1987 by John Hovis, a former Seattle Westinghouse machinist and staff member. Hugh Harley had retired before the move, and was succeeded by Ed Bruno, a young organizer who had served a long apprenticeship in the union in District 6 and in the South.[56]

Another dramatic change was the rise of women to leadership positions in the union. As late as 1984, although one-third of the membership was female, only one woman sat on the 15 member General Executive Board, and there were no women among the general officers. By the next year, three women had been elected to the General Executive Board and one, Amy Newell, the daughter of two longtime UE staffers, a shop worker, longtime staff member and a graduate of the London School of Economics, had been elected UE secretary-treasurer.[57] The number of women on the General Executive Board reached six by 1991, exceeding the female percentage of union membership.[58]

In the hostile environment for trade unions between 1972 and 1990, the exile of the UE, or more accurately its quarantine, largely ended. The old animosities seemed less important at a time when unions of all persuasions were fighting for survival. Nevertheless, in a period when declining unions merged frequently, when the Auto Workers and the Mine Workers returned to the AFL-CIO fold, the UE remained outside. In keeping with its history, this independence was most marked in the political arena.

The UE was one of the first unions to oppose the Vietnam War, attacking the Nixon administration for aggression abroad and repression at home.[59] At a time when the mainstream of the labor movement, including the AFL-CIO, was refusing to endorse the Democratic presidential candidate because of his anti-war stance, UE broke with its nonendorsement policy for the second time in its history to back George McGovern.[60]

The 1972 endorsement was not repeated in 1976. The UE refused to support Jimmy Carter, arguing that the Georgian's policies were an abandonment of even mainstream liberal reforms. When the Democrat won, Albert Fitzgerald warned the membership to "have no illusions about the new administration."[61] Carter, according to the UE, had "contempt for the American people," and his administration was "no more representative of working Americans than either the Nixon or Ford administrations before it."[62] This was hardly the kind of language to endear the UE to George Meany and the AFL-CIO Executive Council; nor was the UE's critique of American military spending or American intervention in Central America, even though many of its members worked in defense industries.[63]

Yet the events of the Reagan eighties, from the firing of the air traffic controllers to the carnage of deindustrialization, sometimes pushed the UE closer to the Democratic Party. In 1984 the leadership was clear that however lukewarm its enthusiasm for the Democrats, Ronald Reagan posed a much greater threat to the labor movement. Though no endorsement was forthcoming, the union tilted strongly toward Walter Mondale and warned its members that "this is no ordinary election because Ronald Reagan is no ordinary president."[64] In 1988, the threshold was crossed. The UE endorsed Michael Dukakis, but the experience did not prove edifying. The electoral humiliation of the Democratic ticket pushed the UE back to its longstanding interest in third-party politics. "To be blunt about it," the *UE News*, told its readers, "a Democratic Party that can't beat Bush-Quayle can't beat anybody."[65]

Some observers argued, as the nineties dawned, that much the same could be said of the labor movement. For the UE, the future looked equally challenging. If, however, it could be said of any union that its past had shown its ability to survive even the most improbable odds, it could certainly be said of the UE.

CONCLUSION:
AN UNCERTAIN LEGACY

As we have seen, the indictment of the left-wing unions formulated in the CIO "trials" of 1950 and advanced by scholars supportive of the CIO position rests on the argument that Communist union leaders were not primarily interested in building strong unions to advance the economic and job-related interests of their members, but rather in using the unions as fronts to advance the interests of the Soviet Union and to radicalize American workers. According to one such observer, Communist labor leaders could not accommodate themselves to the limited function of trade unions in a democratic capitalist society but instead sought "to use the unions for the purpose of achieving a proletarian dictatorship along Soviet lines." Once taken over by the Communists, according to another, "a trade union ceases to be a trade union, for all that it may retain the charter and outward appearances of a trade union."

From the perspective of 1993, it is difficult to take statements such as this seriously, particularly when one looks dispassionately at the record of the UE as a trade union. Nevertheless, precisely the argument that the left-led unions were sham unions dominated the official CIO indictment and the subsequent raids on the UE and other left-led unions.[1]

The argument depends entirely on evidence that Communist labor leaders slavishly followed the twists and turns of the Moscow line on political issues, especially those concerned with foreign policy. The constant emphasis on this line of argument served, ironically, to emphasize the paucity of evidence supporting the main trade union justification—that Communist leaders sacrificed the economic and job-related interests of their members. Without question the leadership of the UE and other left-led unions used dues money to support causes in which the rank and file had little interest or, indeed, little sympathy.[2] They also inspired a steady stream of convention and executive board resolutions that paralleled Communist Party political objectives. But whether this reflected Communist Party Power in the internal workings of the union is open to question. The evidence suggests that the rise of some Communist labor leaders to positions of power in the CIO made them less, not more dependent on party direction. As Ruth Young, the leading woman among the Communist leadership of the UE, put it, many became "Communist trade unionists rather than trade union Communists."[3] Because foreign policy questions dominated the closed, hothouse world of the official party leadership, adherence to party directives on international relations served to mollify the party bureaucrats, who by and large left the running of the unions alone. For their part, the Communist labor leaders knew quite well that the rank and file had little interest in these matters and were quite willing to allow their leaders full latitude in this sphere as long as they performed satisfactorily on bread-and-butter issues.[4] As one anticommunist UE leader later remarked, "the rank and file are only interested in two things: How much do I get in my pay envelope and don't increase the dues." Even James Carey later lamented that his emphasis on the incumbent's political positions evoked only a "what's it to us?" response from the members.[5]

Ironically, the hesitancy of Communist labor leaders to reveal their party membership indicates just how comfortable the CIO's left-wing leaders had become in their roles as progressive, though basically traditional, trade unionists. No doubt, for those UE leaders who were party members, the secrecy surrounding their affiliation created an air of conspiracy and fueled the argument that Communists were wolves in sheep's clothing. But in fact, reluctance to admit party membership was more complex than that. Unquestionably the long history of repression of Communists had built into the party a siege mentality which by the 1930s, a time when open membership made more sense than any other in American history, had become almost impossible to shed. Thus, at a time when they served most effectively in the front ranks of the industrial union drive, Communists chose not to link their militancy to their ideology to try to change workers' attitudes toward communism, or at least toward American Communists.[6]

But if ideology could not be linked to trade union militancy, what good was it? So Communists, because of their ideological commitment, became militant labor leaders. Militancy led to success as trade unionists. But that success could not be translated into an attempt at ideological conversion of the rank and file because of the secrecy deemed necessary to initiate the cycle in the first place. Once success had been achieved, it became too precious to risk by proclaiming either formal party affiliation or intellectual commitment to Marxism. It was a maze with no exit. No other Marxists in the western world faced this dilemma.

The persistant unwillingness to bring the issue before the rank and file did not obviate the left-wing leaders' deep and genuine commitment to that membership. In the UE the results of this commitment were evident in the areas of organizing and collective bargaining. While the general officers contributed a great deal in this area, the major responsibility for bargaining proposals and strategies lay with the local unions. All UE negotiating committees were elected, contracts were ratified by referendum, and strikes were called and concluded by membership votes.[7] This decentralization can be attributed to the role of the established local unions in the creation of the UE, and to the inexperience of the general officers when the union faced its earliest challenges against General Electric and Westinghouse. These early negotiations also revealed the importance of local factors.[8] A recent study shows that UE contracts were consistently more pro-worker on issues such as the right to strike, management prerogatives, and grievance procedure, than those of the United Steelworkers and United Autoworkers.[9] No less an anticommunist scholar than David Saposs granted that the UE was as effective organizationally as any of the "superlatively successful" unions, and its record in terms of wages and working conditions was "at least as favorable as that of any of the outstanding unions."[10] Perhaps the best testimonial to UE's trade union performance lies in the fact that throughout the civil war in the union, the right wing never raiseed a telling criticism in this sphere.

As earlier noted, much of the story of the UE can be explained by the high degree of local autonomy that characterized the union from the beginning. In fact, the decentralization of power in the UE also made it practically impossible for the general officers and the general executive board members to deal autocratically with the rebels. Insurgent locals defiantly disregarded directives from the General Executive Board. They regularly inserted anticommunist clauses in the international constitution. In contested locals, right-wing forces attended membership meetings, regularly ran opposition slates, and battled the incumbents at every turn. No matter how heated, debate was rarely shut off.[11] Bridgeport Local 203, which had been in opposition as early as 1946, actually expelled 26 members for Communist sympathies in 1947. Dismissal meant loss of work as well as loss of union membership. Both the district leadership and the international union used every constitutional weapon at hand to have the workers reinstated, but to no avail.[12]

Contrast the rather benign, or at worst ineffective, policy in the UE with that of the United Auto Workers after Walter Reuther and his supporters captured control of the union from the left wing in 1947. Seventy-seven staff members who had supported the left-wing caucus were dismissed immediately. Reuther sought to gain as complete control of the union at the bottom as he had at the top and used the Taft-Hartley noncommunist affidavits requirement to isolate and drive the Communists out of the union.[13] The victors also employed extra-legal methods. Physical attacks against alleged Communists began in 1948, well after Reuther had overwhelming control of the UAW international executive board. Attacks on left-wing workers took place in Detroit, Flint, Milwaukee, Linden, New Jersey, and Los Angeles. Some of the victims suffered serious injuries, loss of their jobs, or arrest.[14]

In a union in which local autonomy was so well established, the ability of the UE to withstand a decade-long insurgency and two subsequent decades of raids from AFL and CIO unions depended a great deal on the quality of leadership. A major weakness of the insurgents was their inability to find spokespersons of comparable stature to the left-wing leaders. The case of James Carey, who served as titular head of the right wing from 1941 on, illustrates this clearly.[15] The question of Carey's competency is important to an understanding of the anticommunist failure to capture UE from the inside, as well as to the great difficulty that the IUE had in challenging the UE in representational elections after the split. There is substantial evidence that Carey's problems in the UE went beyond his drift toward anticommunism. As early as 1938, during the first General Electric negotiations, the GE conference board, angered by the young president's disruptive public statements, requested that he remove himself from the negotiation. Matles later claimed that the same thing happened at Westinghouse and that Carey, from then on, played no part in UE negotiations with these key companies.[16]

While most of the case for the dissatisfaction with Carey rests on the testimony of his opponents, there is also a significant amount of evidence that even Carey's allies knew of their leader's weaknesses. The Association of Catholic Trade Unionists always had doubts about Carey. As early as 1941, *Labor Leader*, the ACTU paper, charged that Carey was the chief impediment to developing a strong anticommunist opposition and hoped that his defeat would speed up the creation of an "honest rank-and-file movement. . . . " Even after the ACTU and Carey drew closer together, *Labor Leader* noted that Carey lacked the trust of the UE membership. One historian who shares this evaluation in terms of competency, but does not doubt Carey's convictions, claims that by the time he broke with the Communists, Carey had become little more than a figurehead "whose usefulness was declining as suspicions of his ineptitude grew."[17]

Dissatisfaction with Carey carried into the IUE and clearly marked the struggle between the new union and the UE. When they defected from the UE, Districts 3 and 7 chose to go with the IAM, not with IUE. District 8 split between the UAW and the IAM. A number of District 9 locals went into the IAM, IBEW, UAW and the Allied Industrial Workers. As early as 1949 Earl T. Bester, a Steelworkers staff man active in helping IUE raid the UE, wrote to Murray that the workers preferred to go into another union or even into the AFL rather than go into the IUE under Carey.[18]

Carey's troubles in IUE climaxed with the disastrous 1960 General Electric negotiations, when he almost lost the Schenectady local. From 1961 on IUE was plagued by internal strife. Carey managed to out-maneuver his rivals until 1964 when he was ousted from the presidency. Jacob Potofsky, president of the Amalgamated Clothing Workers, who had observed Carey for many years on the AFL-CIO Executive Board, recalled that the generally held view of Carey among his peers was that of an immature braggart.[19]

The right wing also faced a leadership problem at the local level. This stemmed partly from the fact that the UE was a young union, and incumbent local leadership often benefitted from having been instrumental in the formation of the local. This meant that frequently the insurgents had no comparable records of accomplishment. In the majority of cases the insurgents were young, inexperienced members who saw the factional struggle as an opportunity to rise in the union. The credentials that so many Carey-Block people lacked could not be concocted."[20]

Contrast that with the left-wing leadership, most of whom, at the national and local levels, had been with the union from the beginning and could take credit for the very real gains the union had made. This longevity and experience became critically important during the years after the split when the UE and the IUE contested for primacy in the electrical manufacturing industry. At the top of the UE, for example, Matles, Emspak, and Fitzgerald remained as a team until 1962 when Emspak died. By that time the great battles in the electrical chains were over. Matles and Fitzgerald continued on in leadership positions until 1975 and 1978 respectively. Few unions in America could boast of so experienced a leadership team, or one so directly linked to the union's heroic period.

The leadership problems of the right-wing forces made them much more dependent on outside help, thus providing an effective argument for the left wing to use against them. Company statements, congressional hearings, security investigations, and hostile press coverage were of enormous help to the insurgents, but they also provided the UE loyalists with an elan that frequently attaches itself to the embattled.

Carey's testimony before congressional investigating committees enabled the UE leadership to picture him as a tool of reactionary forces. This rang particularly true when hearings coincided with UE elections in contested locals or with important negotiations. Hints of collaboration with employers also hurt the right wing before and after the split. But the most controversial outside help came from Catholic labor activists trained and assisted by a small group of labor priests. The best known were affiliated with the Association of Catholic Trade Unionists, but Catholic-led, anticommunist struggles in UE in cities such as Philadelphia and Bridgeport owed little to that organization, although the goals were identical. It is true that the ACTU played a more significant role in the UE than in any other left-wing union, with the possible exception of the Transport Workers. But it is probably an exaggeration to argue, as did one historian of ACTU, that it "spearheaded the thrust of conservative forces."[21] ACTU always maintained a close working relationship with the UE opposition. But UEMDA remained a religiously and ideologically diverse group, united only by its opposition to the UE leadership. Such diversity required ACTU to take care not to appear to be advancing the interests of its Catholic members. On the other hand, it is also true that Harry Block's and James Click's assertions that ACTU had minimal influence in UEMDA are patently wrong.[22]

Local factors, rather than the existence of a large Catholic membership, sometime proved to be most significant. In the big Erie, Pennsylvania, General Electric local, the pro-administration leadership was heavily Catholic, and the right-wing insurgents "failed utterly" in the words of Father Rice. In Erie, Rice ran into the strong, militant and charismatic leader, John Nelson, a devout Catholic. Add to this the fact that Father Rice was an outsider, even to the Erie clergy, and that the UEMDA group was inexperienced and without credibility, and the challenge failed in a largely Catholic local.[23]

At the East Pittsburgh Westinghouse local on the other hand, ideology and religion, though the ostensible issues, took a back seat to social divisions. Left-wingers tended to be middle-aged, skilled workers, while younger, semi-skilled workers constituted the bulk of the insurgent movement. Their differences had a great deal to do with the rise of a new generation of workers who had come to work during and after the war—a generation with different economic aspirations and eager to share in the power and status of union office. Realizing that the incumbents were most vulnerable because of their radical politics, they made common cause with the ideologues of ACTU.[24]

The most important influence of the Catholic activists was external, not internal, to the UE. It did not take a great deal of strength in the union to create a hostile community climate for loyalist UE locals. In areas with large Catholic populations, such as Pittsburgh, Philadelphia, Pittsfield, Massachusetts, and Bridgeport, priests used the pulpit effectively, often linking the UE leadership with the persecution of Catholics behind the Iron Curtain.[25] In the end it was this kind of community censure, more than trade union considerations, that moved many UE members to vote for the right wing and remove themselves from a controversy that threatened them with social ostracism. The Catholic labor activists' influence in government circles, their ability to bring congressional investigating committees to cities in the midst of certification elections, also helped to create a climate of fear for UE loyalists. Although most members were no doubt generally satisfied with the performance of the UE leadership, the level of satisfaction was probably not high enough in many cases to counteract the fear of being identified with communism in the midst of Cold War America.

Undoubtedly, a key to the success of the Catholic activists lay in their relationship with Philip Murray. While it is clear that Murray did not move with the dispatch that ACTU and others would have liked in ridding the CIO of Communist influence, it is also clear that he shared their vision of the role of the labor as being entirely consistent with Catholic social teaching. He, like the labor priests, drew his inspiration from the Church's social encyclicals. Although he waited until the Progressive Party debacle to formally drive the Communists out of the CIO, there were plenty of indications before that that Murray had no intention of impeding the right-wing forces in their work. Carey, his secretary-treasurer, could not have kept his titular headship of UEMDA without Murray's blessing. Murray did little to protect his friend, R. J. Thomas from defeat by the anticommunist forces in the UAW, as early as 1947 some state CIO councils were changing their constitutions to prohibit Communists from holding office, and finally, he was financing Father Rice's anticommunist activities for several years before the purge. When he finally did decide to take the final step, Murray characterized the effort to destroy the UE as a "good fight, a noble fight, a holy fight."[26]

In the final analysis, the right-wing forces, before and after the split, had no choice but to carry on the struggle as an ideological battle for the hearts and minds of the members. Their left-wing opponents, on the other hand, could make their stand on the record of effective trade unionism. This enabled them to hold on to a substantial majority of the membership until 1949. But as the Cold War progressed, the anticommunist argument began to appeal to more and more workers. Mary Callahan, a UEMDA activist and executive board member at the Philadelphia switchgear factory of General Electric, provided a glimpse into this process when asked if the UE could be faulted on its performance as a trade union. "No, No," she replied, "I think that would be an unfair thing to say." Her reasons for supporting the right wing went beyond the shop floor. "We could see the union had no place in being part of something that was not as democratic as we claimed we were, and that we had just fought this war for democracy [for]," she explained. Hers was "a purely philosophical and idealist argument" that the workers weren't going to have their dues money and their union "dedicated to something that was contrary to what we thought was everybody's democratic right."[27]

The Cold War is over and there can be no question that the collapse of Soviet totalitarianism was a great victory for human liberty. But this overriding truth does not *ipso facto* ennoble all of the means used to achieve it. The larger victory does not absolve the victors from confronting the moral ambiguities and consequences of their own actions.

The domestic Cold War in the United States left many casualties—workers, educators, clergy, artists, writers, actors, government officials and others. Time has healed many of the wounds inflicted during that bitter period, but its effects on the nation's intellectual, political, and economic life were profound and continue to have their effects. Nowhere is this truer than in the labor movement. In addition to the UE and the Farm Equipment Workers, the CIO expelled nine other unions for being Communist-dominated: American Communications Association; Food, Tobacco, Agricultural & Allied Workers; International Fishermen & Allied Workers of America; International Fur and Leather Workers Union; International Longshoremen's and Warehousemen's Union; International Union of Mine, Mill and Smelter Workers; National Union of Marine Cooks & Stewards; United Furniture Workers of America; United Office and Professional Workers of America; United Public Workers of America. In all, the CIO expelled somewhere around 750,000 members, nearly one-fifth of its membership.[28]

With the exception of the UE, the International Longshoremen's Union (ILWU), and the Mine, Mill and Smelter Workers, most of the expelled unions were small and weak. Only the UE and the ILWU managed to stay independent and outside of the AFL-CIO. The others either disappeared or eventually merged with AFL-CIO unions. Irregardless of their numbers, however, the demise of the left-wing unions, and left-wing unionism, had profound implications for American workers and the American labor movement. The Cold War in American labor resulted in the purging of many of the most militant and dedicated activists. Many left-wing, noncommunist progressives who remained were cowed by the experience and learned to trim their sails to remain with the labor movement. The amputation of the left wing of the labor movement also removed a left-wing perspective from the American political arena. The dampening effect on internal opposition to the Cold War and to hot wars such as Korea and Vietnam was incalculable. Much the same could be said for the effect on the nation's attitudes toward civil rights and race relations, areas in which the left-wing unions had played progressive roles. Aggressive organization of the unorganized virtually ground to a halt. The CIO unions in particular settled for the gains they had made during the New Deal and World War II, and the largely unorganized sectors of the economy—sectors with large numbers of minority and women workers—remained nonunion.[29]

It is not too much to say that what was left after the fratricide was labor the bargainer. What had gone was labor the movement. It didn't take long to see that the first was much less effective without the second. With all of their occasional faults—arrogance, intolerance, sectarianism, and sometimes duplicity—many of the militant left-wingers, first among them the Communists, brought with them a genuine commitment to the working class. It would be simplistic to attribute the long decline of the labor movement which began shortly after the purge solely to the removal of the left wing. But it would also be wrong to suggest that it was not a major factor. The tragedy of unionism in the electrical manufacturing industry stands as grim testimony to that truth.

ABBREVIATIONS

ACTU	Association of Catholic Trade Unionists
AEC	Atomic Energy Commission
AFL	American Federation of Labor
ALHUA	Archives of Labor History and Urban Affairs, Wayne State University
CHS	Chicago Historical Society
CIO	Congress of Industrial Organizations
CIO-PAC	CIO Political Action Committee
CUA	Catholic University of America Library
CP	Communist Party of the United States
CRA	Catholic Radical Alliance
FE	Farm Equipment Workers
FBI	Federal Bureau of Investigation
GE	General Electric Corporation
HUAC	House Committee on Un-American Activities
IAM	International Association of Machinists
IBEW	International Brotherhood of Electrical Workers
ICFTU	International Confederation of Free Trade Unions
ILWU	International Longshoremen's and Warehousemen's Union

IUE	International Union of Electrical Workers
IUEA	International Union of Electrical Workers Archives, Rutgers University
NA	National Archives
NRA	National Recovery Administration
NR&AT	National Radio and Allied Trades
NIRA	National Industrial Recovery Act
NLRB	National Labor Relations Board
NYU	New York University Library
PSU	Penn State University Library
RCA	Radio Corporation of America
SACB	Strategic Activities Control Board
TUC	British Trades Union Congress
TUL	Temple University Library
TUUL	Trade Union Unity League
UE	United Electrical, Radio and Machine Workers of America
UEA	United Electrical Workers Archives, University of Pittsburgh
UEMDA	UE Members for Democratic Action
UMW	United Mine Workers
UOPWA	United Office and Professional Workers of America
USWA	United Steelworkers of America
WFTU	World Federation of Trade Unions
WSB	Wage Stabilization Board
WSU	Wright State University Library
WUL	Washington University Library

Notes

Introduction

1. Ellen Schrecker, "McCarthyism and the Labor Movement: The Role of the State," in Steve Rosswurm, ed. *The CIO's Left-Led Unions* (New Brunswick, NJ: Rutgers University Press, 1992), pp. 141–144.

2. David Caute, *The Great Fear: The Anti-Communist Purge Under Truman and Eisenhower* (New York: Simon and Schuster, 1978), pp. 349–350.

3. *Ibid.*, p. 353, 357–358.

4. *New York Times*, September 24, 1949, p. 1

5. J. Edgar Hoover to Rear Admiral Sidney Souers, February 15, 1949, PSF SF-FBI, Communist Party, Harry S. Truman Library, cited in Rosswurm, ed., *The CIO's Left-Led Unions*, p. 6; "200 UE Communists Named," *IUE News*, May 22, 1950, p. 1; Harvey Klehr and John Earl Haynes, *The American Communist Movement* (New York: Twayne Publishers, 1992), p. 83.

6. *Investigation of Un-American Propaganda Activities*, Special Committee on Un-American Activities, House of Representatives, 76th Congress, 1st Session, 1939, Vol 4, pp. 3072–3080; Harvey Klehr, *The Heyday of American Communism* (New York: Basic Books, 1984), pp. 233–234; Louis Budenz, *Men Without Faces: The Communist Conspiracy in the U.S.A.* (New York, Harper and Brothers, 1948, p. 57; *Daily Worker*, March 21, 1934, p. 5; Rosemary Feurer, "William Sentner, the UE, and Civic Unionism in St. Louis," in Rosswurn, *The CIO's Left-Led Unions*, p. 102.

7. Transcript, Oral Interview with Earl Browder, p. 391, Oral History Collection, Columbia University Library; Klehr, *The Heyday of American Communism*, pp. 240–241; Joseph R. Starobin, *American Communism in*

Crisis, 1943–1957 (Cambridge, MA: Harvard University Press, 1972), pp. 39–40; The loosening of the reigns between the party and its trade union influentials resulted primarily from a shift in Soviet policy toward a Popular Front strategy in 1935. The Seventh Comintern Congress of that year, in addition to its call for a popular front with noncommunists against fascism, also ordered a shift in the American Communist Party's position toward support for Franklin Roosevelt and the New Deal. Ironically, the decision also loosened the reigns between Moscow and New York, although American Communists generally stayed in lock step with decisions in Moscow anyway, to the ultimate disaster of the party.

8. Starobin, *American Communism in Crisis,* pp. 97–99.

9. Tape, oral interview with William Santoro; Tape, oral interview with Sadie Rosenberg; Tape, oral interview with Ed Wiese; Tape, oral interview with Rose Podmaka; Tape, oral interview with Walter Barry; Tape, oral interview with Ruth Glassman; Tape, oral interview with Jeannette Dean. All in the Robert Wagner Labor Archives, New York University Library. All of the interviewees were left-wing militants in local unions in District 4 in New Jersey. Most were open Communist Party members. Their recollections constitute a rich record of how dedicated Communists viewed their responsibilities to the rank and file and how they reconciled their essentially "bread and butter" trade union approach with party goals.

10. *Ibid,* p. 39; Joshua B. Freeman, *In Transit: The Transport Workers Union in New York City, 1933–1966* (New York: Oxford University Press, 1989), pp. 129–130.

11. *IUE News,* May 22, 1950, p. 1; Rosswurm, *The CIO's Left-Led Unions,* p. 7

12. Matles to Ernie Roemer, March 5, 1941. Ernest DeMaio Papers, Box 27.

13. Matles Interview, p. 57; Charles Rivers Interview.

14. Lloyd Ulman, *The Government of the Steelworkers Union* (New York: John Wiley, 1962), pp. 51 passim.

Chapter 1

1. Herbert R. Northrup, *Boulwarism: The Labor Relations Policies of the General Electric Company* (Ann Arbor, MI 1964), p. 1

2. Ronald Schatz, *The Electrical Workers: A History of Labor at General Electric and Westinghouse, 1923–60* (Urbana, Ill: University of Illinois Press, 1983), p. 38.

3. Milton Derber, "Electrical Products: in Harry Millis, (ed.), *How Collective Bargaining Works* (New York, 1942), pp. 744,745.

4. *Moody's Manual of Investments, American and Foreign, Industrial Securities* (New York, 1938), pp. 1669–1672, 2965–2929.

5. *Ibid.*

6. Schatz, *The Electrical Workers,* pp. 53, 59–60; National Industrial Conference Board, *Lay-off and Its Prevention* (New York: NICB, 1930)

7. David Loth, *Swope of G.E.: The Story of Gerard Swope and General Electric in American Business* (New York: Simon and Schuster, 1958), pp. 198–199; Schatz, *The Electrical Workers,* p. 55.

8. United Electrical Workers, "Labor Unity in the Electrical Manufacturing Industry," November 1, 1938, p. 2. (Mimeographed report), UE Archives.

9. U.S. Department of Labor, Bureau of Labor Statistics, *Work Stoppages: Electrical Machinery Industry, 1927–1968,* Report 374 (Washington, D.C.: GPO, n.d.), p. 8; Schatz, *The Electrical Workers,* p. 45.

10. Transcript, oral interview with Monsignor Charles Owen Rice, p. 24. The Labor History Collection of the Pennsylvania Historical Collections, Pattee Library, The Pennsylvania State University. (Hereafter cited as the PSU Labor History Collection.)

11. Edwin Young and Milton Derber, *Labor and the New Deal* (Madison, Wisconsin, 1957), p. 83.

12. Dixon Wecter, *The Age of the Great Depression* (New York, 1948), p. 36.

13. Benson Soffer, "A Theory of Trade Union Development: The Role of the Autonomous Workman," *Labor History,* 1 (Spring 1960): 141–143; Schatz, *The Electrical Workers,* p. 86; Ronald Schatz points out that this was particularly true for maintenance workers who traveled throughout the factories—a particularly valuable advantage for organizers in multibuilding industrial sites common to electrical manufacturing. James W. Kuhn, *Bargaining in Grievance Settlements: The Power of Industrial Work Groups* (New York: Columbia University Press, 1961), pp. 138–139.

14. James Matles and James Higgins, *Them and Us: Struggles of a Rank and File Union* (Englewood Cliffs, N.J.: Prentice Hall, 1974), pp. 34–35; Transcript, oral interview with James Matles, p. 37. PSU Labor History Collection; Schatz, *The Electrical Workers,* p. 83.

15. Matles and Higgins, *Them and Us,* pp. 34–35.

16. Millis, *How Collective Bargaining Works,* p. 781.

17. Transcript, oral interview with James B. Carey, p. 13. Oral History Collection, Columbia University Library.

18. Transcript, oral interview with Harry Block, p. 3. PSU Labor History Collection.

19. *Ibid.*, p. 2.

20. Transcript, Oral Interview with Ernest DeMaio, p. 14. Roosevelt University Library, copy in the Ernest DeMaio Papers, folder 1, box 14, Archives and Manuscripts Division, Chicago Historical Society (Hereafter cited as the CHS); Matles Interview, p. 5.

21. Carey Interview, p. 23.

22. *Ibid.*, p. 23.

23. Milton Derber, "Electrical Products," *How Collective Bargaining Works: A Survey of Experience in Leading American Industries*, Harry A. Millis, ed. (New York: Twentieth Century Fund, 1942), pp. 772–801.

24. Block Interview, p. 4.

25. United Electrical Workers, "Labor Unity . . . ," p. 3.

26. *Ibid.*

27. Gerardo Necoechea, "Emergence, Development and Change of a Local Union: Local 201, UE-CIO, at the Lynn G.E. Works," (Unpublished Master's Thesis, University of Massachusetts, 1977), pp. 15–31.

28. Tape, Oral Interview with Charles Rivers, Robert Wagner Labor Archives, New York University Library; Schatz, *The Electrical Workers*, p. 83.

29. Schatz, *The Electrical Workers, p. 83*; Matles and Higgins, *Them and Us*, pp. 34–35.

30. "Minutes, Meeting of Federal Local 18368," December 15, 1933. Harry Block Papers, PSU Labor History Collections.

31. Carey Interview, p. 21.

32. "Minutes, Meeting of the Radio and Allied Trades National Labor Council," December 29, 1933. Block Papers.

33. *By-Laws, National Radio and Allied Trades National Labor Council*. Block Papers.

34. Matles Interview, p. 5; Rivers Interview.

35. Matles Interview, p. 69; "Matles Bibliographical Notes," UE Archives, Red Dot Box, 98; Fact Sheet on UE Officers. District Council 7, IUE: E. J. Kraft, Wesley Steinhilber, Robert Eisner Papers, Box 2, file 2, Wright State University Libraries.

36. Rivers Interview; Matles and Higgins, *Them and Us*, pp. 22–35.

37. Peter Masiko, "A Study of Federal Labor Unions" (unpublished Master's Thesis, Department of Economics, University of Illinois, 1937), p. 59.

38. *Proceedings*, 1934 American Federation of Labor Convention, pp. 53, 54; The AFL's strategy resembled that tried by William Z. Foster in the attempt to organize the steel industry with AFL cooperation in 1919. The plan, called amalgamation, was Foster's solution to the problem of combining the jurisdictional interests of the craft unions with the need for industrial organization in steel.

39. "Minutes, First Meeting of the Federal Trade Union Delegates," October 7, 8, 1934. Block Papers.

40. *Ibid.*

41. Carey Interview, p. 31.

42. IBEW, *Journal of the Electrical Workers and Operators*, XXXV (May, 1936), p. 203.

43. *Proceedings, Meeting of Radio Unions*, December 29, 30, 1934. Block Papers.

44. Matles Interview, p. 9; Although the change in the line had nothing to do with American circumstances, it was welcomed by American Communists for whom it meant an end to working fruitlessly in isolation from the mainstream of the labor movement. The main reason for the change in the line in Moscow, and thus in the overseas parties, was the need for the creation of a "popular front" with noncommunist groups in order to face the growing Nazi threat to the security of the Soviet Union.

45. *Ibid.*, p. 7.

46. *Ibid.*, pp. 6,7; "Minutes of the National Amalgamation Convention of Metal and Allied Unions," May 31, June 1, 2, 1935," Charles Rivers Collection, Robert Wagner Archives, New York University Library, Scrapbook 1.

47. Matles Interview, pp. 8,9; Matles and Higgins, *Them and Us*, pp. 38, 41.

48. Matles to Green, July 19, 1935, Letter reproduced in "Labor Unity in the Electrical Manufacturing Industry," November 1, 1938, p. 6, UE Archives.

49. Green to Matles, August 9, 1935, *Ibid.*, p. 7.

50. John P. Frey to Matles, August 21, 1935, *Ibid.*, p. 8; Matles Interview, pp. 9, 10.

51. Matles to Green, November 14, 1935, *Ibid.*, pp. 10, 11.

52. *Ibid.*

53. William Green to the Delegates to the Convention of the National Radio and Allied Trades, March 30, 31, 1935. Block Papers.

54. "Minutes, Meeting of the National Radio and Allied Trades," March 30, 31, 1935. Block Papers.

55. *Ibid.*

56. "Treasurers Report to the Convention of the National Radio and Allied Trades," March 30, 31, 1934. Block Papers.

57. "Minutes, Meeting of the National Radio and Allied Trades," July 4, 5, 1935. Block Papers.

58. Weldon Caie to Carey, August 8, 1935. Block Papers.

59. Lewis Hines to Carey, August 26, 1935. Block Papers.

60. *Peoples Press*, February 15, 1936, p. 1.

61. *Proceedings*, 1935 American Federation of Labor Convention, p. 752.

62. Carey Interview, p. 34.

63. *Ibid.*, p. 35.

64. "Minutes, Meeting of the Nation Radio and Allied Trades," October 4, 5, 6, 1935. Block Papers.

65. *Ibid.*

66. "Minutes, Conference of the National Radio and Allied Trades," December 27, 28, 29, 1935. Block Papers.

67. *Ibid.*

68. *Ibid.*

69. Carey to Green, December 27, 1935. Block Papers.

70. Green to Carey, December 28, 1935. Block Papers.

71. "Minutes, Conference of the National Radio and Allied Trades," December 27, 28, 29, 1935. Block Papers.

72. Carey Interview, pp. 39, 40.

73. Green to Carey, January 27, 1936. Block Papers.

74. Arthur O. Wharton to Matles, December 10, 1935, "Labor Unity in the Electrical Manufacturing Industry," pp. 18, 19. UE Archives.

75. Carey to Green, February 15, 1936. Block Papers.

76. "Memorandum of Proposed Terms of Affiliation by President Tracy of the International Brotherhood of Electrical Workers to the Radio and/or Television Receiving Set Manufacturing and Assembling Local Unions Operating Under the Federal Labor Union Charters of the American Federation of Labor as of February 5, 1936," Block Papers.

77. "Minutes, Conference of the National Radio and Allied Trades," February 8, 9, 10, 1936, Block Papers.

78. Green to Carey, February 8, 1936. Block Papers.

79. "Minutes, Conference of the National Radio and Allied Trades," February 8, 9, 10, 1936. Block Papers; *Peoples Press*, February 15, 1936, p. 6.

80. Carey Interview, pp. 45, 46.

81. "Unedited Minutes, Founding Convention of the United Electrical, Radio and Machine Workers of America," March 21, 22, 1926. Block Papers.

82. *Ibid.*

83. *Ibid.*; *Peoples Press*, March 28, 1936, p. 6.

84. Brophy to Carey, March 20, 1936. Block Papers; "Unedited Minutes, Founding Convention of the United Electrical, Radio and Machine Workers of America," March 21, 22, 1936. Block Papers; In other action, the convention agreed to use the UE edition of the left-wing *Peoples Press* as its official paper, but more significantly, the delegates defeated by 34 to 10 a motion to adopt a resolution in support of a labor party in the United States. Harry Block, Carey, and Matthew Campbell, three men who were later to become important in the UE's right wing, all from federal locals, voted against the resolution. Julius Emspak, Leo Jandreau, and William Turnbull, all left-wingers and all from the independent electrical workers, voted for it. The split on the vote divided clearly along the lines of the federal and independent groups.

85. Carey Interview, pp. 1–12, 18, 29; FBI Report, "James B. Carey," Sept. 3, 1941, File 62–62426–25, FBI Archives; Gary Fink, ed. *Biographical Dictionary of American Labor Leaders* (Westport, CT: Greenwood Press, 1974), pp. 53–54.

86. Ernest DeMaio, the UE's first staff organizer and later General Executive Board member and vice-president from District 11, claimed that Carey had been given the presidency because his Philco local in Philadelphia had the money to advance $5,000 in per capita payments to the new national union. DeMaio Interview, p. 18.

87. Transcript, oral interview with Julius Emspak, Oral History Collection, Columbia University Library, pp. 27–67; Schatz, *The Electrical Workers*, pp. 92–93; Carey Interview, p. 48; U.S. Congress, House Committee on Un-American Activities, *Hearings Regarding Communism in Labor Unions in the United States*, 80th Congress, 1st session, 1947, vol. 59, (Washington: GPO, 1948), p. 219; Matles Interview, p. 28; Of interest to the question of whether Emspak was a party member or when he became a member is the memoir of Charles Rivers, the TUUL organizer who was sent to Schenectady in 1932 to organize the electrical workers. Rivers claims that Emspak was not known to him during his eight-month tenure in Schenectady. Tape, oral interview with Charles Rivers, Robert Wagner Labor Archives, New York University Library.

88. Matles Interview, p. 28.

89. Carey Interview, p. 48.

90. Emspak Interview, p. 86.

91. *Ibid.*, p. 89.

92. Carey Interview, p. 48.

93. DeMaio Interview, pp. 1–19.

94. Carey to Green, April 13, 1946. Block Papers.

95. Green to Carey, April 14, 1946. Block Papers.

Chapter 2

1. Walter Galenson, *The CIO Challenge to the AFL* (Cambridge, MA 1960), p. 245; *AFL Executive Council Minutes*, January 15–19, 1936, p. 31.

2. *New York Times*, November 8, 1936, p. 2.

3. Millis, *How Collective Bargaining Works*, pp. 716–747, 791–793.

4. *New York Times*, July 21, 1936, p. 7.

5. Emspak Interview, p. 129.

6. *Union News Service*, September 14, 1936.

7. "Report of the Secretary Treasurer to the First Annual UE Convention," 1936. Block Papers.

8. "UE Statement of Cash Receipts and Disbursements, April 1, 1936 to July 31, 1936." Block Papers.

9. "Minutes, First Annual Convention, UE," September 4–7, 1936, p. 26. Block Papers.

10. *Ibid.*, p. 75.

11. *Ibid.*, p. 71.

12. Emspak Interview, pp. 159–160.

13. *Union News Service*, December 21, 1936.

14. Matles and Higgins, *Them and Us*, p. 84; Schatz, *The Electrical Workers*, p. 73.

15. Peter Masiko, "A Study of Federal Labor Unions . . . ," p. 75.

16. Matles Interview, p. 35.

17. Ibid., p. 36; Emspak Interview, p. 222; Matles and Higgins, *Them and Us*, pp. 85, 86.

18. Matles Interview, p. 35.

19. *Ibid.*, pp. 31, 32; Fitzgerald Interview, p. 2; Matles and Higgins, *Them and Us*, p. 80. Matles claims that Carey's action led to a breakdown in the talks that drew out the negotiations for months.

20. Matles Interview, pp. 31, 32; Fitzgerald Interview, p. 3.

21. Fitzgerald Interview, p. 2.

22. Matles Interview, pp. 31–32.

23. *Ibid.*, pp. 31, 32, 37; while this is a difficult episode to document properly, this behavior corroborates the description of Carey as a negotiator later given by GE company representatives in Northrup, *Boulwarism*, pp. 58–60, 165–167, an admittedly hostile study.

24. Robert Manewitz to James Carey and Julius Emspak, November 4, 1936, UEA, D8—500; William Sentner to Carey, December 31, 1936, UEA, O–1288; "Organizer's Report," March 27, 1937, Sentner Papers, Series 1, Box 6, folder 2: Rosemary Feurer, "William Sentner, The UE, and Civic Unionism in St. Louis," in Stephen Rosswurm, ed., *The CIO's Left-Led Unions*, pp. 96, 100; "A Yaleman and a Communist," *Fortune*, November, 1943, p. 213.

25. Lloyd Austin, phone interview, St. Louis, January 5, 1987, quoted in Feurer, "William Sentner, the UE, and Civic Unionism in St. Louis," p. 100.

26. *Ibid.*, pp. 101–102.

27. *Ibid.*, July 19, 1937.

28. Millis, *How Collective Bargaining Works*, pp. 763–764.

29. *Ibid.*

30. "Minutes, UE General Executive Board," June 5, 6, 1937. Block Papers.

31. *Ibid.*

32. *New York Times,* September 4, 1937, p. 7; "Unedited and Unabridged Minutes of the Second Annual UE Convention," September 3–6, 1937. Block Papers.

33. *Proceeding,* 1937 UE Convention, p. 3.

34. *Ibid.*

35. *Ibid.*

36. *Ibid.*

37. *Ibid.*

38. "Unedited and Unabridged Minutes, Second Annual UE Convention," September 3–6, 1937. Block Papers.

39. Matles Interview, p. 14; *New York Times,* December 28, 1935, p. 14.

40. The relationship between the TUUL and the Communist Party was so close that it was difficult to know where one started and the other left off. Top TUUL leaders were also in the highest councils of the party. Unlike the later loose relationship between the party and its CIO union leaders, all decisions affecting the TUUL were made by party officials. Klehr, *The Heyday of American Communism,* p. 39; Klehr and Haynes, *The American Communist Movement,* pp. 72–73; William Z. Foster, "Right Tendencies at the Trade Union Unity Congress," *Communist,* July, 1929, p. 371.

41. Freeman, *In Transit,* p. 88.

42. Matles Interview, p. 12.

43. *Ibid.,* p. 13.

44. Klehr, *The Heyday of American Communism,* pp. 129–130; *Daily Worker,* January 31, 1934, pp. 4–5; *Communist,* May 1934, p. 447.

45. *Ibid.,* pp. 23, 25.

46. *Ibid.,* p. 21.

47. *Ibid.*

48. Arthur O Wharton to General Vice-Presidents, Grand Lodge Rep-

resentatives, Business Agents and General Chairmen, April, 1936, "Labor Unity in the Electrical Manufacturing Industry," p. 24. UEA.

49. Earl Browder, Oral History Interview, cited in Harvey Levenstein, *Communism, Anticommunism and the CIO* (Westport, CT: Greenwood Press, 1981), p. 38.

50. Matles Interview, p. 25; Matles and Higgins, *Them and Us*, pp. 47–50; One historian puts the number closer to 8,000. Mark Perlman, *The Machinists* (Cambridge, MA: Harvard University Press, 1961).

51. *People's Press*, September 4, 1937, p. 5.

52. John Earl Haynes, *Dubious Alliance: The Making of Minnesota's DFL Party* (Minneapolis: University of Minnesota Press, 1984), p. 27.

53. *Proceedings*, 1938 UE Convention, p. 1.

54. Millis, *How Collective Bargaining Works*, pp. 752–760, 787–788; *Union News Service*, June 11, 1938.

55. *Proceedings*, 1938 UE Convention, pp. 226, 228.

56. *Ibid.*, pp. 117–130.

57. *Ibid.*, p. 5.

58. Matles and Higgins, *Them and Us*, p. 124.

59. Emspak Interview, p. 233.

60. Carey Interview, p. 119.

61. Transcript, oral interview with John Brophy, pp. 662, 663. Oral History Collection, Columbia University Library.

62. Transcript, oral interview with Gardner Jackson, p. 764. Oral History Collection, Columbia University Library.

63. *Ibid.*

64. Galenson, *CIO Challenge to the AFL*, p. 255; IBEW, *The Journal of the Electrical Workers and Operators*, February, 1940, p. 63.

65. J.S. Adams to A. Rosen, March 29, 1941; J. Edgar Hoover to Matthew McGuire, September 8, 1941; Matthew McGuire to J. Edgar Hoover, September 12, 1941, "Memorandum" re James B. Carey, FBI Records, File 62–62426.

66. FBI Report, "James B. Carey," (n.d. 1941), File 62–62426–1, FBI Archives; FBI Report, "James B. Carey," Jan. 12, 1942, File 62–62426–26, FBI Archives.

67. Emspak Interview, p. 355.

68. *UE News*, October 14, 1939; Emspak Interview, p. 224.

69. Investigation of Un-American Propaganda Activities, Special Committee on Un-American Activities, House of Representatives, 76th Congress, 1st Session, 1939, Vol. 7, pp. 3072–3080; Emspak Interview; Louis Budenz, *Men Without Faces: The Communist Conspiracy in the U.S.A.* (New York: Harper & Brothers, 1948), p. 57; "The Yaleman and the Communist," *Fortune*, November 1943, pp. 146–148, 212–221; Starobin, *American Communism in Crisis*, p. 39; Klehr, *The Heyday of American Communism*, pp. 233–234.

70. *Proceedings*, 1938 UE Convention, p. 148. Before a UE convention, the various locals and districts of the union passed resolutions and sent them to the international union where they were given to a resolution committee, appointed by the general officers, for consideration. Similar resolutions would often be combined and the committee would arrive at a group of resolutions for consideration of the entire convention. With this system, common to most unions, it was a simple matter for the general officers to have preferred resolutions reach the convention floor. Unless there was a well organized opposition submitting minority resolutions and willing to put on a floor fight, the chances of defeating a resolution reported out of the resolutions committee were practically nonexistent.

71. *UE News*, March 25, 1939, p. 3.

72. *Ibid.*, p. 7.

73. *UE News*, August 12, 1939, p. 8.

74. *The Daily Worker*, September 19, 1939, p. 1; Harvey Klehr, *The Heyday of American Communism*, p. 395.

75. On the effect of the Hitler-Stalin Pact on the Popular Front see Klehr, *The Heyday of American Communism*, pp. 386–409, Klehr and Haynes, *The American Communist Movement*, pp. 92–95, Frank A. Warren, III, *Liberals and Communism, the "Red Decade" Revisited* (Bloomington, IN: University of Indiana Press, 1966) and Philip J. Jaffee, *The Rise and Fall of American Communism* (New York: Horizon Press, 1975); The impact of the Pact on the Popular Front in one state is shown in detail in Haynes, *Dubious Alliance*, pp. 49–52.

76. *UE News*, September 2, 1939, p. 2.

77. *Proceedings*, 1939 UE Convention, p. 45.

78. *UE News*, September 23, 1939, p. 4.

79. *UE News*, September 30, 1939, p. 4.

80. *Ibid.*, p. 8.

81. *UE News*, September 9, 1939, p. 2.

82. *UE News*, October 14, 1939, p. 4.

83. *UE News*, December 23, 1939, p. 3.

84. Carey Interview, pp. 126, 127.

85. *New York Times*, November 27, 1939, p. 5; Carey's statement was blasted the following day by Luigi Antonini, a vice-president of the International Ladies Garment Workers' Union, for its anti-Americanism. Antonini claimed that Carey failed to denounce anti-American statements by Lazaro Pena, the Cuban Communist leader. Antonini called Carey a Communist. *New York Times*, November 28, 1939, p. 12; FBI Report, "James B. Carey," 4/2/41, File 62–62426–6, FBI Archives.

86. *Proceeding*, 1939 UE Convention, pp. 45, 167, 176–179.

87. Millis, *How Collective Bargaining Works*, pp. 760, 761.

88. *UE News*, December 16, 1939; June 22, 1940, p. 1.

89. *UE News*, August 17, 1940, p. 1.

90. *UE News*, January 6, 1940, p. 8.

91. *UE News*, January 13, 1940, p. 2.

92. *UE News*, May 13, 1940, p. 5.

93. *UE News*, June 1, 1940, p. 5.

94. *UE News*, December 7, 1940, p. 5.

95. *New York Times*, August 14, 1938, p. 31.

96. *Ibid.*

97. *New York Times*, October 1, 1939, p. 33.

98. Matles to the Honorable Joe Stearns, Acting Chairman, HUAC, June 12, 1941. Ernest DeMaio Papers, Box 27, folder 1, CHS; *UE News*, October 7, 1939, p. 2.

99. *UE News*, January 13, 1940, p. 5.

100. *UE News*, March 9, 1940, p. 2; U.S., *Congressional Record*, 76th Congr., 3rd Sess., 1940, LXXXVI, Part 1, pp. 582–583, 587, 600.

101. Matles to Sentner, October 18, 1939. Sentner Papers, Series 1, Box 5, folder 3. Washington University Libraries.

102. *Proceedings*, 1940 UE Convention, p. 74.

103. *Ibid.*, p. 215.

104. *Ibid.*, pp. 177, 178.

105. *Ibid.*, pp, 183, 184

106. *Ibid.*, p. 127.

107. Carey to Block, November 25, 1940. Block Papers

108. Carey to Matthew Campbell, November 25, 1940, UEA, District 2, ff 26; Carey's secretary at the inception of the UE in 1936 had been a woman named Stella Abrams. However, she soon became Julius Emspak's secretary and later his wife. All secretarial help in the UE, as in all other CIO unions, came from the ranks of the United Office and Professional Workers Union (CIO), as did Miss Abrams. Carey eventually came to believe that Stella Abrams was a Communist plant. Emspak pointed out, however, that it was Carey who approached her about taking the job when she was acting as recording secretary at the UE's founding convention in Buffalo. Whichever is true, following her marriage to Emspak, she left the employ of the union. The rift over a secretary for James Carey did not involve her, but Carey brought this episode up later to reinforce his contention that his secretaries were loyal to outside forces rather than to him. Carey Interview, p. 48; Emspak Interview, p. 96.

109. U.S. Congress, House, Special Subcommittee of the Committee on Education and Labor, *Hearings, Investigation of Communist Infiltration of UERMWA*, 80th Cong., 2d Sess., 1948, pp. 25, 27, 34.

110. *Ibid.*, p. 25.

111. Julius Emspak to Leo Jandreau, February 15, 1941, UEA, District 3, ff 43.

112. Victor Riesel, "Labor Roundup," *New Leader*, September 6, 1941, p. 1.

113. Emspak to General Executive Board Members, November 30, 1940. Block Papers and UE Papers; U.S. Congress, House, Special Subcommittee of the Committee on Education and Labor, *Hearings, Investigation of Communist Infiltration of UERMWA*, 80th Cong., 2d Sess., 1948, p. 27.

114. Emspak Interview, p. 261.

115. Matles Interview, p. 43.

116. "Minutes, UE General Executive Board," November, 1940. UE National Office Records, UEA.

117. *UE News*, January 18, 1941, p. 5.

118. *UE News*, January 25, 1941, p. 5.

119. *UE News*, January 6, 1940, p. 5.

120. "Minutes, UE General Executive Board," March 22, 23, 1941. UE National Office Records, UEA.

121. *UE News*, March 22, 1941, p. 5.

122. Michael Fitzpatrick to Carey, March 5, 1947, UEA, District 6, ff 91; Carey to Michael Fitzpatrick, March 13, 1941, UEA, District 6, ff 87.

123. Victor Riesel, "Heard on the Left," *New Leader*, March 29, 1941, p. 3.

124. *UE News*, March 22, 1941, p. 5.

125. "Minutes, UE General Executive Board," March 22, 23, 1941. UE National Office Records, UEA.

126. *Ibid.*

127. *Constitution of the United Electrical, Radio and Machine Workers of America.* UE Papers.

128. Matles Interview, pp. 41–43.

129. Block Interview, p. 8.

130. "Minutes, UE General Executive Board," June 21, 1941. UE National Office Records, UEA; Emspak Interview, pp. 256, 257.

131. *UE News*, May 24, 1941, p. 5.

132. Ernest DeMaio to Matles, June 16, 1941, Ernest DeMaio Papers, Box 27; DeMaio Interview, p. 70.

133. FBI Report, "James B. Carey," April 23, 1941, File 62–62426, FBI Archives.

134. *UE News*, May 31, 1941, p. 5.

135. "Minutes, UE General Executive Board," June 21, 1941. UE National Office Records, UEA.

136. *UE News*, June 7, 1941, p. 4.

137. *UE News*, June 21, 1941, p. 2.

138. Steve Rosswurm, "The Catholic Church and the Left-Led Unions: Labor Priests, Labor Schools, and the ACTU," in Rosswurm, ed. *The CIO's Left-Led Unions*, p. 121.

139. *Ibid.*, pp. 122–124; Douglas Seaton, *Catholics and Radicals: The*

Association of Catholic Trade Unionists and the American Labor Movement from Depression to Cold War (Lewisburg, PA: Bucknell University Press, 1981); Patrick J. McGeever, *Rev. Charles Owen Rice: Apostle of Contradiction* (Pittsburgh: Duquesne University Press, 1989), pp. 48, 51, 99; Joshua B. Freeman, *In Transit: The Transport Workers Union in New York City, 1933–1966* (New York: Oxford University Press, 1989), pp. 128–161.

140. Schatz, *The Electrical Workers*, pp. 181–182; Douglas P. Seaton, *Catholics and Radicals*, pp. 141–186; Freeman, *In Transit*, p. 106.

141. "ACTU Statement of Principles," *Labor Leader*, January 3, 1938, p. 1.

142. McGheever, *Reverend Charles Owen Rice*, pp. 1, 23–26.

143. *Ibid.*, pp. 45–51.

144. *Ibid.*, pp. 61–62, 84–86, 93; Rosswurn, "The Catholic Church and the Left-Led Unions," in Rosswurn, *The CIO's Left-Led Unions*, p. 132.

145. *Ibid.*, p. 135; Matles and Higgins, *Them and Us*, p. 258.

146. *Daily Compass*, November 30, 1949, p. 1. The Charles Owen Rice Papers, PSU. Hereafter cited as Rice Papers.

147. Schatz, *The Electrical Workers*, pp. 84, 190–191, 193–194.

148. *Union Generator*, March 1941, pp. 1, 3, publication of UE Local 601, Pittsburgh-Westinghouse. Rice Papers.

149. Emspak to Bishop Hugh Boyle, March 18, 1941. Rice Papers.

150. Ellen Laird to Rice, March 2, 1941. Rice Papers.

151. *Daily Worker*, March 5, 1941, p. 2.

152. Carey to Charles Newell, March 19, 1941. Rice Papers; SAC, Pittsburgh to FBI Headquarters, January 12, 1942, file 62–62426, FBI Archives.

153. Rice to Local 601 members, August 7, 1941. Rice Papers.

154. Schatz, *The Electrical Workers*, pp. 193–194; McGeever, *Reverend Charles Owen Rice*, pp. 113–114. One of the issues over which the election was fought was the desire of the right wing to buy an ambulance to help British victims of Nazi bombings at a time when the Communists were vehemently opposed to any help for Britain. Polish workers, who made up a sizeable voting bloc, and whose country had been divided between Russia and Germany after the signing of the nonaggression pact, voted overwhelmingly for the right-wing slate.

155. *Pittsburgh Press*, February 10, 1942. Local 601 had another

problem as a result of the election. Margaret Darin, an ally of Newell who had been defeated in her bid for retention as local secretary, was demoted by the right-wing forces from office manager to a clerical position. The woman who defeated her was given the office manager's job. Darin's co-workers refused to work until she was reinstated. The issue was settled by eliminating the position and leaving both women as clerks. Rice to Father Thomas Darby, June 13, 1946, Rice Papers.

156. "Minutes, Second National ACTU Convention," 1941. Copy in Rice Papers.

157. *UE News*, June 7, 1941, p. 5.

158. Block Interview, p. 13.

159. Fitzgerald Interview, p. 4.

160. *Ibid.*, p. 7; Block Interview, pp. 14–18.

161. Block Interview, pp. 14, 18.

162. Fitzgerald Interview, p. 7.

163. *Ibid.*, p. 6.

164. *Ibid.*

165. *Ibid.*, p. 4. If this story is true, then Fitzgerald and Coulthard had knowledge of this move before the telephone call with Harry Block and before the New York breakfast with Carey. Matles claimed that Carey became aware of a movement to oust him early in 1941, before Carey raised the issue of local autonomy on the selection of officers qualifications. He says that the move was initiated by the Lynn local. According to Matles they first went to Carey and told him of their decision. They next informed Matles and Emspak. The issue appears to have been neglect of UE duties, according to the Matles version. Matles claims the big Schenectady local supported Lynn. Matles and Emspak then supposedly informed Carey of their neutrality (Matles Interview, pp. 38–40). Julius Emspak agreed with the sequence of events described by Fitzgerald and Matles on the decision to oppose Carey, but he disagrees with Matles on the timing. He noted that the move began with the Lynn people, but dates its inception sometime in the summer, 1941, immediately after the conclusion of the General Electric negotiations. The reasons, according to Emspak, were that Carey had been president in name only, that he took no real part in negotiations, and that his contributions to the unions had ceased. Emspak claimed that for a period of nine months prior to the 1941 convention, Carey was not in the UE New York office at all. Emspak Interview, pp. 259, 270, 271.

166. Carey Interview, p. 147.

167. *U.E. News*, June 21, 1941. p.5.

168. Carey Interview, p. 147.

169. Maurice Isserman, *Which Side Are You On?: The American Communist Party During the Second World War* (Middletown, CT: Wesleyan University Press, 1982), pp. 103–126.

170. *UE News*, July 12, 1941, p. 5.

171. *UE News*, July 26, 1941, p. 5.

172. *UE News*, August 3, 1941, p. 5.

173. Sentner to Matles, September 29, 1941. Sentner Papers, Series 6, Box 1, folder 6.

174. *Proceedings*, 1941 UE Convention, p. 11.

175. *Ibid.*, p. 5.

176. Block Interview, p. 19.

177. *PM*, November 13, 1940, p. 1; Robert Sherrill and Harry Ernst, *The Drugstore Liberal* (New York: Grossman Publishers, 1968), p. 81; U.S., Congress, Senate, Subcommittee of the Committee on Labor and Public Welfare, *Hearings, Communist Domination of Unions and National Security*, 82d Cong., 2d Sess., 1952, pp. 489–491.

178. Matles to Joe Stearns, Acting Chairman, HUAC, June 12, 1941. Ernest DeMaio Papers, Box 27; *New York Times*, June 12, 1941, pp. 1, 13.

179. Emspak Interview, pp. 275, 276.

180. Carey Interview, pp. 140, 141; FBI Report, "James B. Carey," January 12, 1942, File 62–62426, FBI Archives.

181. *Proceedings*, 1941 UE Convention, p. 22.

182. *New York Times*, September 2, 1941, p. 1.

183. *UE News*, September 6, 1941, p. 1.

184. *Proceedings*, 1941 UE Convention, p. 172; *UE News*, September 13, 1941, p. 2.

185. *UE News*, September 13, 1941, pp. 1, 2.

186. Carey Interview, p. 129.

187. Block Interview, p. 47. While this may be true of some unions, UE may have been an exception. The union always looked upon its officers as first among equals. They were expected above all to give service to the districts and locals. One indication of how UE expected its officers to perform is found in the fact that the UE constitution restricted the salaries of

the officers to the top wage paid to workers in the industry over which UE claimed jurisdiction. This is still true of the UE.

188. *Labor Leader*, September 12, 1941, p. 1.

189. James Weschler, "Carey and the Communists," *Nation*, CLIII (September 13, 1941), pp. 224, 225.

190. Levenstein, *Communism, Anticommunism and the CIO*, pp. 157–158.

191. Carey Interview, p. 142; Matles and Higgins, *Them and Us*, pp. 134–135. Matles claimed that not long after the convention, he, Emspak, and Fitzgerald visited Murray and urged the CIO leader to help Carey find himself as a trade union leader by teaching him the things he had failed to learn as president of UE.

192. Matles Interview, p. 48.

193. Levenstein, *Communism, Anticommunism and the CIO*, pp. 157–158; Ernest DeMaio claimed that the decision to support Carey for the CIO post resulted from a desire to not destroy him as a person. DeMaio later saw it as a major mistake on the part of the UE officers. DeMaio Interview, p. 42.

194. UE Local 105 General Membership Minutes, September 26, 1941, IUE Local 105 Papers, Box 1, TUL.

195. *UE News*, September 13, 1941, p. 2.

196. *New York Times*, September 4, 1941, p. 1.

197. Block Interview, p. 18; Carey Interview, p. 143; Fact sheet on UE officers. District Council 7, IUE: E. J. Kraft, Wesley Steinhilber, Robert Eisner Papers, Box 2, file 2, WSUL.

198. U.S. Congress, House, Special Subcommittee of the Committee on Education and Labor, *Hearing, Investigation of Communist Infiltration of UERMWA*, 80th Cong. 2nd Sess., 1948, p. 83.

199. Block Interview, pp. 14, 18.

200. Ellington Smith, "The Electrical Workers Meet," *New Republic*, XII (September 19, 1949), p. 15.

201. Bert Cochrane, *Labor and Communism* (Princeton, NJ: Princeton University Press, 1977), pp. 280–282, 289, 290.

Chapter 3

1. Matles Interview, p. 64.

2. "Minutes, UE General Executive Board," September 6, 1941. UE National Office Records, UEA.

3. "Minutes, UE General Executive Board," November, 1941. UE National Office Records, UEA.

4. *Ibid.*

5. *Ibid.*

6. Block Interview, pp. 20, 21.

7. "Minutes, UE General Executive Board," November, 1941. UE National Office Records, UEA.

8. "Minutes, District Council 1," November 6, 1941. Block Papers.

9. *UE News*, January 17, 1942, p. 1.

10. "Minutes, UE General Executive Board," November, 1941. UE National Office Records, UEA.

11. *Ibid.*

12. "Minutes, District Council 1," November 6, 1941. Block Papers.

13. *New York Times*, December 12, 1941, p. 23.

14. *UE News*, December 13, 1941, p. 1.

15. *Ibid.*

16. "Minutes, UE General Executive Board," December 15, 1941. UE National Office Records, UEA.

17. *UE News*, December 20, 1941, p. 1.

18. *New York Times*, December 18, 1941, p. 16; *Pittsburgh Press*, December 18, 1941, p. 1.

19. *UE News*, January 17, 1942, p. 6.

20. "Minutes, UE General Executive Board," March 20, 21, 1942. UE National Office Records, UEA.

21. "Minutes, District Council 1," April 9, 1942. Block Papers.

22. Maurice Isserman, *Which Side Were You On?*, pp. 85–87, 130–132. On May 16, 1942, on the eve of a visit from Soviet foreign minister Molotov, Roosevelt commuted Browder's sentence to time served. He did it in the service of national unity and with the recognition that his four-year sentence for passport fraud was by way of a penalty because of his political views.

23. *New York Times*, May 17, 1942, p. 1.

24. U.S., *Congressional Record*, 77th Cong., 2d Sess., 1942, LXXXVIII, Part 6, 7687.

25. *New York Times*, May 29, 1942, p. 1.

26. *Ibid.*, pp. 1. 9.

27. *Ibid.*

28. "Minutes, UE General Executive Board," May 29, 30, 1942. UE National Office Records, UEA.

29. *District Six Journal*, June 18, 1942, p. 3. Rice Papers; McGeever, *Rev. Charles Owen Rice*, pp. 98–99.

30. *New York Times*, September 10, 1942, p. 16.

31. *UE News*, September 12, 1942, p. 4; *Proceedings*, 1942 UE Convention, pp. 120, 121, 127.

32. *Ibid.*

33. *Ibid., p.* 208.

34. "Minutes, District Council 1," June 4, 1942. Block Papers.

35. Block Interview, pp. 12, 13; Carey Interview, p. 60.

36. Victor Decavitch to Julius Emspak, June 27, 1942, UEA, District 7, Local 801, ff 1009; Matles and Higgins, *Them and Us*, pp. 125–126; William Sentner to James Matles, Oct. 16, 1941, UEA, District 8, ff 69.

37. "Minutes, UE General Executive Board," May 29, 30, 1942. UE National Office Records, UEA.

38. "Minutes, District Council 1," September 3, 1942. Block Papers.

39. *UE News*, September 26, 1942, p. 6.

40. *Ibid.*

41. Matles to Ernest DeMaio, February 26, 1941; Matles to Ernest DeMaio, April 25, 1941. Ernest DeMaio Papers, Box 27.

42. *Ibid.*, pp. 1, 6. Actually this was a very low number of staff men to have delegates' credentials. In a union like the United Steelworkers of America, practically the entire staff receives credentials. LLoyd Ulman, *The Government of the Steelworkers Union* (New York: John Wiley and Sons, 1962), pp. 106–110. This is also true of the United Mine Workers and numerous other unions. Right-wing critics later claimed that all new UE staff members had to be approved by the Communist Party. The local county chairman of the Party would make recommendations to the state chairman who would then confer with the international representative of the UE in that district. If all agreed that the person was suited for the job, their recommendation would be passed on to James Matles for approval. Fact sheet on UE officers. District Council 7, IUE: E. J. Kraft, Wesley Steinhilber, Robert Eisner Papers, Box 2, file 2, WSUL.

43. *Ibid.*, p. 7.

44. "Minutes, District Council 1," November 5, 1942. Block Papers.

45. "Minutes, UE General Executive Board," December 15, 16, 1942. UE National Office Records, UEA.

46. *Washington Post*, February 25, 1943, p. 16; Kampelman, *Communist Party vs. CIO*, p. 125.

47. *UE News*, March 6, 1943, p. 6.

48. *UE News*, January 13, 1942, p. 6.

49. *New York Times*, June 8, 1942, p. 22.

50. *New York Times*, June 2, 1943, p. 13.

51. *UE News*, June 12, 1943, p. 1.

52. *UE News*, June 26, 1942. p. 3.

53. *UE News*, July 24, 1943, p. 3.

54. *UE News*, September 25, 1943, p. 12; *Proceedings*, 1943 UE Convention, pp. 40–99.

55. *UE News*, September 18, 1943, p. 1; *Proceedings*, 1943 UE Convention, p. 112.

56. *New York Times*, September 14, 1943, p. 12; *New York Times*, September 15, 1943, p. 31.

57. Harry Block, "Report on the 1943 UE Convention," (unpublished report). Block Papers.

58. "Minutes, District Council 1," October 7, 1943, Block Papers.

59. Block to Emspak, December 21, 1943. Block Papers.

60. Emspak to Block, December 27, 1943. Block Papers.

61. Carl Bersing to Emspak, February 5, 1944. Block Papers.

62. "Minutes, UE General Executive Board," March 16, 17, 1944. UE National Office Records, UEA.

63. *New York Times*, September 26, 1944, p. 24; *Proceedings*, 1944 UE Convention, pp. 31–44.

64. "Minutes, UE General Executive Board," June 8, 9, 1944. UE National Office Records, UEA.

65. *Ibid.*

66. *Ibid.*

67. *UE News,* June 10, 1944. p. 1.

68. *New York Times,* September 27, 1944, p. 38; *Proceedings,* 1944 UE Convention, p. 78.

69. *New York Times,* September 27, 1944, p. 38; *Proceedings,* 1944 UE Convention, p. 78.

70. *New York Times,* September 29, 1944, p. 17; *Proceedings,* 1944 UE Convention, pp. 79, 80.

71. *Ibid.*

72. *New York Times,* September 28, 1944, p. 36; *Proceedings,* 1944 UE Convention, pp. 131–149.

73. Johnson, p. 29.

74. William Sentner to James Matles, October 16, 1941, UEA, District 8, ff 69.

75. Harry [Fleischman] to Bill [Becker], May 8, 1945, Socialist Party Papers, reel 52; William Pratt, "The Socialist Party, Socialist Unionists, and Organized Labor, 1936–1950," in Maurice Zeitlin and Howard Kimeldorf, eds., *Political Power and Social Theory,* vol. 4 (Greenwich, CT: JAI Press), p. 81.

76. "Minutes, District Council 8," October 14, 15, 1944. Block Papers.

77. *New York Times* November 5, 1944, p. 1.

78. *UE News,* November 25, 1944, pp. 7, 12.

79. *Ibid.*

80. Charles Rivers to James Matles, July 31, 1942, O–1182; Charles Rivers to Julius Emspak, February 21, 1942, O–1181; District 2 Connecticut Report, December 1943, District 2–15, UEA; Ronald Schatz, "Connecticut's Working Class in the 1950s: A Catholic Perspective," *Labor History,* Vol. 25, No. 1 (Winter 1984), p. 83; Seaton, *Catholics and Radicals,* pp. 171–172; *Labor Leader,* September 30, 1944, p. 1. The Connecticut Valley proved to be an early and durable right-wing stronghold. Connecticut locals supported right-wing resolutions at the 1942 and 1944 UE Conventions and Martin Hogan, from Hartford Local 251, ran against Fitzgerald at the 1944 UE convention. In addition to the presence of strong ACTU chapters in Bridgeport and Hartford, the Connecticut right-wingers benefitted from the already established right wing insurgency in Connecticut's "Brass Valley" against the left-wing leadership of the Mine, Mill, and Smelter Workers Union.

81. *UE News*, December 9, 1944, p. 4.

82. *Proceedings*, 1942 UE Convention, p. 47. The Little Steel Formula established January 1, 1941, as the base date in terms of cost of living and stipulated that workers were entitled to a 15 percent increase over that date's rate of pay because of the cost of living rise and then could only have wage claims considered on the grounds of inequalities or substandards of living.

83. *Proceedings*, 1943 UE Convention, p. 53.

84. *Ibid.*

85. *War Labor Reports*, vol. 23, Bureau of National Affairs, Washington, DC, 1945, Westinghouse Electric Co. (Pittsburgh) and UERMWA (CIO), Case no. 111–8213, April 11, 1945, pp. 153–166.

86. *Ibid.*

87. Earl Browder Interview, pp. 390–391; *Communist*, Vol. 22 (January 1943), pp. 19–23; Earl Browder, *Wage Policy in War Production* (New York: Workers Library, 1943), p. 7; Maurice Isserman, *Which Side Were You On: The American Communist Party During the Second World War* (Middletown, CT: Wesleyan University Press, 1982), p. 162.

88. Irving Howe and Lewis Coser, *The American Communist Party: A Critical History, 1919–1957* (Boston: Beacon Press, 1957), pp. 408–414; Joel Seidman, "Labor Policy of the Communist Party During World War II," *Industrial and Labor Relations Review*, Vol. 4 (October 1950), pp. 59–65; Art Preis, *Labor's Giant Step: Twenty Years of the CIO* (New York: Pathfinder, 1972), pp. 185–186, 212–213; Schatz, *The Electrical Workers*, p. 142; *UE News*, October 3, 1941, p. 2; March 27, 1942, p. 1; Necoecha, "Emergence, Development and Change . . . ," p. 99.

89. Schatz, *The Electrical Workers*, pp. 138–139, 141–142; Roger Keeran, *The Communist Party and the Auto Workers Unions* (Bloomington, IN: Indiana University Press, 1980), pp. 237–240; *UE Guide to Wage Payment Plans*; Finn Theodore Malm, "Local 201, UE-CIO: A Case Study of a Local Industrial Union," (Unpublished Ph.D. Dissertation, Massachusetts Institute of Technology, 1946).

90. Nelson Lichtenstein, *Labor's War at Home: The CIO in World War II* (Cambridge, England: Cambridge University Press, 1982), pp. 148–149.

91. Judith Stepan-Norris & Maurice Zeitlin, "'Red Unions' and 'Bourgeois' Contracts? The Effects of Political Leadership on the 'Political Regime of production'," *American Journal of Sociology*, Vol. 96, no. 5 (March 1991), pp. 1184–1188.

92. Clifford McAvoy to Louis Budenz, January 29, 1945, in the Earl Browder Papers, Syracuse University, cited in Starobin, *American Communism in Crisis*, p. 258.

93. Rosenberg Interview.

94. *War Labor Reports*, vol. 28, Bureau of National Affairs, Washington, DC, 1946, General Electric Co. and Westinghouse and UERMWA (CIO), Case nos. 111–17208–D and 111–17204–D, November 27, 1945, pp. 357–359.

95. *UE News*, August 18, 1945, p. 5.

96. "Resolution: Women's Wage Differential," May 25, 1941, UE District 6, quoted in Ruth Milkman, *Gender at Work: The Dynamics of Job Segregation by Sex During World War II* (Urbana, IL: University of Illinois Press, 1987), pp. 51, 78.

97. "History of UE Local 601," UE Archives, District 6, ff 320b; *War Labor Board Reports*, Vol. 28, p. 690; "Program of Local 601 for Women Workers of Westinghouse, to be submitted to Westinghouse Conference," October 1941, UE Archives, District 6, ff 310; *Proceedings*, 1941 UE Convention, p. 184; Milkman, *Gender at Work*, p. 78; Schatz, *The Electrical Workers*, pp. 30–31, 121–127; Donald T. Critchlow, "Communist Unions and Racism: A Comparative Study of the Responses of the United Electrical Radio and Machine Workers and the National Maritime Union to the Black Question During World War II," *Labor History*, Vol. 17, No. 2 (Spring 1976), pp. 231–233.

98. UE, *UE Guide to Wage Payment Plans, Time Study, and Job Evaluation* (1943), cited in Milkman, *Gender at Work*, p. 79; "Women Doing Men's Work at Lower Pay in Transmitter," *Electrical Union News*, UE Archives, District 3, ff 237; *UE News*, July 15, 1944, p. 12.

99. *War Labor Board Report*, Vol. 28, pp. 357–359, 668, 680, 683, 686; Milkman, *Gender at Work*, p. 80.

100. *UE News*, January 5, 1946, p. 3, March 23, 1946, p. 1; May 11, 1946, pp. 5, 12; Milkman, *Gender at Work*, pp. 148–149; "Against the Mainstream: Interview with James Matles of the UE," *Studies on the Left*, vol. 5 (Winter 1965), p. 45; In addition to the 18.5 cent increase at General Electric, UE negotiated a 4.5 cent increase for two-thirds of the company's female employees. At Westinghouse the contract called for an 18 cents increase, with an additional cent per hour per worker to be applied to reducing the female differential. General Motors agreed to an identical minimum hiring rate for men and women in its electrical division.

101. Milkman, *Gender at Work*, p. 89.

102. *St. Louis American*, April 2, 1943, p. 1, cited in Feurer, "William Sentner, the UE, and Civic Unionism in St. Louis," p. 115.

103. Schatz, *The Electrical Workers*, pp. 106–132; Critchlow, "Communist Unions and Racism," pp. 231–237.

104. James Matles, *UE: The Members Run This Union: An Answer to the Saturday Evening Post* (UE Pamphlet Series, 1947), pp. 24, 26.

105. *UE News*, August 18, 1945, p. 5; Matles and Higgins, *Them and Us*, p. 138.

106. Carey Interview, pp. 160–162.

107. *UE News*, September 29, 1945, p. 3.

108. *UE News*, October 6, 1945, p. 7.

109. Philip Taft, *Organized Labor in American History* (New York: Harper and Row, 1964), p. 600.

110. *UE News*, October 13, 1945, p. 7.

111. *UE News*, September 15, 1945, p. 1.

112. *UE News*, September 22, 1945, p. 7.

113. *UE News*, December 8, 1945, p. 8.

114. *New York Times*, December 4, 1945, p. 1.

115. "Minutes, UE General Executive Board," December 6, 7, 1945. UE National Office Records, UEA.

116. *New York Times*, December 4, 1945, p. 1.

117. *New York Times*, December 5, 1945, p. 1.

118. "Minutes, UE General Executive Board," December 6, 7, 1945. UE National Office Records, UEA.

119. *UE News*, December 22, 1945, p. 1.

Chapter 4

1. Klehr and Haynes, *The American Communist Movement*, p. 101.

2. *Political Affairs*, September 1946, p. 795; Starobin, *American Communism in Crisis*, p. 138.

3. U.S., Department of Labor, *Monthly Labor Review*, May, 1946, p. 883; Taft, Organized Labor in American History, p. 567.

4. Irving Howe and B. J. Widick, *The UAW and Walter Reuther* (New York: Random House, 1949); Taft, *Organized Labor in American History*, p. 70; Art Preis, *Labor's Giant Step* (New York: Pathfinder, 1964), p. 262.

5. *New York Times*, March 11, 1946, p. 1.

6. Preis, *Labor's Giant Step*, p. 269.

7. *New York Times*, January 16, 1946, p. 1.

8. Preis, *Labor's Giant Step*, pp. 269–279; Taft, *Organized Labor in American History*, p. 570.

9. *New York Times*, January 27, 1946, p. 1.

10. *UE News*, February 16, 1946, p. 1; *New York Times*, February 13, 1946, p. 1.

11. Preis, *Labor's Giant Step*, p. 279.

12. *New York Times*, February 16, 1946. p. 1.

13. *New York Times*, March 14, 1946, p. 1.

14. *New York Times*, March 15, 1946, p. 1; *New York Times*, May 11, 1946, p. 1.

15. Preis, *Labor's Giant Step*, pp. 281, 282; At the eight-day convention of the UAW in March 1946, Murray appeared in person to throw his support behind Thomas. Even so, Reuther won by 124 votes out of 8,800 cast.

16. *UE News*, March 16, 1946, p. 3; FBI Report, "Ernest DeMaio," 10/11/43, File 100–35152–33, FBI Archives. The FBI report on Anthony DeMaio contained the information that he had allegedly shot to death American and Canadian members of the Abraham Lincoln Brigade in a Barcelona cafe to prevent their exposure of Communist atrocities.

17. *New York Times*, April 8, 1946, p. 15.

18. UE, *In Defense of Labor* (UE Pamphlet Series, 1952), p. 43.

19. DeMaio Interview, pp. 83–84.

20. *Steel Labor*, June, 1946, p. 4.

21. Rice to Darby, June 13, 1946. Rice Papers.

22. Darby to Rice, June 14, 1946. Rice Papers.

23. Block Interview, p. 29.

24. *New York Times*, June 7, 1947, p. 3.

25. William Bailey and Howard Kelly to "to whom it may concern," September 1, 1942, UEA, District 7, Local 801, ff 993.

26. "Special Meeting," Statement by Lem Markland, District 7, Local

801, ff 1009; Arthur Garfield to James Matles, March 8, 1943, District 7, Local 801, ff 1009; Arthur Garfield to Robert Elsner, March 18, 1943, District 7, Local 801, ff 985; Robert Elsner to James Matles, April 30, 1946, District 7, Local 801, ff 987, all in UEA.

27. *New York Times*, July 23, 1946, p. 23.

28. *New York Times*, August 20, 1946, p. 19.

29. "Thoroughly disgusted group of UE Members in Hartford to General Officers," November 27, 1942, UE District 2, ff 89; Richard Linsley to Julius Emspak, October 30, 1944, UE District 2, ff 81, both in UE Archives.

30. Schatz, "Connecticut's Working Class in the 1950s . . . ," p. 83; Seaton, *Catholics and Radicals*, p. 172; Amy Heller, "The Perennial Nightmare": Anti-communism Inside and Outside UE Local 203, Bridgeport, 1944–1950," Unpublished paper, UEA; Rosswurm, "The Catholic Church and the Left-Led Unions," in Rosswurn, ed. *The CIO's Left-Led Unions*, pp. 127–128; In 1944 the right-wing president of the local appointed a political action committee of five opponents of CIO-PAC. "Connecticut May–June Report," July 1, 1944, Charles Rivers Collection, Scrapbook 1, NYU.

31. UE District 2, "Statement of Policy," August 3, 1946. Block Papers.

32. *New York Times*, August 12, 1946, p. 14; UE Local 105 Executive Board Minutes, August 14, 1946, IUE Local 105 Papers, Box 1, TUL; IUE Local 801 Executive Board Minutes, November 13, 1946, IUE Local 801 Papers, File 8, WSUL.

33. William C. Pratt, "The Socialist Party, Socialist Unionists, and Organized Labor, 1936–1950," *Political Power and Social Theory*, Vol. 4 (1984), Maurice Zeitlin and Howard Kimmeldorf, eds. (Greenwich, CT: JAI Press, 1985), pp. 63–100.

34. Sam Horn to Arthur G. McDowell, April 30, 1940, Socialist Party Papers, reel 38; Pratt, "The Socialist Party, Socialist Unionists, and Organized Labor," in Zeitlin, *Political Power and Social Theory*, p. 94

35. William Becker to Victor Reuther, July 12, 1946, Socialist Party Papers, Reel 55; William Becker to William Gausmann, July 19, 1946, Socialist Party Papers, Reel 55; Pratt, "The Socialist Party, Socialist Unionists, and Organized Labor," in Zeitlin, *Political Power and Social Theory*, p. 82.

36. William Becker to Socialists in UER-CIO, August 1946, Socialist Party Papers, Reel 55; "Confidential Memorandum," [circa 1947], Socialist Party papers, Reel 541; Pratt, "The Socialist Party, Socialist Unionists, and Organized Labor," in Zeitlin, *Political Power and Social Theory*, p. 82.

37. Fitzgerald to All Local Unions, August 13, 1946. Block Papers.

38. Seaton, *Catholics and Radicals*, pp. 197–199.

39. John Byrne to Rice, not dated. Rice Papers.

40. Gojack to Matles, August 30, 1946. UEA, District 9, ff 57; Gojack to All Local Unions and Staff Members in District 9, September 6, 1946. Block Papers.

41. "Minutes, UE General Executive Board Meeting," September 7, 14, 1946. UE National Office Records, UEA.

42. James Matles, "Report of the UE Director of Organization for the Months of August, September and October, 1946." UE National Office Records, UEA and Block Papers; "Disruption in District Eight, A Report by Robert B. Logsdon on the Activities of UE Members for Democratic Action," September 20, 1947. Sentner Papers, Series 1, Box 4, ff 8. WUL.

43. *New York Times*, November 17, 1946, p. 5; Clipping [paper not identified], "Charges Reds Wrecking UE," UE Archives, UE District 6, ff 63.

44. "Report of the General Officers to the 11th International Convention of UE," *Proceedings*, 1946 UE Convention, pp. 1–30.

45. Block Interview, p. 19.

46. *New York Times*, September 10, 1946, p. 3; *New York Times*, September 11, 1946, p. 2; *Proceedings*, 1946 UE Convention, p. 229.

47. *Ibid.*, pp. 236–253; After the disappointing results of the 1946 convention, UEMDA met in Dayton, Ohio, to draw up a trade-union program to complement their anti-communism. They came up with organizing the unorganized, more aggressive union actions, support for the re-election of CIO president Philip Murray, a shorter work week, and the guaranteed annual wage. The effort proved disappointing and was more or less wasted. UEMDA did little to push or publicize the program. Seaton, *Catholics and Radicals*, p. 200.

48. *New York Times*, September 11, 1946, p. 2.

49. *Ibid.*; *Proceedings*, 1946 UE Convention, p. 59.

50. Curtis MacDougall, *Gideon's Army*, Vol. 1 (New York: Marzani & Munsell, 1965), p. 109; Starobin, *American Communism in Crisis*, p. 147.

51. *Proceedings*, 1946 UE Convention, p. 119.

52. *Ibid.*, pp. 152, 157, 161; *UE News*, September 21, 1946, pp. 1, 12.

53. *UE News*, September 28, 1946, p. 1; *Proceedings*, 1946 UE Convention, p. 111.

54. *UE News*, September 21, 1946, p. 11.

55. *Proceedings*, 1946 UE Convention, p. 288; John Gojack, "Summary of the 11th International UE Convention," (unpublished report). Block Papers.

56. *UE News*, October 17, 1946, p. 3.

57. *UE News*, September 28, 1946, pp. 1, 5.

58. *Ibid.* The 1946 UE convention called for the establishment of a "People's Party in 1948 if the two major parties refused to heed the will of the American people." This predated the December 1947 meeting called by the Communist Party to instruct the CP labor leaders on the decision to support a third party.

59. "Minutes, District Council 4 Executive Board," September 23, 1946. Block Papers.

60. Kampelman, *Communist Party vs. the CIO*, p. 129.

61. "Disruption in District Eight, A Report by Robert B. Logsdon on the Activities of the UE Members for Democratic Action," September 20, 1947, p. 1. Sentner Papers, Series 1, Box 4, ff 8. WUL.

62. *New York times*, November 16, 1946, p. 1; Taft, *Organized Labor in American History*, pp. 624. 625.

63. *Proceedings*, 1946 CIO Convention, p. 112.

64. *New Leader*, March 1, 1946, p. 5.

65. Robert Bendiner, "CIO Tightrope Act," *Nation*, Vol 63 (November 30, 1946), p. 601.

66. *Proceedings*, 1946 CIO Convention, p. 114; Starobin, *American Communism in Crisis*, pp. 147–148; Matles later claimed that Emil Rieve and George Baldanzi of the Textile Workers, who were then heading the CIO's Southern Organizing Drive, put pressure on Murray to support the "resent and reject" resolution on communism because they believed that they couldn't organize the South without it. Matles and Higgins, *Them and Us*, pp. 161, 162.

67. *Proceedings*, 1946 CIO Convention, *Ibid.*

68. *Ibid.*, p. 112.

69. *Ibid.*, pp. 112–113.

70. *Ibid.*, pp. 111–114.

71. John Cort, "The CIO Convention," *Commonweal*, XXXXV (December 13, 1946), p. 231.

72. *UE News*, November 2, 1946, p. 8.

73. Seaton, *Catholics and Radicals*, p. 200.

74. *Labor Leader*, December 13, 1946, p. 3.

75. *New York Times*, December 22, 1946, p. 29.

76. *Boston Traveler*, February 10, 1947, pp. 1, 8; UE Archives, UE District 2, ff 84.

77. *Labor Leader*, December 27, 1946, p. 1.

78. Seaton, *Catholics and Radicals*, p. 208.

79. Charles Rivers to Julius Emspak, February 21, 1942, UE Archives, O–1181; Heller, "The Perennial Nightmare, p. 1; Rivers was speaking of organizing workers in a large electrical plant while preventing the various factions from going to war with each other.

80. U.S. Congress, House, Committee on Un-American Activities, *Hearings, Regarding Communism in the United States*, 80th Cong., 1st Sess., 1946, pp. 148–149.

81. *UE News*, February 15, 1947, pp. 4, 5; "Minutes, UE General Executive Board," February 10–11, 1947. UE National Records, UEA.

82. Fitzgerald to Berescik and Julianelle, February 4, 1947, reprinted in *UE News*, February 15, 1947. p. 4; "Minutes, UE General Executive Board," February 10–11, 1947. UE National Office Records, UEA; Seaton, *Catholics and Radicals*, p. 208.

83. *New York Times*, February 11, 1947, p. 22; James Matles to International Staff Members in New England, February 7, 1947, UEA. District 2, ff 44; "Minutes, UE General Executive Board," February 10–11, 1947. UE National Office Records, UEA; Paul Seymour to Julius Emspak, February 21, 1947. UE Archives, District 2, ff 54.

84. *UE News*, February 15, 1947, p. 4; *Labor Leader*, February, 28, 1947, p. 4.

85. *New York Times*, March 27, 1947, p. 2.

86. U.S. Congress, House, Committee on Un-American Activities, *Hearings, Regarding Communism in the United States*, 80th Cong., 1st Sess., 1947, p. 171.

87. *Bridgeport Telegram*, August 9, 1944, UEA, District 2–215; *Bridgeport Post*, October 29, 1944; *Bridgeport Sunday Herald*, December 24, 1944, all cited in Heller, "The Perennial Nightmare," pp. 16, 19, 20. (Unpublished term paper, Yale University), Copy in UEA.

88. U.S. Congress, House, Committee on Un-American Activities, *The CIO Political Action Committee,* Report No. 1311, 78th Cong., 2d Sess., 1944, pp. 44–50; Haynes, *Dubious Alliance,* p. 157–159.

89. DeMaio Interview, pp. 62–65.

90. Kampelman, *Communist Party vs. the CIO,* p. 115; Haynes, *Ibid.*

91. U.S. Congress, House, Committee on Un-American Activities, *The CIO Political Action Committee,* Report No. 1311, 78th Cong., 2d Sess., 1944, p. 66; Kampelman, *Communist Party vs. the CIO,* p. 113.

92. U.S. Congress, House, Committee on Un-American Activities, *Hearings, Regarding Communist in Labor Unions in the United States,* 80th Cong., 1st Sess., 1947, pp. 128–140.

93. Haynes, *Dubious Alliance,* pp. 144–172.

94. Philip Taft, *The Structure of Government of Labor Unions* (Cambridge, MA: Harvard University Press, 1954), pp. 199–205; After Curran broke with the left wing, he, with Murray's support, and the help of Michael Quill, another left-wing defector of the Transport Workers Union, carried out a thorough purge of all left-wing elements in the NMU.

95. *UE News,* March 15, 1947, p. 10.

96. "Statement from Harry Block to Committee Investigating Article in the UE News." Block Papers.

97. *UE News,* April 5, 1947, p. 9.

98. *New York Times,* February 11, 1947, p. 22.

99. *Labor Leader,* January 17, 1947, p. 2.

100. "Comrade Juniper" became something of a celebrity after Louis Budenz mentioned him in testimony before HUAC. According to Budenz, Juniper was the secret party name for Julius Emspak. Juniper was supposedly the only higher-up in the Communist Party whose identity was not known even to many in the higher councils of the party. U.S. Congress, House, Committee on Education and Labor, *Hearings, Investigation of Communist Infiltration of UERMWA,* 80th Cong., 2d Sess., 1948, pp. 352–356; The only other reference to a secret, high placed Communist labor leader who might have been "Juniper" came during a debate on the Duclos letter at the party's National Board meeting on June 2, 1945, when one of the leading Communists to take part was referred to in the minutes only as "Comrade J." Starobin, *American Communism in Crisis,* p. 87.

101. Joseph Alsop and Stewart Alsop, "Will the CIO Shake the Communists Loose?" Part 1, *Saturday Evening Post,* Vol. 219 (February 22,

1947), pp. 15–16, 105–106, 108; Part 2, *Saturday Evening Post*, Vol. 219 (March 1, 1947), pp. 26, 117, 118.

102. *New York Times*, February 23, 1947, p. E7.

103. "Address of Albert Fitzgerald to the Semi-Annual Convention of UE District 9," March 28, 1947. Block Papers.

104. *New York Times*, February 28, 1947, p. 4.

105. *New York Times*, March 14, 1947, p. 16.

106. *UE News*, March 22, 1947, p. 1

107. *UE News*, June 21, 1947, p. 5.

108. *UE News*, July 19, 1947, p. 5.

109. U.S. Congress House Committee on Un-American Activities, *Hearings, Regarding Communism in the Labor Movement in the United States*, 80th Cong., 1st Sess., 1947, p. 145.

110. *Ibid.*, pp. 176–177.

111. *Ibid.*, pp. 154–158; As a footnote to the Berescik and Julianelle testimony, the members of the Bridgeport Local 203 voted both out of office in favor of a group of pro-administration candidates in December. The victory followed a split between the men over charges by Berescik that Julianelle was trying to turn the local into a company union and was collaborating with the bosses. In reply, Julianelle charged Berescik with "gang control" of the local. *UE News*, December 20, 1947, pp. 1, 10.

112. *Ibid.*, p. 219.

113. *Ibid.*, p. 193.

114. *UE News*, August 2, 1947, p. 3.

115. John Carrington to Harry Block, August 26, 1946. Block Papers.

116. Block to Carrington, August 20, 1946. Block Papers.

117. Block Interview, p. 24.

118. Kampelman, *Communist Party vs. the CIO*, pp.. 131–132.

119. *New York Times*, August 26, 1946, p. 12.

120. "Disruption in District Eight, A Report by Robert B. Logsdon on the Activities of the UE Members for Democratic Action," September 20, 1947, p. 6. Sentner Papers, Series 1, Box 4, ff 8. WUL.

121. "Minutes, UE General Executive Board," August 7, 1947. Block Papers and UE Archives.

122. *New York Times,* June 5, 1947, p. 1.

123. Preis, *Labor's Giant Step,* p. 316.

124. "Minutes, UE General Executive Board," June 28, 1947. UE National Office Records, UEA.

125. Preis, *Labor's Giant Step,* p. 318; *Proceedings,* 1947 CIO Convention, pp. 202, 203.

126. *Ibid.,* p. 317; Preis, *Labor's Giant Step,* p. 317.

127. Preis, *Labor's Giant Step,* p. 318.

128. Schatz, *The Electrical Workers,* p. 179.

129. Matles and Higgins, *Them and Us,* p. 170.

130. *Bridgeport Herald,* July 6, 1947, reprinted in *UE News,* July 19, 1947, p. 5.

131. *CIO News,* January 28, 1947, p. 1.

132. *New York Times,* March 13, 1947, p. 1.

133. "Minutes, UE District Council 6," March 23, 1947. Rice Papers; *UE News,* March 29, 1947, p. 7.

134. *UE News,* March 29, 1947, p. 7.

135. *UE News,* March 17, 1947, p. 3.

136. "Inside the CIO," *New Republic,* Vol. 116 (March 24, 1947), pp. 38, 39.

137. Carey to Mrs. James Pascoe, April 3, 1947. Block Papers.

138. *Labor Leader,* April 30, 1947, p. 1; *Pittsburgh Press,* April 16, 1947, p. 1; McGeever, *The Rev. Charles Owen Rice.* p. 106.

139. *Pittsburgh Press,* August 10, 1947, p. 1.

140. Rice to Bishop Hugh Boyle, June 7, 1947. Rice Papers; ACTU was becoming an increasing powerful adversary. Often, as in the case of Father Rice, they were out in the open; however, this was not always true. In St. Louis the Reverend Leo Brown led the ACTU forces from behind the scenes with no exposure. Leo Brown to Rice, June 18, 1946, Rice Papers; McGeever, *The Rev. Charles Owen Rice,* pp. 115–116.

141. *Labor Leader,* May 30, 1947, p. 1.

142. *New York Times,* June 28, 1947, p. 7; UE Local 105 General Membership Minutes, May 16, 1947. IUE Local 105 Papers, Box 1. TUL; *Labor Leader,* July 25, 1947, p. 1.

143. Matles and Higgins, *Them and Us*, p. 170.

144. *New York Times*, September 23, 1947, p. 7.

145. *Proceedings*, 1947 UE Convention, pp. 79, 80.

146. John Gojack, "Summary of the 12th International UE Convention, 1947." Block Papers; *New York Times*, September 22, 1947, p. 10.

147. Starobin, *American Communism in Crisis*, pp. 109,: Freeman, *In Transit*, p. 292; Norman Markowitz, *The Rise and Fall of the People's Century: Henry A. Wallace and American Liberalism, 1941–1948* (New York: Free Press, 1973), pp. 200–265; MacDougall, *Gideon's Army*, Vol. 1, pp. 172–175; Nevertheless, talk of an independent third party candidacy by Wallace was discussed at the District Council 7 PAC Conference held on December 14, 1947. "Minutes," District Council 7 PAC Conference, December 14, 1947. IUE Local 755 Papers, Box 31, file 2.

148. Starobin, *American Communism in Crisis*, p. 170; Klehr and Haynes, *The American Communist Movement*, p. 114; The Popular Front alliance started to weaken in the middle of 1945 when the publication of the "Duclos Letter" in a French Communist theoretical journal revealed that the Soviet Union no longer sanctioned American Communist Party chairman Earl Browder's policy of blending the Communist movement into mainstream American politics. With Browder's fall the Communist Political Association reverted to its prior title of Communist Party and the American Youth for Democracy re-emerged as the Young Communist League. This change did not end the Popular Front, but dramatically altered the demands Communists made on their allies. After 1945 allies were expected to oppose Truman's anti-Soviet foreign policy and the front's defense of the Soviet Union became increasingly strident. Haynes, *Dubious Alliance*, pp. 126, 127.

149. *UE News*, October 4, 1947, p. 3.

150. *New York Times*, September 22, 1947, p. 10.

151. "UEMDA Statement to the 1947 UE Convention" (unpublished report). Block Papers.

152. *Proceedings*, 1947 UE Convention, pp. 171, 177, 183; *UE News*, October 4, 1947, p. 2; Nor did the left-wing convention victory have much effect on its opponents. Local 105 in Philadelphia simply voted to disregard the constitutional amendments passed at the convention. UE Local 105 Executive Board Minutes, October 15, 1947. IUE Local 105 Papers, Box 1, TUL.

153. *New York Times*, September 26, 1947, p. 19; One scholar estimates that under the three major government personnel security programs—the Industrial Personnel Security Program, the Atomic Energy

Commission Program, and the Port Security Program—plus the private industry security program, some 6,000 workers failed to get clearance to work in classified areas. Many of these lost their jobs. Caute, *The Great Fear*, pp. 364, 373.

154. Preis, *Labor's Giant Step*, p. 340; *Proceedings*, 1947 CIO Convention, pp. 274–276.

155. *New York Times*, October 16, 1947, pp. 1, 3.

156. *Proceedings*, 1947 CIO Convention, p. 202.

157. *Labor Leader*, October 31, 1947, p. 1.

158. *New York Times*, October 17, 1947, p. 1; Matles Interview, p. 68. Another explanation put forth for Murray's decision not to sign the noncommunist affidavit was the decision of his old mentor, and new competitor, John L. Lewis not to sign. Lewis had attacked the AFL leadership for signing and pulled his miners out of the Federation. James Matles believed that Lewis's action had considerable influence on Murray.

159. *Proceedings*, 1947 CIO Convention, p. 197.

160. Preis, *Labor's Giant Step*, p. 320; *New York Times*, November 1, 1947, p. 1.

161. *New York Times*, November 11, 1947, p. 1.

162. *Pittsburgh Catholic*, November 20, 1947, p. 11. Rice Papers.

163. *New York Times*, December 11, 1947, p. 11.

164. *Ibid*.

165. Schatz, *The Electrical Workers*, pp. 148–149, 151, 168–169, 199; Herbert Northrup, *Boulwarism: The Labor Relations Policies of the General Electric Company* (Ann Arbor, MI: Bureau of Industrial Relations, University of Michigan, 1964), pp. 25–38.

Chapter 5

1. For a thorough explanation of American labor's role in the reconstruction of the labor movements in Western Europe see, Frederico Romero, *The United States and the European Trade Union Movement* (Chapel Hill: Univeristy of North Carolina Press, 1992); Ronald Filippelli, *American Labor and Postwar Italy* (Stanford, CA: Stanford University Press, 1989); Roy Godson, *American Labor and European Politics* (Los Angeles: Crane, Russak and Co., 1976); Ronald Radosh, *American Labor and Foreign Policy* (New York: Random House, 1969).

2. Freeman, *In Transit*, p. 292, 496fn; Levenstein, *Communism*,

Anti-Communism, and the CIO, pp. 260–261; Starobin, *The Crisis of American Communism*, p. 176, 293fn.

3. *UE News*, January 3, 1948, p. 2.

4. "Minutes, CIO Executive Board," January 22–23, 1948, pp. 12–244, CIO Executive Board Minutes, Reel 4, ALHUA; *New York Times*, January 23, 1948, p. 1.

5. *Labor Leader*, January 31, 1948, p. 1.

6. "Minutes, CIO Executive Board," pp. 12–244; CIO Executive Board Minutes, Reel 4, ALHUA; *UE News*, January 31, 1948, p. 3.

7. Preis, *Labor's Giant Step*, p. 345.

8. *New York Times*, March 25, 1948, p. 1.

9. "Minutes, CIO Executive Board," January 22–23, 1948, pp. 12–244. CIO Executive Board Minutes, Reel 4, ALHUA; Klehr and Haynes, *The American Communist Movement*, pp. 116–117; Levenstein, *Communism, Anti-Communism, and the CIO*, pp. 244–245; O.J. Dekom, "The Washington Reporter," *Plain Talk*, April 1948, p. 34.

10. Klehr and Haynes, *The American Communist Movement*, pp. 117–118; According to Matles, the members weren't so much pro-Truman as they were anti-Wallace. Matles Interview, p. 69.

11. "Minutes, Meeting of the Voluntary Association of the UE Independent Political Committee of Ohio and Kentucky, June 14, 1948." IUE Local 755 Papers, Box 31, ff 2; "Minutes, Executive Board Meeting, October 27, 1948." IUE Local 755 Papers, Box 5, ff 6; "Minutes, Membership Meeting, February 18, 1948." IUE Local 768 Papers, ff 2 & 3; "Minutes, Executive Board Meeting, June 17, 1948." IUE Local 768 Papers, ff 2 & 3; "Minutes, Special Executive Board Meeting, October 22, 1948." IUE Local 801 Papers, ff 8; "Minutes, Membership Meeting, January 5, 1949." IUE Local 801 Papers, ff 9. All in WSU.

12. Emspak and Fitzgerald to Murray, March 11, 1948. UEA.

13. "Minutes, UE General Executive Board," March 11–12, 1948. UE National Office Records, UEA; *New York Times*, March 12, 1948, p. 16.

14. "Minutes, UE General Executive Board," March 11–12, 1948. UE National Office Records, UEA; *New York Times*, March 15, 1948, p. 24.

15. *New York Times*, March 16, 1948, p. 10.

16. *UE News*, March 20, 1948, p. 1; An extensive discussion on the issue of freedom of speech in the CIO with regard to political action took place at the August meeting of the CIO Executive Board with Fitzgerald making a strong statement in favor of autonomy on the part of the affili-

ates. "Minutes, CIO Executive Board, August 30, September 1, 1948." CIO Executive Board Minutes, Reel 4, ALHUA.

17. *New York Times*, January 3, 1948, p. 5; January 14, 1948, p. 14; *New Leader*, January 3, 1948, p. 15.

18. *Labor Leader*, February 18, 1948, p. 4.

19. Haywood to Bridges, February 18, 1948, cited in Taft, *Organized Labor in American History*, p. 626; Freeman, *In Transit*, p. 294; Levenstein, *Communism, Anti-Communism, and the CIO*, pp. 225–226; McGeever, *The Rev. Charles Owen Rice*, p. 115.

20. *Labor Leader*, February 29, 1948, p. 3.

21. "Minutes, UE General Executive Board, March 11–12, 1948." UE National Office Records, UEA; Kampelman, *Communist Party vs. the CIO*, pp. 156–158.

22. *Steel Labor*, June, 1948, p. 1.

23. *New York Times*, June 25, 1948, p. 28.

24. *CIO News*, September 6, 1948, p. 5.

25. Fitzgerald Interview, p. 17.

26. Rice Interview, pp. 21, 22; McGeever, *Rev. Charles Owen Rice*, p. 119; Harry Block denied that the UEMDA or ACTU received money from the United Steelworkers. He claimed that the only assistance came in the form of Carey's CIO salary. The rest of the money came from the proceeds of "fifty-fifty raffles" which UEMDA ran to finance its organizers. Block Interview, p. 25.

27. "Minutes, UE District Council 1, January 8, 1948." Block Papers.

28. Stanley Loney to Members, January 30, 1948, District 6, ff 5; Thomas Fitzpatrick to Julius Emspak, December 10, 1947, District 6, ff 100; Stanley Loney to Julius Emspak, December 14, 1948, ff 107; "Findings as to John Duffy," District 6, ff 107; "Minutes, UE General Executive Board, September 4, 1948, December 11, 1948." UE National Office Records, UEA.

29. *UE News*, February 14, 1948, p. 7; Seaton, *Catholics and Radicals*, p. 215.

30. *New York Times*, March 16, 1948, p. 24; Seaton, *Catholics and Radicals, Ibid.*

31. Rice Interview, p. 25.

32. UE Organizational Report, February–April, 1948, May–July, 1948. UE National Office Records, UEA; Frank Cormier and William J. Eaton, *Reuther* (Englewood Cliffs, NJ: Prentice Hall, 1971), p. 253.

33. *New York Times*, March 20, 1948, pp. 1, 14.

34. *New York Times*, March 21, 1948, p. 39.

35. *Ibid.*; "Minutes, UE General Executive Board, March 12, 1948." UE National Office Records, UEA.

36. *Ibid.*

37. *Ibid.*

38. *New York Times*, March 23, 1948, p. 28.

39. *New York Times*, March 25, 1948, p. 22.

40. *New York Times*, April 11, 1948, p. 36.

41. Frank Dombrowski, President, Local 51, UAW-CIO to Walter Reuther, April 7, 1948. UEA.

42. Dave Miller, President, Local 22, UAW-CIO to Albert Fitzgerald, April 10, 1948. UEA; UE Organizational Report, February–April, 1948. UE National Office Records, UEA.

43. *New York Times*, April 2, 1948, p. 15.

44. *New York Times*, April 19, 1948, p. 15.

45. UE Organizational Report, Feb–April, 1948, November–December, 1948. UE National Office Records, UEA; *UE News*, April 3, 1948, p. 4.

46. *Ibid.*; *UE News*, May 22, 1948, p. 5.

47. *UE News*, June 12, 1948, p. 7.

48. *UE News*, June 26, 1948, p. 8.

49. UE Organizational Reports, 1947–1949. UE National Office Records, UEA.

50. *UE News*, August 7, 1948, p. 4.

51. *Hoover Company Pamphlet*, May 5, 1948. Rice Papers.

52. Felix Hinkle, "One Man's Opinion," *Canton Public Opinion*, April 30, 1948. Clipping in Rice Papers.

53. "Minutes, District Council 1," October 7, 1948. Block Papers.

54. *Ibid.*

55. IUE Local 768 Executive Board Minutes, April 1, 1948, ff 2 & 3. WSU.

56. Fitzgerald Interview, p. 21.

57. Charles Owen Rice, "How to De-Control Your Union of Communists," (pamphlet). Rice Papers.

58. Matles to General Executive Board Members, September 21, 1948. PM-151, UEA.

59. *UE News*, March 6, 1948, p. 8.

60. "Minutes, District Council 1," August 12, 1948, Block Papers.

61. Fitzgerald to Truman, August 30, 1948, reprinted in *UE News*, September 4, 1948, p. 10.

62. W. Manly Sheppard, Clerk, House Committee on Education and Labor, to Fitzgerald, August 23, 1948. UEA.

63. *New York Times*, August 31, 1948, p. 1.

64. Block Interview, p. 49; Not all of the right-wing locals saw this in the same light. The executive board of Local 801 in Dayton authorized the sending of a telegram to the Kersten Committee condemning the investigation of union officials during the period of a national convention. IUE Local 801 Executive Board Minutes, September 1, 1948. IUE Local 801 Papers, ff 8. WSU.

65. Under Hoover's custodial detention program begun in 1939, persons whose presence at liberty constituted a menace to the "public peace and safety of the United States Government," were subject to forced detention. In 1943, Attorney General Francis Biddle ordered immediate cessation of the program, but Hoover reinstituted it under a new name—the Security Index. U.S. Senate, Select Committee to Study Governmental operations with Respect to Intelligence Activities, Hearings, 94th Cong. 1st Sess., 1975, Vol. 6, *Federal Bureau of Investigation* (Washington: GPO, 1975), pp. 409–411, 412–427, 645–668.

66. J. Edgar Hoover to SAC, FBI, Seattle, January 7, 1942; J. Edgar Hoover to SAC, New York, January 28, 1942, File 62–62426; Correlation Summary, December 9, 1960, Main File 962–62426, James Barron Carey, p. 24; E.A. Tamm to J. Edgar Hoover, March 14, 1944, File 62–62426; Correlation Summary, December 9, 1960, Main File 962–62426, p. 45; Memo, August 24, 1948, August 31, 1948, File 62–62426; Memo, A. H. Belmont to D. M. Ladd, January 7, 1954, File 62–62426; Hoover to Clyde Tolson, April 13, 1949, File 62–62426. FBI Archives. Throughout their relationship, Carey cautioned Hoover to keep their contacts secret because its revelation would be fatal to his efforts in UE. Carey's meetings with Hoover and his staff, as well as FBI meetings with Carey's staff at the CIO, continued until 1953, when the men had a falling out over public statements by Carey that were critical of Hoover. Carey tried hard to restore relations, but Hoover never relented, calling Carey a "Phoney" and an opportunist.

67. "Minutes, District Council 1," September 2, 1948. Block Papers; *UE News*, September 4, 1948, pp. 1, 4.

68. U.S. Congress House Subcommittee of the Committee on Education and Labor, *Hearings, Investigation of Communist Infiltration of UERMWA*, 80th Cong., 2d Sess., 1948, pp. 40, 41.

69. *Ibid.*, p. 11.

70. Block Interview, p. 22; U.S. Congress, House, Subcommittee of the Committee on Education and Labor, *Hearings, Investigation of Communist Infiltration of UERMWA*, 80th Cong., 2d Sess., 1948, pp. 11–13.

71. *Ibid.*, pp. 110, 111; *UE News*, September 11, 1948, p. 3; *Proceedings*, 1948 UE Convention, pp. 110–111.

72. U.S., Congress, Senate, Committee on Labor and Public Welfare, *Hearings, Communist Domination of Unions and National Security*, 82d Cong., 2d Sess., 1952, p. 426; *New York Times*, September 4, 1948, p. 26.

73. *UE News*, July 31, 1948, pp. 1, 6, 7.

74. *CIO News*, September 6, 1948, p. 2.

75. *Proceedings*, 1948 UE Convention, p. 9.

76. Fitzgerald Interview, p. 18; McGeever, *The Rev. Charles Owen Rice*, p. 100.

77. *Proceedings*, 1948 UE Convention, pp. 20, 21, and P. 66 of Appendix 1.

78. *New York Times*, September 8, 1948, p. 1.

79. Matles Interview, p. 69.

80. *Proceedings*, 1948 UE Convention, pp. 46, 47, 59, 66; Carey spoke for the minority resolution. Matles replied that Carey and his supporters had little room to talk since they had repeatedly violated the UE's policy on the matter of the constitutional right of anyone to hold office regardless of political belief.

81. *Ibid.*, p. 93.

82. *New York Times*, September 10, 1948, p. 15.

83. *Proceedings*, 1948 UE Convention, pp. 116–119; *New York Times*, September 9, 1948, p. 16.

84. *New York Times*, September 8, 1948, p. 1; *UE News*, September 11, 1948, p. 9.

85. David Lilienthal to Charles C. Wilson, November 1, 1948, in

U.S. Congress, House, Committee on Un-American Activities, *Hearings, Investigation of Local 601, UERMWA*, 81st Cong., 1st Sess., 1949, pp. 542, 543.

86. U.S., Congress, Senate, Committee on the Judiciary, *Hearings, Subversive Influence of the United Electrical, Radio and Machine Workers of America*, 82d Cong., 2d Sess., 1952, p. 58.

87. Preis, *Labor's Giant Step*, p. 373.

88. Robert Bendiner, "Murray's Limited Purge," *Nation*, Vol. 167 (December 18, 1948), pp. 685–686.

89. Preis, *Labor's Giant Step*, p. 373.

90. *UE News*, December 4, 1948, p. 2.

91. Robert Bendiner, "Showdown in the CIO," *Nation*, Vol. 169 (October 15, 1949), p. 363; *Labor Leader*, January 17, 1949, p. 1.

92. Fitzgerald Interview, p. 28.

93. *Proceedings*, 1947 UE Convention, pp. 23, 31; UE Organizing Report, February–April, 1947, May–July, 1947, September–October, 1947. UE National Office Records, UEA.

94. *Ibid.*, p. 32.

95. *Proceedings*, 1948 UE Convention, p. 42; UE Organizing Report, February–April, 1948, May–July, 1948, November–December, 1948. UE National Office Records, UEA.

96. *Ibid.*, pp. 39, 40.

97. *Ibid.*, p. 21.

98. *Proceedings*, 1947 UE Convention, pp. 26–30.

99. James Youtsler, *Labor's Wage Policies in the Twentieth Century* (New York: Twayne, 1956), pp. 250, 251.

100. *Ibid*; Settlements once again compared favorably to the auto and steel industries where at General Motors six cents were added to base rates and eight cents in cost of living float that could move up or down, and in the steel industry where United States Steel agreed to a package which gave the steelworkers nine and one half cents an hour in general wage increases. Nathan Spero, "The Facts Behind the Fiction in Professor Youtsler's Book: An Expose of the IUE Propaganda by Professor Youtsler in His Book, *Labor's Wage Policies in the Twentieth Century*," (unpublished report by the UE Director of Research). UE National Office Records, "Red Dot," Box 127, file: "UE Publications re IUE [1954–1960], UEA.

101. *Ibid.*

102. *New York Times*, February 17, 1949, p. 20.

103. *Proceedings*, 1948 CIO Convention, pp. 119, 120; Filippelli, *American Labor and Postwar Italy*, pp. 177–180; Romero, *The United States and the European Trade Union Movement*, pp. 131–137.

104. *UE News*, January 1, 1949, p. 10.

105. *District Six Progress*, January, 1949, pp. 6–9. Rice Papers; "Minutes, UE General Executive Board, September 4, 1948, December 10–11, 1948," UE National Office Records, UEA; McGeever, *The Rev. Charles Owen Rice*, p. 119.

106. "Minutes, UE General Executive Board, December 10, 11, 1948." UE National Office Records, UEA.

107. Frank Emspak, "The Breakup of the Congress of Industrial Organizations," Unpublished Ph.D. dissertation, University of Wisconsin, 1972.

108. *New York Times*, May 23, 1948, p. 48; Johnson, "Organized Labor's Postwar Red Scare: The UE in St. Louis," p. 33. Sentner's weakness in his own local stemmed from several sources. Exasperated with the right-wing faction, he had previously tried to expel the local from the district. His involvement with the Wallace campaign in 1948 meant that he was expelled from the CIO's Missouri PAC, and, as an open Communist, he could not sign the Taft-Hartley loyalty oath.

109. "Minutes, UE General Executive Board, September 4, 1948, December 10, 11, 1948." UE National Office Records, UEA.

110. "Statement by Opal Cline," Sept. 30, 1948; William Sentner to Lt. Col. E. H. Farr, Oct. 5, 1948; Helen A. Sage, Memo, quoted in David Caute, *The Great Fear*, pp. 383–384.

111. Joseph Bacon to Father Rice, January 19, 1949. Rice Papers.

112. *Ibid.*

113. "Minutes, District Council 1," March 3, 1949. Block Papers.

114. Rice to Fitzgerald, March 13, 1949. Rice Papers.

115. *Labor Leader*, January 17, 1949, p. 1.

116. *Pittsburgh Press*, April 14, 1949, p. 1.

117. *CIO News*, April 15, 1949, p. 1: *UE News*, May 2, 1949, p. 7.

118. *UE News*, May 2, 1949, p. 7; *Pittsburgh Press*, April 17, 1949, p. 1.

119. *UE News*, April 18, 1949, p. 2.

120. "Minutes, UE General Executive Board, April 24, 1949." UE National Office Records, UEA. FE had been engaged in a jurisdictional battle with the UAW from 1941 on. In that year the UAW added "agricultural implement workers" to its name and its jurisdiction. After World War II, when Walter Reuther came to power, the fight between the left-wing FE and Reuther's UAW became particularly bitter. The UAW launched a massive raiding campaign, particularly at the International Harvester plants. In the spring of 1949, Murray ordered FE to merge with the UAW, but they refused and began merger talks with UE, with whom they later merged. Steve Rosswurm and Toni Gilpin, "The FBI and the Farm Equipment Workers: FBI Surveillance Records as a Source for CIO Union History," *Labor History*, Vol. 27 (Fall 1986), pp. 485–505.

121. *CIO News*, May 23, 1949, p. 3; By fall of 1949, in addition to UE, the CIO left wing unions included the Farm Equipment Workers, the Mine, Mill, and Smelter Workers, the United Office and Professional Workers, the United Public Workers, the American Communications Association, the International Longshormen's and Warehousemen's Union; the National Union of Marine Cooks and Stewards; the Food, Tobacco, Agricultural and Allied Workers Union, and the Fur and Leather Workers Union.

122. *UE News*, April 2, 1949, p. 4; The issue of a merger between the Farm Equipment Workers and the UAW had been ongoing since early 1947 when the Farm Equipment Workers, fearing the effects of the Taft-Hartley Act on their small union, sought a merger with the UAW. At that time, in the midst of the right-left struggle for control of the Auto Workers, the Reuther forces argued against the merger and defeated it. Once Reuther gained effective control of the UA in 1947, serious raids on FE shops and continual jurisdictional battles marked relations between the two unions. The matter was discussed at some length at a CIO Executive Board meeting in November of 1948. "Minutes, CIO Executive Board, November, 1948," pp. 318–358. CIO Executive Board Minutes, Reel 4, ALHUA; Halpern, *UAW Politics in the Cold War Era*, pp. 205–206, 261.

123. *New York Times*, July 28, 1941, p. 1; *New York Times*, July 29, 1949, p. 9.

124. "Minutes, UE District Council 1," August 4, 1949. Block Papers.

125. *UE News*, August 22, 1949, p. 1.

126. *UE News*, August 8, 1949, p. 1.

127. U.S. Congress, House, Committee on Un-American Activities, *Hearings, Investigation of Local 601, UERMWA*, 81st Cong., 1st Sess., 1949, pp. 605, 606; *UE News*, August 24, 1949, p. 4; McGeever, *The Rev. Charles Owen Rice*, pp. 124–125.

128. "Text of a Statement Read in the Pittsburgh Diocese Concerning

the UE Local 601 Election." Rice Papers; "Sunday Bulletin," St. Regis Church, Trafford, Pennsylvania, August 14, 1949. UEA, District 6, ff 12.

129. Charles Newell to National Officers et al, August 16, 1949, UE Archives, District 6, ff 12; McGeever, *The Rev. Charles Owen Rice,* pp. 123, 124; Seaton, *Catholics and Radicals,* pp. 226, 227.

130. Figures compiled by the UE Director of Research, Nathan Spero, from NLRB election reports and from organizers in the field. This information was received from Mr. Spero in conversation with him on April 4, 1969, in New York. He contended that the figures are probably an underestimate.

131. *UE News,* October 3, 1949, p. 6.

132. "Minutes, UE General Executive Board, August 10, 11, 1949." UE National Office Records, UEA.

133. *Ibid.* This turned out to be a tactical error. At its September council meeting, District Council 1 voted by 158 to 149 to instruct its delegates to the convention to vote against the amendment. It was the first right-wing victory in the District since Harry Block's defeat in 1946. One month later Block missed being elected to the post of recording secretary by one vote in an election the right wing claimed had been stolen. "Minutes, District Council 1," September 8, 1949; Block to Price, October 11, 1949; Minutes, District Council 1," October 6, 1949. All in Block Papers.

134. "Minutes, UE General Executive Board, August 10, 11, 1949." UE National Office Records, UEA.

135. "Minutes, District Council 1," September 8, 1949. Block Papers.

136. Ellington Smith, "The Electrical Workers Meet," *New Republic,* Vol. 121 (September 19, 1949), pp. 14, 15.

137. Frank Emspak, "The Breakup of the Congress of Industrial Organizations," pp. 314, 324.

138. *New York Times,* May 8, 1949, p. 42; *New York Times,* May 9, 1949, p. 11.

139. Rice to ACTU-UE members, August, 1949. Rice Papers.

140. *Proceedings,* 1949 UE Convention, p. 44. The 1949 UE wage package offers an interesting study in attitude toward UE. While James Carey called the $500 package "feeble," James Youtsler in his anti-UE book, *Labor's Wage Policies in the Twentieth Century,* termed it "ridiculous," (p. 253) meaning exorbitant and unrealistic. It is interesting that on the same page Youtsler lists IUE demands for 1949 which totaled more the $600. Elsewhere in the book (p. 191) the author cites a UAW demand the same year totaling $620 a year and a USWA demand which totaled $600 per year.

Why he did not find these demands as ridiculous as UE's is something of a mystery.

141. *Ibid.*, p. 48.

142. *Ibid.*, p. 91.

143. *Ibid.*, pp. 103–105; *UE News*, October 3, 1949, p. 2; Matles and Higgins, *Them and Us*, p. 194.

144. *Proceedings*, 1949 UE Convention, p. 44.

145. *Ibid.*, pp. 205–225.

146. *Ibid.*, pp. 147, 156.

147. Block Interview, pp. 34, 35.

148. Fitzgerald Interview, p. 22.

149. *Ibid.*, pp. 25, 26.

150. It is interesting to note that the right wing expected a degree of ethics from the left-wing delegates that it was not willing to exercise itself in the light of Father Rice's pre-convention instructions to the right-wing delegates.

151. Block Interview, pp. 34, 35.

152. Harry Block, "Tentative Draft Report of the UE Convention, 1949" (unpublished report). Block Papers.

153. *Proceedings*, 1949 UE Convention, pp. 147–150. These figures are compiled from the roll call vote totals printed in the convention proceedings and from the locals listed by Harry Block in his "Tentative Report of the UE Convention, 1949," Block Papers.

154. *Ibid.*, p. 200.

155. *UE News*, October 3, 1949, p. 6.

156. *New York Times*, October 18, 1949, p. 30.

157. "Minutes, UE General Executive Board, September 17–18, 1949," UE National Office Records, UEA; *New York Times*, September 24, 1949, p. 5; *UE News*, October 3, 1949, p. 2.

158. *UE News*, October 3, 1949, p. 5; Seaton, *Catholics and Radicals*, p. 227.

159. Les Finnegan to E. J. Kraft, October 14, 1949. District Council 7, IUE: E. J. Kraft, Wesley Steinhilber, Robert Eisner Papers, Box 1, ff 7; "Minutes, Special Executive Board Meeting, October 20, 1949." IUE Local 801 Papers, ff 9, WSU.

160. Emspak to Murray, October 24, 1949. UEA.

161. Fitzgerald Interview, p. 27; Matles Interview, pp. 77, 78; "UE Stewards Bulletin: Report on UE Meeting with Murray," n.d. District Council 7, IUE: E. J. Kraft, Wesley Steinhilber, Robert Eisner Papers, Box 1, ff 8. WSU.

162. Agreements Between United Electrical, Radio, and Machine Workers of America and Congress of Industrial Organizations, United Steelworkers of America, and United Auto Workers, October 30, 1949. Sentner Papers, Series 5, Box 11, ff 2, WUL; Matles Interview, p. 77; "Minutes, UE General Executive Board, October 30, 31, 1949." UE National Office Records, UEA; *UE News*, November 14, 1949, p. 1.

163. "Minutes, UE General Executive Board, December 16, 17, 1949." UE National Office Records, UEA. FE members had voted to join UE in a referendum during the summer of 1949, although the CIO later erroneously claimed that the FE board's decision to join the UE was taken without any sanction from the membership. Sixty three UE charters were issued to FE at the December GEB meeting. UE Organizational Report, August–October 1949, UE Archives; CIO Press Release, October 11, 1949. District Council 7, IUE: E. J. Kraft, Wesley Steinhilber, Robert Eisner Papers, Box 2, ff 2, WSU; *UE News*, November 14, 1949, p. 6.

164. Benjamin Mosse, "Communism at Cleveland," *America*, Vol. 82 (October 22, 1949), pp. 66–68.

165. Robert Bendiner, "Showdown in the CIO," *Nation*, Vol. 169 (October 15, 1949), p. 362.

166. Victor Riesel, "Inside Labor," *New York Post*, October 13, 1949.

167. *Proceedings*, 1949 CIO Convention, pp. 266, 267.

168. *Ibid.*, p. 314. Some 20 years later, in 1968, Walter Reuther withheld per capita payments to the AFL-CIO in a dispute over the goals of the organization. In the same year Reuther's Auto Workers did not attend the AFL-CIO convention in Miami which was to take up the issue of the Auto Workers withholding of per capita. At that convention the UAW was expelled from the Federation. If Reuther remembered his words at the 1949 CIO convention, he must have found them somewhat embarrassing in 1968.

169. *Ibid.*, pp. 302–305.

170. *Ibid.*, p. 359.

171. James Matles to GEB Members, International Representatives, and Field Organizers, November 1, 1949. Sentner Papers, Series 5, Box 11, ff 3, WUL. All of the members of the right-wing "Committee of Ten" which

had been announced after the 1949 UE convention held delegates credentials at the CIO convention in Cleveland.

172. *Ibid.,* pp. 240, 288.

173. *New Leader,* November 19, 1949, p. 1.

Chapter 6

1. Transcript, Oral Interview with Edward Houchins, pp. 4–8. PSU.

2. "Minutes, UE District 7 Executive Board, November 1, 1949." IUE District Council 7, MS–116, WSU.

3. *UE News,* December 17, 1949, p. 5; *IUE-CIO News,* November 21, 1949, p. 3; Bert Cochran, *Labor and Communism: The Conflict That Shaped American Unions,* p. 291; James "Memorandum," December, 1949. Carey Papers, Box 9, Folder 6, ALHUA.

4. *New York Times,* January 8, 1950, p. 31.

5. *IUE-CIO News,* January 3, 1950, p. 15; January 9, 1950, p. 3; James Matles to GE Locals, January 3, 1950. UEA, PM-195.

6. *New York Times,* January 23, 1950, p. 5; Matles to General Vice-presidents, December 7, 1949. UEA, PM-193; UE, Organizational Report, January 21, 1950. UEA Blue Dot Box; "Minutes, UE General Executive Board, December 16, 1949." UE General Office Records, UEA; Julius Emspak to UE Locals, December 27, 1949. UEA, PM-194.

7. *IUE-CIO News,* February 6, 1950, p. 1; February 20, 1950, p. 1; March 26, 1950, p. 1; "Minutes, Local 801 IUE Executive Board, January 26, 1950." IUE Local 801 Papers, ff 9, WSU.

8. Emspak to UE Locals, November 23, 1949. UEA, PM-190.

9. *UE News,* December 26, 1949, p. 1; "One Union, One Contract, 1950." UEA, PM-238.

10. *IUE-CIO News,* April 7, 1950, p. 3.

11. "It Took Fifteen Years to Build," 1950. UEA, D/6–181.

12. *Pittsburgh Press,* April 17, 1950, p. 1; Matles to UE Locals, April 20, 1950. UEA, PM-209; *Union Generator,* February 14, 1950. UEA, DD6–PP37; *Pittsburgh Post-Gazette,* November 3, 1949, p. 1; *Pittsburgh Press,* April 27, 1950, p. 15.

13. *Pittsburgh Post-Gazette,* April 15, 1950, p. 1; Hearings, Committee on Un-American Activities, House of Representatives, 81st Congress, Second Session, *Expose of the Communist Party of Western Pennsylvania, Based on the Testimony of Matthew Cvetic, Undercover Agent.*

14. *UE News,* May 1, 1950, p. 9; "Bulletin," St. Williams Church, April 16, 1950. UEA, Quinn 1–L.

15. *IUE-News,* May 8, 1950, p. 12; Matles to General Vice-presidents, May 29, 1950. UEA, PM-213.

16. *Pittsburgh Post-Gazette,* May 29, 1950, p. 1.

17. *Pittsburgh Post-Gazette,* May 27, 1950, p. 1; Tom Quinn, "To Swing a Union Election," in Bud Schultz and Ruth Schultz, *It Did Happen Here* (Berkeley: University of California Press, 1989), p. 122. Musmanno, who had worked closely with leftists in the 1920s and 1930s on campaigns such as Sacco and Vanzetti and the Scotsboro Boys, reoriented his political career around a virulent and colorful anticommunism in the decade after 1955. See Michael Musmanno, *Across the Street from the Courthouse,* (Philadelphia: Dorrance, 1954).

18. *IUE-CIO News,* June 5, 1950, p. 1.

19. Jake Staas to Edward Matthews, November 11, 1949. UEA, CBW-1601.

20. *Pittsburgh Post-Gazette,* November 7, 1949, p. 1.

21. "Charles Zuber Report," February 1, 1950. UEA, 0–1662.

22. Matles to GE and Westinghouse Locals, May 6, 1950. UEA, PM-211; *IUE-CIO News,* May 8, 1950, p. 12.

23. Matles to GE and Westinghouse Locals, May 6, 1950. UEA, PM-211; *UE News,* April 17, 1950, p. 10.

24. Joseph Dermody to All GE Locals, January 12, 1950. UEA, CBGE–78; *IUE-CIO News,* May 8, 1950, p. 1; Carey had called top GE officials in mid-November 1949 for "an off the record meeting" to "discuss the plans of the IUE prior to the filing of a petition for election," GE stated that they had rebuffed this request. Charles E. Wilson to James Carey, November 28, 1949. James Carey Papers, Box 11, ff 11, ALHUA.

25. Matles to General Electric Board, January 11, 1950. UEA, PM-196; Victor Pasche to William Cahn, April 11, 1950. UEA, D/3–74; Dermody to all UE-GE Locals, May 13, 1950. UEA, CBGE–85; UE Organizational Report, June 15, 1950. UEA, Blue Dot Box.

26. *IUE-CIO News,* June 5, 1950, p. 12.

27. Dermody to Jack Davis, January 18, 1950. UEA, CBGE–561; UE Organizational Report, June 15, 1950. UEA, Blue Dot Box.

28. *New York Times,* May 22, 1950, p. 8.

29. *IUE-CIO News,* June 5, 1950, p. 12.

30. *Ibid;* "GE Local 203," 1950. UEA, CBGE–616.

31. Transcript, Oral Interview with Joseph Hughes, p. 6. PSU; Houchins Interview, pp. 4–8.

32. Hughes Interview, p. 7.

33. *IUE-CIO News,* June 5, 1950, p. 12.

34. Ibid; Schatz, *The Electrical Workers,* pp. 204–217.

35. *IUE-CIO News,* June 5, 1950, p. 12; UE Organizational Report, June 15, 1950. UEA, Blue Dot Box.

36. Benjamin Riskin to Albert Fitzgerald, March 22, 1950. UEA, CBS–333; Riskin to Matles, April 25, 1950. UEA, CBS–334.

37. "Background to Pulaski Incident," November 14, 1949. UEA, CBRCA–194; Henry Rhine to Tom Wright, January 10, 1950. UEA, CBRCA–195; Rhine to Matles, January 26, 1950. UEA, CBRCA–195.

38. Ted Smorodin to Riskin, December 9, 1949. UEA, CBRCA–88.

39. *IUE-CIO News,* May 22, 1950, p. 3.

40. Riskin to Fitzgerald, March 2, 1950; Cole Pilcher to Robert Denham, August 25, 1950. UEA, CBS–333; *IUE-CIO News,* June 5, 1950, p. 2; June 19, 1950, p. 6; Matles to General Executive Board, June 22, 1950. UEA, PM-212.

41. Emspak to Locals, December 1, 1949. UEA, PM-191.

42. Matles to General Vice Presidents, December 22, 1949. UEA, PM-194.

43. Organizational Report, January 21, 1950. UEA, Blue Dot Box; Klehr and Haynes, *The American Communist Movement: Storming Heaven Itself,* p. 123. Klehr and Haynes summarize the bitter six year struggle of the FE-UE by ignoring the referenda, describing the CIO's award to the UAW of jurisdiction and noting, "the FE resisted, but UAW raids took most of its membership and it ceased to function."

44. Matles to UE General Executive Board, June 22, 1950. UEA, PM-212; "NLRB Scoreboard," *IUE-CIO News,* June 13, 1950, p. 12.

45. Matles to General Executive Board, June 22, 1950. UEA, PM-212.

46. "UE Shows the Way," 1950. UEA, D/6–450.

47. UE Organizational Report, June 15, 1950. UEA, Blue Dot Box.

48. Schatz, *Electrical Workers.* Schatz studied this question closely at the East Pittsburgh Westinghouse plant and at the Erie GE plant.

49. Walter McCabe to Joseph Turkowski, December 6, 1949. UEA, CBGE–741.

50. Smorodin to Riskin, December 9, 1949. UEA, CBRCA–88; *UE News*, April 3, 1950, p. 4.

51. *United Front*, March 23, 1950, D/2-120, UEA; Charles Zuber Report, April 1, 1950, 0-1662, UEA; "Westinghouse in Mansfield," Westinghouse Collection, Mansfield Public Library, Mansfield, Ohio.

52. Ruth Milkman, *Gender at Work*, pp. 144–151; *Voice of the UE*, April 25, 1950; *UE News*, May 1, 1950, p. 4; Matles to Westinghouse Staff, April 19, 1950. UEA, PM-209.

53. "Program on Job Rights," 1950. UEA, CBW-1199.

54. *Lima News*, April 26, 1950, p. 14, CBW-870, UEA; Daily UE Organizers' Report, unsigned, March 20, 1950. UEA, CBW-852.

55. Stanley Aronowitz, *False Promises* (New York: McGraw Hill, 1973), pp. 347–348.

56. General Electric Conference Board Minutes, August 27, 1951. UEA, GECB–16; *IUE–CIO News*, August 3, 1951, p. 1.

57. *IUE-CIO News*, August 3, 1951, p. 1; "Objections of UE Local 201 to Election, August 22, 1951. UEA, CBGE-563.

58. *IUE-News*, August 27, 1951, p. 1; Matles to International Representatives, September 15, 1951. UEA, PM-238; *New York Times*, March 1, 1951, p. 19.

59. "Minutes, UE General Executive Board, June 13, 1951." UE National Office Records, UEA; UE Organizational Report, March 16, 1951. UEA, Blue Dot Box; Mark McColloch, "The Shop Floor Dimension of Inter-Union Rivalry," in Rosswurm, *The CIO's Left-Led Unions*, pp. 183–240.

60. Robert Logsdon to Matles, March 14, 1951; March 20, 1951. UEA, Box 61; Matles to General Executive Board, July 14, 1950. UEA, PM-217.

61. "A Program for East Pittsburgh Workers." UEA, CBW1122; "A Trail of Broken Promises," 1952. UEA, POL–36; William Peeler to Matles, August 10, 1952. UEA, D/6–308.

62. Matles to General Executive Board, August 19, 1952. UEA–PM-263; *Pittsburgh Press*, July 10, 1952, p. 14; August 17, 1952, p. 1; *IUE Generator*, August 12, 1952, p. 1.

63. "Statement of William Peeler, August 28, 1952. UEA, D/6–308; *UE News*. September 1, 1952, p. 3.

64. *IUE-CIO News*, April 21, 1952, p. 1.

65. *IUE-CIO News*, July 14, 1952, p. 1.

66. Fitzgerald to UE Locals, July 19, 1950. UEA, PM-217; Russ Nixon to UE Locals, July 12, 1950. UEA, PM-216.

67. Fitzgerald to UE Locals, July 19, 1950; August 14, 1950. UEA–PM-217; *UE News*, November 27, 1950, p. 9.

68. Fitzgerald to UE Locals, August 9, 1950. UEA, PM-218; *UE News*, August 21, 1950, p. 9.

69. "Minutes, UE General Executive Board, March 16, 1951." UE General Office Records, UEA; Fitzgerald to UE Locals, February 26, 1951. UEA, PM-231; August 8, 1951. UEA, PM-239.

70. Fitzgerald to UE Locals, February 26, 1951. UEA, PM-231.

71. Quinn, "To Swing a Union Election," p. 122.

72. Matles to General Executive Board, March 3, 1951. UEA, POM–232.

73. Quinn, "To Swing a Union Election," pp. 123–125.

74. Fitzgerald to UE Locals, August 8, 1951. UEA, PM-239.

75. Matles to General Executive Board, November 18, 1952. UEA, POM–269; Matles to International Representatives, February 2, 1952. UEA, PM-270.

76. "Minutes, UE General Executive Board, December 8, 1952." UE General Office Records, UEA; Matles to International Representatives, January 28, 1953. UEA, PM-275; *New York Times*, November 26, 1952, p. 15.

77. Matles to UE Locals, October 15, 1952. UEA, PM-267; Matles to UE Locals, December 15, 1952. UEA, PM-271.

78. Matles to UE Locals, October 27, 1952. UEA, PM-267; Matles to UE Locals, December 11, 1952. UEA, PM-271; Emspak to General Vice-presidents, March 20, 1953. UEA, PM-280.

79. Matles to General Executive Board, June 19, 1952. UEA, PM-259; Matles to General Executive Board, June 30, 1952. UEA, POM–260; Edward Matthews to Westinghouse Locals, May 7, 1952. UEA, CBW-152; Carey to Averell Harriman, October 2, 1952. James Carey Papers, Box 10, ff 9, ALHUA.

80. Charles H. Kersten, "How Spies are Protected in U.S. Defense Plants," *Reader's Digest*, Vol. 62 (January, 1953), pp. 28–30; Leslie Velie,

"Red Pipeline Into Our Defense Plants," *Saturday Evening Post*, Vol. 225 (October 18, 1952), pp. 19–21.

81. Fitzgerald to UE Locals, November 14, 1953. UEA, PM-295.

82. "Stop Union Busters." UEA, DD6-PL8; *New York Times*, November 11, 1953, p. 24; November 15, 1953, p. 24.

83. Emspak to General Vice-presidents, March 20, 1953, UEA,PM-272; Fitzgerald to UE Locals, November, 1953. UEA, PM-294; *UE Information Bulletin*, March 16, 1954, UEA, DD6–P12.

84. Emspak to UE Locals, December 10, 1953. UEA, PM-295.

85. *IUE-CIO News*, March 29, 1954, p. 7; *UE Organizational Bulletin*, April 5, 1954, UEA, PP–157; Westinghouse Grievance Reply, March 31, 1954. UEA, DD6–118.

86. "Westinghouse Dismisses Two Employees," 1954. UEA, DD6–PL11; Tom Quinn to David Scribner, September 29, 1954. UEA, DD6–D47.

87. Quinn to Scribner, *Ibid.*

88. "Minutes, IUE Local 610 Executive Board, January 4, 1955. UEA, IUE: 89: 16, Box 4; Report on Discharge of East Pittsburgh Workers, 1955. UEA, DD6–L18; Tom Quinn to John Torquato, February 7, 1956. UEA, DD6–D49.

89. Matles to General Executive Board, July 6, 1955. UEA, PM-317; Emspak to General Vice-presidents, October 5, 1955. UEA, PM-320; Fitzgerald to General Executive Board, December 21, 1955. UEA, PM-324.

90. Matles to International Representatives, January 6, 1956, UEA, PM-325; *New York Times*, December 21, 1955, p. 18; Subversive Activities Control Board files, Reel 10, NA. The hearings did not begin immediately, because the government decided to await the Supreme Court's ruling on the legality of its proceedings against the Communist Party. Hearings resumed briefly in May–July 1957, when they were again suspended.

91. Matles to UE General Executive Board, October 22, 1957. UEA, PM-346.

92. Matles to UE General Executive Board, July 3, 1957. UEA, PM-344; Emspak to UE General Executive Board, October 7, 1957. UEA–PM-346; *New York Times*, January 11, 1958, p. 3; Strategic Activities Control Board Files, Reel 10, NA.

93. Matles to UE General Executive Board, February 13, 1959. UEA, PM-364; Matles to UE General Executive Board, March 23, 1959. UEA, PM-365; Matles to General Executive Board, March 31, 1959. UEA,

PM-366; *UE News*, March 30, 1959, p. 1; *New York Times*, March 25, 1959, p. 78; Strategic Activities Control Board Files, Reel 10, NA.

94. Emspak to Presidents, January 29, 1957. UEA, PM-339.

95. Emspak to UE Locals, October 23, 1957. UEA, PM-347; *New York Times*, August 27, 1957, p. 19. Killian was retried and again convicted, only to be later released on appeal.

96. "Minutes, UE General Executive Board, December 11, 1958." UE General Office Records, UEA.

97. Aronowitz, *False Promises*, p. 347.

98. UE Organizational Report, September 1954, UEA, Blue Dot Box.

99. UE General Executive Board Minutes, April 5, 1955; June, 1955. UEA, Blue Dot Box.

100. "Minutes, UE General Executive Board, June, 1955." UE General Office Records, UEA; *UE Organizers' Bulletin*, August 2, 1955. UEA, PP–187; "Minutes, UE General Executive Board, July 27, 1955." UE General Office Records, UEA; Matles to UE General Executive Board, September 26, 1955. UEA, PM-320; *IUE-CIO News*, October 10, 1955, p. 9; Emspak to UE Locals, October 25, 1955. UEA, PM-321; "Minutes, UE General Executive Board, November 10, 1955." UE General Office Records, UEA; *New York Times*, September 20, 1956, p. 16; *UE News*, September 17, 1956, p. 1. Among the national officers, Matles leaned towards a merger with the UAW or IAM, while Emspak and Fitzgerald favored uniting with the IUE.

101. Aronowitz, *False Promises*, pp. 349–350; Cochran, *Labor and Communism*, p. 294. Cochran claims that, as early as 1951, Matles had met with Communist Party officials and, in "a stormy session" had rejected their advice to enter the IUE. At this same meeting Cochran claims that Matles told the CP officials that he had "no confidence" in the Party leadership. There is no citation for these claims; Klehr and Haynes, *Storming Heaven*, p. 141.

102. "Minutes, UE General Executive Board, November 29, 1955." UE General Office Records, UEA; UE Organizational Report, June, 1955, UEA, Blue Dot Box. The old FE locals had been pounded by years of pressure, notably during the 1952 International Harvester strike. District President Don Harris now believed that further negotiations against Harvester were futile, if attempted alone, and that the individual locals would be lost to the UAW, if the district did not merge.

103. District Four Locals Meeting Minutes, June 27, 1956. UEA, D/4–184; *IUE Westinghouse News*, March 4, 1957, p. 1. IUEA, 410, Box 23; "UE Demands Renewed," July 23, 1956. UEA, CBW-101; "Secession Flops,"

1956. UEA, PL–46; *New York Times*, January 25, 1957, p. 1; May 13, 1956, p. 78; Aronowitz, *False Promises*, p. 349.

104. Matles to District 7 Locals, September 5, 1956. UEA, PM-334; UE Organizational Report, June 1956, UE Organizational Report, September, 1956. UEA, Blue Dot Box; Matles to UE General Executive Board, March 28, 1957. UEA, PM-341; UE Organizational Report, August 1957. UEA, Blue Dot Box; "Minutes, UE General Executive Board, December 10, 1957." UE General Office Records, UEA; UE Organizational Report, August, 1957. UEA, Blue Dot Box; UE Organizational Report, March, 1958. UEA, Blue Dot Box.

105. UE Organizational Report, August, 1957. UEA, Blue Dot Box; "Minutes, UE General Executive Board, December 10, 1957." UE General Office Records, UEA.

106. Abraham Cohen, "Coordinated Bargaining at General Electric: An Analysis." Unpublished Ph.D. Dissertation, Cornell University, 1973, p. 67; Jules Backman, *The Economics of the Electrical Machinery Industry* (New York: New York University Press, 1962), p. 241; Lemuel Boulware, *The Truth About Boulwarism: Trying to Do Right Voluntarily* (Washington: Bureau of National Affairs, 1969).

107. UE Organizational Report, September 15, 1950. UEA, Blue Dot Box; *New York Times*, June 28, 1950, p. 28; September 21, 1950, p. 32.

108. Dermody to UE GE Locals, May 18, 1951. UEA, CBGE–92.

109. *Ibid*; An important factor in the success of Boulwarism was the IUE's refusal to agree to joint negotiations with the UE. Consequently, while each union hoped and claimed to outdo its rival at the bargaining table, each lacked the clout to carry out a truly effective strike alone.

110. "Minutes, UE General Executive Board, June 13, 1951." UE General Office Records, UEA; Dermody to UE GE Locals, November 9, 1951; Dermody to UE GE Locals, December 6, 1951. UEA, CBGE–96.

111. "Stop Stalling," January, 1952. UEA, PL–34; Matles to International Representatives, September 25, 1952. UEA, PM-265; Nixon to General Officers, November 10, 1952. UEA, PM-268; *UE News*, December 12, 1952, p. 5.

112. Cohen, "Coordinated Bargaining at GE," p. 88; *New York Times*, June 17, 1953, p. 38.

113. Backman, *The Economics of the Electrical Machinery Industry*, pp. 218–219; *IUE-CIO News*, November 7, 1955, p. 10.

114. Press Release, November 13, 1950. UEA, PR–35.

115. Matthews to Locals, October 16, 1950. UEA, CB–143; *UE News*,

November 13, 1950, p. 1; Also see the discussion in Mark McColloch, "The Shopfloor Dimension of Inter-union Rivalry," in Rosswurn, *The CIO's Left-Led Unions*, pp. 183–199.

116. *UE News*, March 17, 1952; McColloch, "The Shop Floor Dimension of Inter-union Rivalry," p. 7; Matthews to Westinghouse Locals, April 24, 1952. UEA, CBW-152; unsigned to GE Locals, November, 1952. UEA, PM-268.

117. Matthews to Westinghouse Locals, February 20, 1952. UEA, CBW-150; Matles to UE General Executive Board, April 10, 1952. UEA, PM-253; Elizabeth Hencken letter, April, 1952. UEA, D/4–778.

118. L. Botsai to All Employees of the Nuttal Works, April 19, 1952. UEA, CBW-1096; *UE News*, July 21, 1952, p. 1; Strike Settlement Agreement, September 5, 1952. UEA, CBW-1183.

119. *IUE-CIO News*, July 2, 1953, p. 12.

120. *UE News*, July 26, 1954, p. 1.

121. Matles to UE General Executive Board, October 26, 1955. UEA, PM-322; *UE News*, October 31, 1955, p. 1; *IUE-CIO News*, November 25, 1955, p. 10; *New York Times*, October 18, 1955, p. 42; October 26, 1955, p. 6. While negotiations and strike plans were not coordinated, the two unions did experience temporarily improved relations.

122. Matles to Westinghouse Locals, January 12, 1956. UEA, PM-235; *Westinghouse Picket*, January 23, 1956, UEA, DD6–P45.

123. Matles to UE General Executive Board, 1956. UEA, PM-326; Garret Keaster to Local 1105, March 14, 1956. UEA, DD11–L4; Carey to John Kane, March 22, 1956. IUEA, C1.21.

124. *UE News*, April 2, 1956, p. 1; *New York Times*, March 21, 1956, p. 1. The Times noted that "Carey finally yielded on time study and production standards."

125. *UE News*, March 5, 1956, p. 1; April 2, 1956, p. 3; *UE Information Bulletin*, April 12, 1956. UEA, DD6–P12; Steve Kuzio Report, April 22, 1956. UEA, Red Box 61; *UE News*, December 26, 1955, p. 3.

126. Matles to UE Locals, August 8, 1956. UEA, PM-333; *New York Times*, August 7, 1956, p. 11; *UE News*, August 20, 1956, p. 4.

127. McColloch, "The Shopfloor Dimension of Inter-union Rivalry," in Rosswurn, *The CIO's Left-Led Unions*, p. 185–186.

128. "1950 UE Policy," p. 13. UEA, PC–17.

129. UE Westinghouse Contract, April 1, 1948. UEA, CB–W9.

130. *UE News*, May 15, 1950, p. 11.

131. "Charles Zuber Report," April 15, 1950. UEA, 0–1662.

132. McColloch, "The Shopfloor Dimension of Inter-union Rivalry," in Rosswurn, *The CIO's Left-Led Unions*, p. 188.

133. *UE News*, June 11, 1951, p. 9.

134. *IUE-CIO News*, April 23, 1951, p. 1; "Mike Fitzpatrick Report to the IUE Westinghouse Conference Board," 1951. IUEA, F1.221.

135. *Local 107 News*, August, 1953, p. 3; East Pittsburgh Twenty-Seventh Keysheet, July 1, 1953. UEA, DD6–L11; Earl Kipp to David Lasser, January 13, 1951. IUEA, G1.05.

136. *IUE-CIO News*, October 10, 1955, p. 3; Peter Abbondi to UE Westinghouse Locals, August 17, 1955. UEA, DD6–M2; "Company Proposal," 1955. IUEP, C1.121, IUEA.

137. "Comparison between present UE and IUE Contracts," March, 1956. UEA, DD6–M3.

138. *Ibid*; "The Westinghouse Strike and Westinghouse Peace," 1956. IUEP, G1.072, IUEA.

139. UE Westinghouse Contract, April 1, 1948; Schatz, *Electrical Workers*, pp. 116–117.

140. Schatz, *The Electrical Workers*, p. 127; Milkman, *Gender at Work*, p. 146.

141. *UE News*, July 10, 1950, p. 11; "To Westinghouse Locals of IUE-CIO," June, 1950. IUEP, G1.05, IUEA.

142. Westinghouse Conference Board Minutes, October 7, 1950. UEA, CBW-36.

143. Westinghouse-IUE Contract, July 19, 1950. IUEA.

144. Westinghouse-IUE Local 202 Contract, 1950. IUEA, G1.09.

145. UE Organizational Report, December 8, 1950. UEA, Blue Dot Box; *New York Times*, August 31, 1950, p. 26.

146. UE Organizational Report, September 12, 1952. UEA, Blue Dot Box; Matles to International Representatives, November 17, 1952. UEA, PM-268; *New York Times*, October 4, 1952, p. 18; See daily front-page coverage in the *Chicago Tribune* from October 5 to 10.

147. UE Organizational Report, March, 1953. UEA, Blue Dot Box; *New York Times*, November 16, 1952, p. 43. Ward was found not guilty in December 1952, see *New York Times*, December 3, 1952, p. 50.

148. *New York Times*, September 3, 1954, p. 24; UE Organizational Report, September 1954; December, 1954. UEA, Blue Dot Box.

149. Matles to International Representatives, July 29, 1954. UEA, PM-306; Emspak to UE Locals, November 8, 1954; November 26, 1954. UEA, PM-309; George Kirschner, "What Happens to the People," unpublished M.A. Thesis, City University of New York (Queens), 1973; *New York Times*, October 1, 1954, p. 8; October 5, 1954, p. 4; November 5, 1954, p. 5.

150. Backman, *The Economics of the Machinery Industry*, p. 297.

Chapter 7

1. Herbert Northrup, *Boulwarism*, pp. 74–76; *Proceedings*, 1958 IUE Convention, p. 154; Organizational Report, March, 1959. UEA, Blue Dot Box; Organizational Report, June, 1959. UEA, Blue Dot Box.

2. *Wall Street Journal*, September 27, 1960, p. 1; Northrup, *Boulwarism*, p. 86; IUE-GE Negotiating Committee Minutes, August 10, 1960, James Carey Papers, Box 11, ff 15, ALHUA. IUE GE Conference Board Chairman John Callahan warned Carey that "We've got just about everything we're going to get." Carey replied that the negotiating committee should not "try to frighten me or itself with a strike. I don't think there's a strike there."

3. *Local 301 News*, October 21, 1960, p. 1; Northrup, *Boulwarism*, p. 88.

4. *New York Times*, October 25, 1960, p. 1; Northrup, *Boulwarism*, pp. 89–90.

5. Northrup, *Boulwarism*, p. 47; *Wall Street Journal*, July 25, 1963; *UE News*, May 21, 1962, p. 2; *UE News*, January 28, 1963, p. 2; Joseph Curran to James Carey, no date, James Carey Papers, Box 3, ff 13, ALHUA. Meany referred to Carey at an AFL-CIO meeting as "irresponsible and neurotic," and refused to name him as even an alternate to an international labor body.

6. *IUE News*, December 3, 1964, p. 1; December 17, 1964, p. 1; *UE News*, October 5, 1964, p. 2.

7. Matles to General Executive Board, April 6, 1965. UEA, PM432; *IUE News*, April 15, 1965, p. 3.

8. Matles to UE Locals, February 12, 1965. UEA, PM430.

9. Robert Kirkwood to Field Organizers, February 24, 1965. UEA, PM431; Matles to General Executive Board, June 3, 1965, UEA, PM433; *UE News*, July 12, 1965, p. 2.

10. *New York Times*, March 22, 1960, p. 74; Matles to GEB, March 28, 1960. UEA PM377.

11. Matles to General Executive Board, March 28, 1960. UEA, PM377.

12. *Ibid.*

13. *New York Times*, March 26, 1960, p. 22; "UE Officers Report, 1960," p. 51. UEA.

14. *UE News*, August 15, 1960, p. 2.

15. *New York Times*, March 26, 1960, p. 22; Matles to General Executive Board, March 28, 1960. UEA, PM377.

16. Matles to International Representatives, August 9, 1960. UEA, PM377; *New York Times*, March 26, 1960, p. 22; *The Machinist*, April 7, 1960, p. 2.

17. *UE News*, September 9, 1963, p. 2; *IUE News*, July 11, 1963, p. 6.

18. See, for example, "UE Plots," *Pittsburgh Catholic*, March 5, 1960, p. 4.

19. *UE News*, February 1, 1960, p. 3; *New York Times*, January 13, 1960, p. 11; *IUE News*, August 24, 1961, p. 7. The UE defended the right of individual political associations, but did pass a resolution stating that no staff member may serve on an outside body without permission of the GEB. In early 1962, Nixon left the union to become manager of the *National Guardian* and Lustig became general manager of the *Worker*.

20. Matles and Higgins, *Them and Us*, pp. 258–59. Rice agrees that this took place as described. McGeever, *The Rev. Charles Owen Rice*, pp. 228, 229.

21. *UE News*, August 10, 1964, p. 1; October 5, 1964, pp. 1,3; February 8, 1965, p. 1; June 14, 1965, p. 9; October 17, 1966, p. 6; April 7, 1969, p. 1.

22. Kirkwood to GEB, May 10, 1965. UEA, PM433; *UE News*, May 17, 1965, p. 2.

23. *UE News*, October 16, 1967, p. 1.

24. *New York Times*, September 1964, p. 25; "UE Policy," 1964. UEA, PC, p. 53.

25. "Minutes, UE General Executive Board, December 13, 1963," UE General Office Records, UEA; Emspak to UE Locals, December 27, 1961. UEA, PM400, for example; Fitzgerald to UE Locals, July 11, 1962. UEA, PM487; "UE Policy," 1962, p. 33.

26. Fitzgerald to General Executive Board, July 26, 1963. UEA, PM417; *UE News*, September 9, 1963, p. 6; Fitzgerald to UE Legislative Committees, February 6, 1964. UEA, PM421; Matles to UE Locals, June 21, 1965. UEA, PM434.

27. UE Officers' Report, 1964, p. 70. UEA, PC; UE Officers' Report,

1966, p. 11, UEA, PC; See for example, *UE News,* November 27, 1967, p. 6; *Proceedings,* 1968 UE Convention, p. 114, UEA, PC.

28. Emspak to Locals, November 13, 1961. UEA, PM398; *UE News,* January 29, 1962, p. 1.

29. "Minutes, UE General Executive Board, December 13, 1962." UEA, BLue Dot Box.

30. *UE News,* May 7, 1962, p. 1.

31. *UE News,* September 17, 1962; *IUE News,* September 6, 1962, p. 6.

32. *UE News,* September 17, 1962, p. 4.

33. *New York Times,* October 26, 1965, p. 21; Abraham Cohen, *Coordinated Bargaining at General Electric,* Unpublished Dissertation, Cornell University, 1973, p. 109.

34. Cohen, *Ibid.,* p. 58; UE Officers Report, 1965, p. 33. UEA, PC.

35. *New York Times,* October 15, 1966, p. 34; Matles to General Executive Board, September 19, 1966. UEA, PM446.

36. Cohen, *Coordinated Bargaining at General Electric,* p. 145.

37. *UE News,* October 17, 1966, p. 1.

38. *UE News,* August 8, 1966, p. 1.

39. *New York Times,* October 19, 1966, p. 41; *UE News,* November 14, 1966, p. 1; October 31, 1966, p. 1.

40. *New York Times,* February 2, 1969, p. 53; June 29, 1969, p. 52, October 27, 1969, p. 1; Cohen, *Coordinated Bargaining at General Electric,* pp. 193, 196, 238.

41. Cohen, *Ibid.,* p. 247; *New York Times,* January 31, 1970, p. 24; December 22, 1969.

Chapter 8

1. *UE News,* March 9, 1970, pp. 1,3.

2. *Ibid.*

3. *UE News,* September 7, 1970, p. 1; December 28, 1970, p. 2; February 8, 1971, p. 2.

4. *IUE News,* June, 1971, p. 3.

5. *Ibid.*

6. "Minutes, UE General Executive Board, June 17, 1971." UEA, Blue Dot Box; *IUE News*, June 7, 1971, p. 3; October, 1971, p. 2; *Wall Street Journal*, September 7, 1971, p. 1.

7. "Minutes, UE General Executive Board, May 9, 1970, September 23, 1970, August 28, 1971," UE General Office Records, UEA; *Milwaukee Labor*, June 28, 1971, p. 3; *UE News*, December 25, 1972, p. 4.

8. *UE News*, November 17, 1969; September 14, 1973, p. 6; "Minutes, UE General Executive Board, June 17, 1971." UE General Office Records, UEA.

9. *UE News*, September 23, 1974, p. 5.

10. *Wall Street Journal*, June 18, 1973, p. 9.

11. *UE News*, July 6, 1976, p. 6; *Wall Street Journal*, July 9, 1976, p. 2.

12. *UE News*, July 26, 1976, p. 6; *Wall Street Journal*, July 19, 1976, p. 3; July 21, 1976, p. 4

13. *UE News*, December 29, 1969, p. 2. The Basic-Witz plant in Staunton, VA was won from a non-functioning Carpenters local; *UE News*, September 7, 1970, p. 6. Foster-Wheeler, a former UE shop of 600 workers, was won back from the Boilermakers. See *UE News*, June 15, 1970, for an example of the smaller shops won in the period.

14. UE Officers Report, 1971. UEA, PC–3, p. 35.

15. *Ibid*, pp. 35–38; "Minutes, UE General Executive Board, December 9, 1971." UE General Office Files, UEA.

16. *UE News*, January 8, 1973, p. 1; "Minutes, UE General Executive Board, December 10, 1970." UE General Office Files, UEA.

17. *Ibid*.

18. "Minutes, UE General Executive Board, June 22, 1972; March 16, 1972." UE General Office Records, UEA; UE Organizational Report, April 1972. UEA, Blue Dot Box; *Proceedings*, 1972 UE Convention, p. 271; *UE News*, January 8, 1973, p. 1; July 23, 1973, p. 3; September 3, 1973, p. 3; *Proceedings*, 1970 UE Convention, p. 248; "Minutes, UE General Executive Board, December 10, 1970." UE General Office Records, UEA; *Proceedings*, 1974 UE Convention, p. 225. UEA, Blue; *UE News*, December 15, 1975, p. 1; "Minutes, UE General Executive Board, December 17, 1972." UE General Office Files, UEA; *UE News*, December 15, 1975, p. 6; September 7, 1976, p. 1; *Proceedings*, 1976 UE Convention, p. 212. UEA, Blue.

19. *UE News*, May 15, 1972, p. 4; *UE News*, July 10, 1972, p. 3.

20. *UE News*, December 2, 1974, p. 6; "Minutes, UE General Executive Board, December 9, 1974." UE General Office Records, UEA.

21. *Proceedings*, 1974 UE Convention, p. 166; *UE News*, October 21, 1974, p. 2.

22. *UE News*, January 13, 1975, p. 2; June 16, 1975, p. 6; *UE News*, December 1, 1975, p. 8.

23. *UE News*, February 2, 1976, p. 2; *UE News*, June 21, 1976, pp. 6–7.

24. *UE News*, August 8, 1980, p. 5; July 21, 1980, p. 6; December 8, 1980, p. 6; February 9, 1981, p. 2; April 13, 1981, p. 3.

25. *UE News*, July 21, 1980, p. 6; December 8, 1980, p. 6.

26. *UE News*, August 29, 1980, p. 2

27. *UE News*, February 9, 1981, p. 3; February 23, 1981, p. 3, April 13, 1981, p. 7.

28. *UE News*, November 15, 1982, p. 2; March 21, 1983, p. 9; December 26, 1983, p. 6; March 19, 1984, p. 1; September 10, 1984, p. 2.

29. *UE News*, October 27, 1980, p. 3, November 24, 1980, p. 3.

30. *UE News*, June 11, 1984, p. 4; February 2, 1987, p. 3.

31. *UE News*, June 2, 1980, p. 7; October 27, 1980, p. 3; September 8, 1980, p. 3.

32. *UE News*, November 10, 1980, pp. 2, 7; August 13, 1980, p. 5; January 21, 1980, p. 6; April 7, 1980, p. 3.

33. *UE News*, August 27, 1990, p. 2; GE sold its Allentown plant to Black and Decker, who then moved the work to South Africa and Brazil, see *UE News*, May 21, 1984, p. 3; *UE News*, April 8, 1985, p. 3.

34. *UE News*, May 21, 1984, p. 3; *UE News*, April 8, 1985, p. 3.

35. *UE News*, January 20, 1986, p. 2.

36. *UE News*, February 23, 1987, p. 2.

37. *UE News*, March 30, 1990, p. 3.

38. Barbara Doherty, *The Struggle To Save Morse Cutting Tool* (New Bedford, MA: Southeastern Massachusetts University Labor Education Center, 1986).

39. *New York Times*, June 15, 1986, p. 31.

40. *Wall Street Journal*, June 18, 1973, p. 3.

41. *UE News*, July 6, 1976, p. 6; *Wall Street Journal*, July 9, 1976, p. 2.

42. *Wall Street Journal,* July 19, 1976, p. 3; *Wall Street Journal,* July 21, 1976, p. 4.

43. *UE News,* July 2, 1979, p. 6.

44. *UE News,* July 23, 1979, p. 6; *UE News,* September 10, 1979, p. 3.

45. *UE News,* July 12, 1982, p. 6; *UE News,* August 2, 1982, p. 2.

46. *UE News,* November 9, 1981, p. 3.

47. *UE News,* December 7, 1981, p. 3.

48. *UE News,* April 19, 1982, p. 3; *UE News,* June 7, 1982, p. 6.

49. *UE News,* July 22, 1985, p. 1.

50. *UE News,* April 1, 1988, p. 6; July 15, 1988, p. 1.

51. *UE News,* June 21, 1991, p. 5; *UE News,* July 12, 1991, p. 1.

52. *UE News,* October 13, 1986, p. 1.

53. "Minutes, UE General Executive Board, March 18, 1971." UE General Office Files, UEA; *UE News,* September 13, 1971, p. 2; *Proceedings,* 1971 UE Convention, p. 264. UEA, Blue Dot Box.

54. *Proceedings,* 1974 UE Convention, p. 265; *UE News,* September 22, 1975, p. 3, 6.

55. *UE News,* September 25, 1978, p. 1, 6.

56. *UE News,* September 18, 1987, p. 2; October 30, 1987, p. 4.

57. *UE News,* June 11, 1984, p. 6; December 30, 1985, p. 3; *New York Times,* September 19, 1985, p. 30.

58. *UE News,* December 7, 1990, p. 4; *UE News,* June 21, 1991, p. 4.

59. *UE News,* December 1, 1969, p. 5.

60. *UE News,* December 8, 1980, p. 6.

61. "Minutes, UE General Executive Board, December 1, 1976." UE General Office Records, UEA.

62. *UE News,* November 26, 1977, p. 6; "1977 UE Convention Resolutions," p. 103, UEA, Blue Dot Box.

63. *UE News,* April 27, 1981, p. 6; October 25, 1982, p. 6; December 6, 1982, p. 6; May 3, 1982, p. 4.

64. *UE News,* March 19, 1984, p. 6; October 22, 1984, p. 1.

65. *UE News,* November 18, 1988, p. 1.

Conclusion

1. Galenson, *The CIO Challenge to the AFL*, p. 228; Kampelman, *The Communist Party vs. the CIO*, p. 249; CIO, *Official Reports on the Expulsion of Communist Dominated Organizations from the CIO* (1951).

2. The phenomenon of elected union leaders taking public and private stances on issues with which the rank and file is either unconcerned, unaware of, or in opposition to is not restricted to Communistwelcome datacomps. For example, the AFL-CIO's involvement in State Department and CIA attempts to undermine Communist-led unions in Europe and elsewhere since World War II was largely carried on without the membership's knowledge or direct approval. Ronald Radosh, *American Labor and Foreign Policy*; Roy Godson, *American Labor and European Politics*; Ronald Filippelli, *American Labor and Postwar Italy, 1943–1953*; Federico Romero, *The United States and the European Trade Union Movement, 1944–1951*.

3. "Ruth Young's Speech at June 18–20, 1945, meeting of the National Committee of the Communist Political Association," Philip Jaffe Papers, Reel 3, Woodruff Library, Emory University, cited in Rosswurm, *The CIO's Left-Led Unions*, p. 8.

4. This was an old story in the American trade union movement. Gompers always had a great deal of latitude on political pronouncements, especially with regard to foreign policy. Simeon Larson, *Labor and Foreign Policy* (Rutherford, NJ: Fairleigh Dickenson University Press, 1975). Levenstein argues that Communist Party directives had little effect on the day-to-day activities of Communist labor leaders. He also argues that had the party tried to exert more control it probably would have failed because the appeal of the CIO to radicals would have overwhelmed any attempt by the party to control it. Levenstein, *Communism, Anti-Communism and the CIO*, p. 40.

5. Block Interview, p. 19; Carey Interview, pp. 213–214; Levenstein, *Communism, Anti-Communism and the CIO*, p. 144.

6. Levenstein, *Communism, Anti-Communism and the CIO*, p. 42–46.

7. Matles and Higgins, *Them and Us*, pp. 10, 11.

8. Matles Interview, pp. 35–76; Emspak Interview, p. 222.

9. Stepan-Norris & Zeitlin, "'Red Unions' and 'Bourgeoise' Contracts," p. 1172.

10. Cochrane, *Labor and Communism*, p. 285; Saposs, *Communism in American Unions* (New York: McGraw Hill, 1959), pp. 184–185.

11. Santoro interview; Ed Wiese Interview.

12. *New York Times,* March 27, 1947, p. 2; U.S. Congress, House, Committee on Un-American Activities, *Hearings Regarding Communism in the United States.* 80th Cong., 2nd Session, 1947.

13. For a good discussion of the consequences of Reuther's victory for the internal workings of the UAW see, Martin Halpern, *UAW Politics in the Cold War Era* (Albany: State University of New York Press, 1988), pp. 237–264.

14. *Ibid.,* p. 262.

15. Levenstein, *Communism, Anti-Communism, and the CIO,* pp. 55–57; Cochran, *Labor and Communism,* pp. 280–282, 289, 290.

16. Fitzgerald Interview, pp. 2–3; Matles Interview, pp. 31–32; James Matles, *The Members Run this Union* (UE, 1947); Matles and Higgins, *Them and Us,* pp. 79–82.

17. Harrington, "Catholics in the Labor Movement," pp. 237, 238; Thomas Darby to Charles Owen Rice, August 12, 1946, Rice Papers; Charles Owen Rice to Thomas Darby, June 13, 1946, Rice Papers; Levenstein, *Communism, Anti-Communism and the CIO,* p. 143.

18. Frank Emspak, "The Breakup of the Congress of Industrial Organizations," p. 341.

19. McColloch, "The United Electrical Workers and the International Union of Electrical Workers, 1949–1960: The Struggle for Control," Unpublished Master's Thesis, Pennsylvania State University, 1972, pp. 85–102; Potofsky Interview, pp. 634–638, cited in Levenstein, *Communism, Anti-Communism, and the CIO,* p. 143.

20. Cochran, *Labor and Communism,* pp. 289–290; cf. Harrington, "Catholics in the Labor Movement," p. 269.

21. Neil Betten, *Catholic Activism and the Catholic Worker* (Gainesville, FL: University of Florida Press, 1976), p. 145.

22. Block Interview, p. 29; Harrington, "Catholics in the Labor Movement," p. 29.

23. Rice Interview, pp. 18–19; Schatz, *The Electrical Workers,* pp. 189–217.

24. Schatz, *Ibid.*

25. One clear example of this appears in the "Text of a Statement Read in the Pittsburgh Diocese Concerning the Local 601 Election," which can be found in the Charles Owen Rice Papers.

26. Joseph Donnelly, "The Junior Clergy Look at Organized Labor," *American Ecclesiastical Review,* 115 (1946), p. 1; Rosswurn, "The Catholic

Church and the Left-Led Unions," in Rosswurn, *The CIO's Left-Led Unions,* p. 130; *Proceedings,* 1950 IUE Convention, p. 21.

27. Transcript, oral interview with Mary Callahan, pp. 32–34, III. PSU; UE Local 105 Executive Board Minutes. IUE Local 105 Papers, Box 31, TUL.

28. Rosswurn, "Introduction," in Rosswurn, ed., *The CIO's Left-Led Unions,* pp. 1–2.

29. Rosswurn, *Ibid.,* pp. 14–17; Halpern, *UAW Politics in the Cold War Era,* pp. 266–270.

Bibliography

Manuscript Collections

Harry Block Papers. Historical Collections and Labor Archives, The Pennsylvania State University Libraries. (PSU)

James Carey Papers. Archives of Labor History and Urban Affairs, Wayne State University. (ALHUA)

Congress of Industrial Organizations Papers. Special Collections, Catholic University of America Libraries. (CUA)

Congress of Industrial Organizations papers. Archives of Labor History and Urban Affairs, Wayne State University. (ALHUA)

Ernest DeMaio Papers, Chicago Historical Society. (CHS)

Federal Bureau of Investigation Archives. Federal Bureau of Investigation, Washington D.C. (FBI)

International Union of Electrical Workers Archives. Special Collections, Rutgers University Libraries. (IUEA)

International Union of Electrical Workers, Local 463 Collection. Robert Wagner Labor Archives, New York University Libraries. (NYU)

International Union of Electrical Workers, District 7 Archives. Special Collections, Paul Laurence Dunbar Library, Wright State University. (WSU)

International Union of Electrical Workers, Local 755 Papers. Special Collections, Paul Laurence Dunbar Library, Wright State University. (WSU)

International Union of Electrical Workers, Local 768 Papers. Special Collections, Paul Laurence Dunbar Library, Wright State University. (WSU)

International Union of Electrical Workers, Local 801 Papers. Special Collections, Paul Laurence Dunbar Library, Wright State University. (WSU)

International Union of Electrical Workers, Local 105, Urban Archives, Temple University Libraries. (TUL)

Philip Murray Papers. Special Collections, Catholic University of America Libraries. (CUA)

Philadelphia Council AFL-CIO Papers, Urban Archives, Temple University Libraries. (TUL)

Charles Owen Rice Papers. Historical Collections and Labor Archives, The Pennsylvania State University Libraries. (PSU)

Charles Rivers Collection. Robert Wagner Labor Archives, New York University Libraries. (NYU)

William Sentner Papers. Special Collections, Washington University Libraries. (WUL)

Socialist Party of America Papers. Microfilming Corporation of America edition.

Subversive Activities Control Board Files. National Archives. (NA)

United Electrical, Radio and Machine Workers of America Archives. Archives of Industrial Society, University of Pittsburgh Libraries. (UEA)

Westinghouse Collection. Sherman Room. Mansfield, Ohio Public Library.

Oral History Interviews

Walter Barry, Tape of Oral Interview. Robert Wagner Labor Archives, New York University Libraries.

Harry Block, Transcript of Oral Interview. Historical Collections and Labor Archives, The Pennsylvania State University Libraries.

John Brophy, Transcript of Oral Interview. Oral History Collection, Columbia University Libraries.

Earl Browder, Transcript of Oral Interview. Oral History Collection, Columbia University Libraries.

Mary Callahan, Transcript of Oral Interview. Historical Collections and Labor Archives, Pennsylvania State University Libraries.

James B. Carey, Transcript of Oral Interview. Oral History Collection, Columbia University Libraries.

Jeanette Dean, Tape of Oral Interview. Robert Wagner Labor Archives, New York University Libraries.

Ernest DeMaio, Transcript of Oral Interview. Roosevelt University Library.

Julius Emspak, Transcript of Oral Interview. Oral History Collection, Columbia University Libraries.

Albert Fitzgerald, Transcript of Oral Interview. Historical Collections and Labor Archives, The Pennsylvania State University Libraries.

Ruth Glassman, Tape of Oral Interview. Robert Wagner Labor Archives, New York University Libraries.

Gardner Jackson, Transcript of Oral Interview. Oral History Collection, Columbia University Libraries.

James Matles, Transcript of Oral Interview. Historical Collections and Labor Archives, The Pennsylvania State University Libraries.

Rose Podmaka, Tape of Oral Interview. Robert Wagner Labor Archives, New York University Libraries.

Charles Owen Rice, Transcript of Oral Interview. Historical Collections and Labor Archives, The Pennsylvania State University Libraries.

Charles Rivers, Tape of Oral Interview. Robert Wagner Labor Archives, New York University Libraries.

Sadie Rosenberg, Tape of Oral Interview. Robert Wagner Labor Archives, New York University Libraries.

William Santoro, Tape of Oral Interview. Robert Wagner Labor Archives, New York University Libraries.

Edward Weise, Tape of Oral Interview. Robert Wagner Labor Archives, New York University Libraries.

Public Documents

U.S., Bureau of National Affairs. War Labor Reports. XXIII, 1945.
———. War Labor Reports. XXVIII, 1945.
U.S., *Congressional Record.* LXXXVI.
U.S., *Congressional Record.* LXXXVIII.
U.S., Department of Labor. "Collective Bargaining by United Electrical, Radio and Machine Workers," *Monthly Labor Review.* July 1938.
———. *Monthly Labor Review.* May 1946.
———. *Monthly Labor Review.* October 1954.
U.S., House of Representatives. Committee on Un-American Activities. *Hearings, Investigation of Local 601, UERMWA.* 81st Cong., 1st Sess., 1949.
U.S., House of Representives. Committee on Un-American Activities. *Hearings, Expose of the Communist Party of Western Pennsylvania.* 81st Cong., 2nd Sess., 1950.

————. *Hearings, Regarding Communism in Labor Unions in the United States.* 80th Cong., 1st Sess., 1947.

————. *The CIO Political Action Committee.* Report No. 1311. 78th Cong., 2d Sess., 1944.

U.S., House of Representatives. Special Subcommittee of the Committee on Education and Labor. *Hearings, Investigation of Communist Infiltration of UERMWA.* 80th Cong., 2d Sess., 1948.

U.S., Senate. Committee on the Judiciary. *Hearings, Subversive Influence of the United Electrical, Radio and Machine Workers of America.* 82d Cong., 2d Sess., 1949.

————. Subcommittee of the Committee on Labor and Public Welfare. *Hearings, Communist Domination of Unions and National Security.* 82d Cong., 2d Sess., 1952.

Union Publications

American Federation of Labor. Convention Proceedings, 1934–1936.

Congress of Industrial Organizations. *Convention Proceedings,* 1946–1950.

Congress of Industrial Organizations. *Official Reports on the Expulsion of Communist Dominated Organizations From the CIO.* CIO, 1954.

Fitzgerald, Albert and James Matles. *A Little Bit of UE History You Should Know.* UE, 1968.

International Union of Electrical Workers. *Convention Proceedings,* 1952–1990.

Matles, James. *UE: The Members Run This Union: An Answer to the Saturday Evening Post.* UE, 1947.

UERMWA. *CIO Needs Unity—Not Raiding.* UE, 1948.

————. *Convention Proceedings.* 1935–1990.

————. *In Defense of Labor.* UE, 1952.

————. *Thirty-Four Million: The CIO Can't Organize Them By Raiding UE.* UE, 1950.

————. *UE Acts Against Raiding and Dictatorship in the CIO.* UE, 1950.

Books

Alinsky, Saul. *John L. Lewis.* New York: G. P. Putnam's Sons, 1949.

Aronowitz, Stanley. *False Promises.* New York: McGraw-Hill, 1973.

Backman, Jules. *The Economics of the Electrical Machinery Industry.* New York: New York University Press, 1962.

Barbash, Jack. *Labor Unions in Action*. New York: Harper and Brothers, 1948.

————. *Unions and Union Leadership*. New York: Harper and Brothers, 1959.

Beal, Fred E. *The Red Fraud: An Exposé of Stalinism*. New York: Tempo Publishers, 1949.

Betten, Neil. *Catholic Activism and the Catholic Worker*. Gainesville: University of Florida Press, 1976.

Boulware, Lemuel. *The Truth About Boulwarism: Trying to Do Right Voluntarily*. Washington: Bureau of National Affairs, 1969.

Budenz, Louis. *Men Without Faces: The Communist Conspiracy in the United States*. New York: Harper and Brothers, 1948.

Carr, Robert K. *The House Committee on Un-American Activities*. Ithaca, NY: Cornell University Press, 1952.

Caute, David. *The Great Fear*. New York: Simon and Schuster, 1978.

Chapin, Ralph. *American Labor's Case Against Communism: How the Operations of Stalin's Red Quislings Look From Inside the Labor Movement*. Seattle: Education Publishing Co., 1947.

Cochrane, Bert. *Labor and Communism*. Princeton, NJ: Princeton University Press, 1977.

Cormier, Frank and Eaton, William. *Reuther*. Englewood Cliffs, NJ: Prentice Hall, 1971.

Crosser, Paul K. *Ideologies and American Labor*. New York: Oxford University Press, 1941.

Dies, Martin. *Martin Dies' Story*. New York: Bookmailer, 1963.

Doherty, Barbara. *The Struggle To Save Morse Cutting Tool* New Bedford, MA: Southeastern Massachusetts University Labor Education Center, 1986.

Draper, Theodore. *The Roots of American Communism*. New York: The Viking Press, 1957.

Dulles, Foster Rhea. *Labor in America*. New York: Thomas Y. Crowell Co., 1960.

Filippelli, Ronald. *American Labor and Postwar Italy, 1943–1953*. Stanford, CA: Stanford University Press, 1989.

Fink, Gary, ed. *Biographical Dictionary of American Labor Leaders*. Westport, CT: Greenwood Press, 1974.

Foster, William Z. *American Trade Unionism*. New York: International Publishers, 1947.

Freeman, Joshua. *In Transit: The Transport Workers Union in New York*. New York: Oxford University Press, 1989.

Galenson, Walter. *The CIO Challenge to the AFL.* Cambridge, MA: Harvard University Press, 1960.

Gitlow, Benjamin. *The Whole of Their Lives.* New York: Charles Scribner's Sons, 1948.

Godson, Roy. *American Labor and European Politics.* Los Angeles: Crane, Russak and Co., 1976.

Halpern, Martin. *UAW Politics in the Cold War Era.* Albany: State University of New York Press, 1988.

Harris, Herbert. *Labor's Civil War.* New York: Alfred Knopf, 1940.

Haynes, John Earl. *Dubious Alliance: The Making of Minnesota's DFL Party.* Minneapolis: University of Minnesota Press, 1981.

Howe, Irving and Coser, Lewis. *The American Communist Party: A Critical History, 1919–1957.* Boston: Beacon Press, 1957.

—— and Widick, B. J. *The UAW and Walter Reuther.* New York: Random House, 1949.

Isserman, Maurice. *Which Side Are You On?: The American Communist Party During the Second World War.* Middletown, CT: Wesleyan University Press, 1982.

Jaffee, Philip. *The Rise and Fall of American Communism.* New York: Horizon Press, 1975.

Kampelman, Max. *The Communist Party vs. the CIO.* New York: Frederick Praeger, 1957.

Keeran, Roger. *The Communist Party and the Auto Workers Union.* Bloomington: Indiana University Press, 1980.

Klehr, Harvey. *The Heyday of American Communism.* New York: Basic Books, 1984.

—— and Haynes, John Earl. *The American Communist Movement.* New York: Twayne Publishers, 1992.

Kuhn, James. *Bargaining in Grievance Settlements: The Power of Industrial Work Groups* New York: Columbia University Press, 1961.

Larson, Simion. *Labor and Foreign Policy.* Rutherford, NJ: Fairleigh Dickinson University Press, 1975.

Lens, Sidney. *Left, Right and Center; Conflicting Forces in American Labor.* Hinsdale, IL: H. Regnery, 1949.

Leuchtenberg, William E. *Franklin Roosevelt and the New Deal.* New York: Harper and Row, 1963.

Levenstein, Nelson. *Communism Anti-Communism and the CIO.* Westport, CT: Greenwood Press, 1981.

Lichtenstein, Nelson. *Labor's War at Home: The CIO in World War II.* Cambridge, England: Cambridge University Press, 1982.

MacDougall, Curtis. *Gideon's Army.* 2 Vols. New York: Marzani and Munsell, 1965.

Madison, Charles A. *American Labor Leaders*. New York: Frederick Ungar Publishing Co., 1962.

Markowitz, Norman. *The Rise and Fall of the People's Century: Henry A. Wallace and American Liberalism, 1941–1948*. New York: Free Press, 1973.

Matles, James and Higgins, James. *Them and Us: Struggles of a Rank and File Union*. Englewood Cliffs, NJ: Prentice Hall, 1974.

McGeever, Patrick. *Rev. Charles Owen Rice: Apostle of Contradiction*. Pittsburgh: Duquesne University Press, 1989.

Milkman, Ruth. *Gender at Work: The Dynamics of Job Segregation by Sex During World War II*. Urbana: University of Illinois Press, 1987.

Millis, Harry (ed.). *How Collective Bargaining Works*. New York: The Twentieth Century Fund, 1942.

———, and Emily Clark Brown. *From the Wagner Act to Taft-Hartley*. Chicago: University of Chicago Press, 1950.

Mills, C. Wright. *The New Men of Power, America's Labor Leaders*. New York: Harcourt, Brace, 1948.

Mitchell, George S. and Horace R. Cayton. *Black Workers and the New Unions*. Chapel Hill: University of North Carolina Press, 1939.

Moody's Manual of Investments, American and Foreign, Industrial Securities. New York, 1938.

Morris, George. *The Trotskyite 5th Column in the Labor Movement*. New York: New Century Publishers, 1945.

Murray, Philip and John Brophy, James Carey, I. F. Stone. *The CIO and National Defense*. Washington, D.C.: American Council on Public Affairs, 1941.

Murray, Robert K. *Red Scare*. Minneapolis: University of Minnesota Press, 1955.

Musmanno, Michael. *Across the Street from the Courthouse*. Philadelphia: Dorrance, 1954.

Northrup, Herbert. *Boulwarism: The Labor Relations Policies of the General Electric Company*. Ann Arbor: University of Michigan Press, 1964.

Perlman, Mark. *The Machinists*. Cambridge, MA: Harvard University Press, 1961.

Preis, Arthur. *Labor's Giant Step*. New York: Pathfinder, 1972.

Radosh, Ronald. *American Labor and United States Foreign Policy*. New York: Random House, 1969.

Rice, Charles Owen. *How to De-Control Your Union of Communists*. Published by the Author, 1948.

Romero, Frederico. *The United States and the European Trade Union Movement, 1944–1951*. Chapel Hill: University of North Carolina Press, 1992,

Rosswurn, Steven, ed. *The CIO's Left-Led Unions.* New Brunswick, NJ: Rutgers University Press, 1992.

Saposs, David J. *Communism in American Politics.* Washington: Public Affairs Press, 1960.

———. *Communism in American Unions.* New York: McGraw-Hill, 1959.

———. *Left Wing Unionism.* New York: International Publishers, 1926.

Schatz, Ronald. *The Electrical Workers: A History of Labor at General Electric and Westinghouse.* Urbana: University of Illinois Press, 1983.

Seaton, Douglas. *Catholics and Radicals: The Association of Catholic Trade Unionists and the American Labor Movement from Depression to Cold War.* Lewisburg, PA: Bucknell University Press, 1981.

Schneider, David. *The Workers Party and American Trade Unions.* Baltimore: Johns Hopkins Press, 1928.

Seidman, Joel. *American Labor from Defense to Reconversion.* Chicago: University of Chicago Press, 1953.

Sherril, Robert. *The Drugstore Liberal.* New York: Grossman Publishers, 1968.

Starobin, Joseph. *American Communism in Crisis, 1943–1957.* Cambridge, MA: Harvard University Press, 1972.

Stolberg, Benjamin. *The Story of the CIO.* New York: Viking Press, 1938.

Stouffer, Samuel A. *Communism, Conformity and Civil Liberties: A Cross-Section of the Nation Speaks Its Mind.* New York: Doubleday and Company, 1955.

Taft, Philip. *Organized Labor in American History.* New York: Harper and Row, 1964.

———. *The Structure of Government of Labor Unions.* Cambridge: Harvard University Press, 1956.

Ulman, Lloyd. *The Government of the Steelworkers' Union.* New York: John Wiley, 1962.

Warren, Frank A. *Liberals and Communism: The "Red Decade" Revisited.* Bloomington: Indiana University Press, 1966.

Wecter, Dixon. *The Age of the Great Depression.* New York: MacMillan Company, 1948.

Young, Edwin and Milton Derber. *Labor and the New Deal.* Madison: University of Wisconsin Press, 1957.

Youtsler, James. *Labor's Wage Policies in the Twentieth Century.* New York: Twayne Publishers, 1956.

Zeitlin, Maurice and Kimeldorf, Howard, eds. *Political Power and Social Theory,* Vol. 4. Greenwich, CT: JAI Press, 1984.

Articles

Alsop, Joseph and Stewart Alsop. "Will the CIO Shake the Communists Loose?" *Saturday Evening Post,* Vol. 219 (February 22, 1947; March 1, 1947), 15–16, 105–106, 108; 26, 117–118.

"Alternating Currents in UE—The CP's Last Base," *Fortune,* Vol. 39 (March 1949), 175–177.

Bell, Daniel. "The Coming Tragedy of American Labor," *Politics,* Vol. 1 (March 1944), 37–42.

Bendiner, Robert. "CIO Tightrope Act," *Nation,* Vol. 163 (November 30, 1946), 601.

———. "Murray's Limited Purge," *Nation,* Vol. 167 (December 18, 1948), 685.

———. "Showdown in the CIO," *Nation,* Vol. 169 (October 15, 1949), 361–363.

———. "Surgery in the CIO," *Nation,* Vol. 169 (November 12, 1949), 458–459.

Broun, Heywood. "Dr. Dewey Finds Communists in the CIO," *New Republic,* Vol. 113 (January 12, 1938), 280–281.

Carey, James B. "Why the CIO Bowed Out," *Saturday Evening Post,* Vol. 221 (June 11, 1949), 28, 128–132.

"Carey vs. Boulware," *Fortune,* Vol. 46 (October 1952), 92, 93.

"Civil War in the CIO," *Fortune,* Vol. 40 (November 1949), 204, 206.

Conn, Harry. "Communist Led Unions and U.S. Security," *New Republic,* Vol. 126 (February 18, 1952), 16, 17.

Cort, John C. "Another Split in U.S. Labor," *Commonweal,* Vol. 55 (October 14, 1949), 12, 13.

———. "Anti-CP's are Hotter," *Commonweal,* Vol. 45 (October 25, 1946), 49.

———. "CIO Expels Its Communist Unions," *Commonweal,* Vol. 11 (November 25, 1949), 211–212.

———. "Hillman, C.P.A. and PAC—What's It All About," *Commonweal,* Vol. 41 (October 20, 1944), 6–9.

———. "Mundt-Nixon Bill," *Commonweal,* Vol. 48 (July 2, 1948), 285–286.

———. "One Thing and Another," *Commonweal,* Vol. 44 (June 28, 1946), 264.

———. "Swing in the CIO," *Commonweal,* Vol. 45 (January 17, 1947), 355.

———. "The CIO Convention," *Commonweal,* Vol. 45 (December 13, 1946), 231–232.

———. "WFTU Hits the Ricks," *Commonweal,* Vol. 49 (February 4, 1949), 423–424.

Donald T. Critchlow. "Communist Unions and Racism: A Comparative Study of the Responses of the United Electrical Radio and Machine Workers and the National Maritime Union to the Black Question During World War II," Labor History, Vol. 17 (Spring 1976), 231–233.

Donnelly, Joseph. "The Junior Clergy Look at Organized Labor," American Ecclesiastical Review. Vol. 115 (1946), 1.

Dubinsky, David. "Warning Against Communists in Unions," New York Times Magazine (May 11, 1947), 61–65.

Ebon, Martin. "Why is the CIO in a Soviet Front Outfit?" Saturday Evening Post, Vol. 221 (September 25, 1948), 172.

Epstein, Albert and Nathan Goldfinger. "Communist Tactics in American Unions," Labor and Nation, Vol. 6 (Fall 1950), 36–43.

Filippelli, Ronald. "UE: The Formative Years, 1933–1937," Labor History, Vol. 17 (Summer 1976), 351–371.

Fisher, Hilda. "Labor and the Communists," Current History, Vol. 12 (March 1947), 199–204.

Foster, William Z. "Danger Ahead for Organized Labor," Masses and Mainstream, Vol. 1 (July 1948), 24–34.

———. "Organized Labor and the Marshall Plan," Political Affairs, Vol. 27 (February 1948), 99–109.

———. "The Wage and Strike Movement," Political Affairs, Vol. 25 (February 1946), 121–129.

Friedman, Robert. "UE—Ten Years Strong," New Masses, Vol. 61 (September 17, 1946), 3–5.

Hard, William and Frederick Blackly. "Communists Invited Out," Reader's Digest, Vol. 49 (November 1946), 17–21.

High, Stanley. "What and Who Inspired the Allis Chalmers Strike," Reader's Digest, Vol. 38 (June 1941), 89–93.

Kannenberg, Lisa. "The Impact of the Cold War on Women's Trade Union Activism: The UE Experience," Labor History, Vol. 34 (Spring–Summer 1993), 309–323.

Kersten, Charles. "How Spies are Protected in U.S. Defense Plants," Reader's Digest, Vol. 62 (January 1953), 27–31.

Levenstein, Aaron. "Troubles in the CIO," American Mercury, Vol. 62 (June 1946), 706–712.

"Luck to the CIO," Colliers, Vol. 119 (May 3, 1947), 94.

Masse, Benjamin L. "Communism at Cleveland," America, Vol. 82 (October 22, 1949), 66–68.

———. "Dies Committee Reports on the CIO," America, Vol. 71 (April 8, 1944), 11–12.

———. "Is Congress Framing UE?" America, Vol. 84 (November 11, 1950), 159–161.

————. "Is the CIO Ready to Resolve to Rid Itself of the Reds?" *America*, Vol. 66 (November 15, 1941), 152–153.

————. "Reds on the Run in the CIO," *America*, Vol. 79 (July 24, 1948), 265–267.

————. "Stalinist Strength in the CIO," *America*, Vol. 80 (January 8, 1949), 373–374.

Matles, James. "Against the Mainstream," *Studies on the Left*, Vol. 5 (Winter 1965), 43–54.

McFarland, Dalton E. "Left-Wing Domination of Labor Unions: A Case Study of Local Union Leadership," *ILR Research*, Vol. 1 (June 1955), 2, 3.

Morris, George. "The Vatican Conspiracy in the American Trade-Union Movement," *Political Affairs*, Vol. 29 (June 1950), 46–57.

Obrien, F. S. "The 'Communist Dominated' Unions in the United States Since 1950," *Labor History*, Vol. 9 (Spring 1968), 184–209.

Porter, Paul. "Factions and Unity in the CIO," *American Scholar*, Vol. 8 (April 1939), 131–143.

Reuther, Walter P. "How to Beat the Communists," *Colliers*, Vol. 121 (February 28, 1948), 11, 44, 48, 49.

Rice, Charles Owen. "Philip Murray and the Reds," *Catholic Digest*, Vol. 1 (May 1947), 97–101.

Rosswurn, Steve and Gilpin, Toni. "The FBI and the Farm Equipment Workers: FBI Surveillance Records as a Source for CIO Union History," *Labor History*, Vol. 27 (Fall 1986), 485–505.

Schatz, Ronald. "American Labor and the Catholic Church, 1919–1950," *International Labor and Working Class History*, Vol. 20 (1981). 46–53.

————. "Connecticut's Working Class in the 1950s: A Catholic Perspective," *Labor History*, Vol. 25 (Winter 1984), 83–101.

————. "The End of Corporate Liberalism: Class Struggle in the Electrical Manufacturing Industry," *Radical America*, Vol. 9 (July–August 1975), 197–201.

Schlesinger, Arthur M., Jr. "U.S. Communist Party," *Life*, Vol. 21 (July 29, 1946), 84, 86–88, 90, 93–94, 96.

Seidman, Joel. "Labor Policy of the Communist Party During World War II," *Industrial and Labor Relations Review*, Vol. 4 (October 1950), 55–69.

Seligman, Daniel. "UE, The Biggest Communist Union," *American Mercury*, Vol. 69 (July 1949), 35–45.

Shaw, David I. "How Effective is the Non-Communist Affidavit?" *Labor Law Journal*, Vol. 1 (September 1950), 935–944.

Shelton, Willard. "Labor; Inside the CIO," *New Republic*, Vol. 116 (March 24, 1947), 38, 39.

Smith, Ellington. "Electrical Workers Meet," *New Republic*, Vol. 71 (September 19, 1949), 14–15.

Soffer, Benson. "A Theory of Trade Union Development: The Role of the Autonomous Workman," *Labor History*, Vol. 1 (Spring 1960), 141–163.

Stepan-Norris, Judith and Zeitlin, Morris. "The Effects of Political Leadership on the 'Political Regime of Production'" *American Journal of Sociology*, Vol. 96, (March 1991), 1184–1188.

Stolberg, Benjamin. "Communist Wreckers in American Labor," *Saturday Evening Post*, Vol. 212 (September 2, 1939), 5–7, 32, 34, 36.

———. "Inside Labor," *American Mercury*, Vol. 53 (August 1941), 174–183.

Stein, Bruno. "Loyalty and Security Cases in Arbitration," *Industrial and Labor Relations Review*, Vol. 16 (October 1963), 96–113.

Stein, Sid. "The CIO Convention and the Struggle for Labor Unity," *Political Affairs*, Vol. 28 (December 1949), 35–45.

Sullivan, Edward F. "Stay Out of the UERMWA," *American Flint*, Vol. 35 (September 1946), 31.

U.S. News and World Report, Vol. 22 (February 21, 1947), 30–32.

Velie, Leslie. "Red Pipeline Into Our Defense Plants," *Saturday Evening Post*, Vol. 225 (October 18, 1952), 19–21.

Weinberg, Jules. "Priests, Workers, and Communists," *Harpers Magazine*, Vol. 247 (November 1948), 49–56.

Weschler, James. "Carey and the Communists," *Nation*, Vol. 153 (September 13, 1941), 224–225.

West, George P. "Communists and Liberals," *New Republic*, Vol. 108 (May 10, 1943), 631–633.

Williamson, John. "The AFL and CIO Conventions," *Political Affairs*, Vol. 26 (December 1947), 1077–1089.

———. "The Situation in the Trade Unions," *Political Affairs*, Vol. 26 (January 1947), 20–36.

———. "Trade Union Problems and the Third Party Movement," *Political Affairs*, Vol. 27 (March 1948), 224–237.

———. "Two Conventions of Labor; the Situation in the Trade Union Movement," *Political Affairs*, Vol. 28 (January 1949), 23–44.

Unpublished Materials

Cohen, Abraham. "Coordinated Bargaining at General Electric: An Analysis." Unpublished Ph.D. Dissertation, Cornell University, 1973.

Heller, Amy. "The Perennial Nightmare: Anti-Communism Inside and Outside UE Local 203, Bridgeport, 1944–1950." Unpublished paper. UE Archives.

Kirschner, "What Happens to the People." Unpublished Master's Thesis, City University of New York (Queens), 1973.

Malm, Finn Theodore. "Local 201, UE-CIO: A Case Study of a Local Industrial Union." Unpublished Ph. D. Dissertation, Massachusetts Institute of Technology, 1946.

Masiko, Peter. "A Study of Federal Labor Unions." Unpublished Dissertation, University of Illinois, 1937.

McColloch, Mark. "The United Electrical Workers and the International Union of Electrical Workers, 1949–1960." Unpublished Master's Thesis, Pennsylvania State University, 1972.

Necoechea, Gerardo. "Emergence, Development and Change of a Local Union: Local 201, UE-CIO, at the Lynn G.E. Works." Unpublished Master's Thesis, University of Massachusetts, 1977.

Riker, William H. "The CIO in Politics, 1936–1946." Unpublished Ph.D. Dissertation, Harvard University, 1948.

Index